WORLD MISSION

An Analysis
of the World Christian Movement

SECOND EDITION
Full revision of the original work

The Biblical / Historical
Foundation

Part One of a Manual in Three Parts

Jonathan Lewis, Ph.D., Editor

WILLIAM CAREY LIBRARY
Pasadena, California

Published by: William Carey Library, P.O. Box 40129, Pasadena, CA 91114, telephone (818) 798-0819

ISBN 0-87808-237-9
Printed in the United States of America

Editor: Jonathan Lewis, Ph.D.
Assistant Editors: Meg Crossman and Stephen Hoke, Ph.D.
Technical Editor: Susan Peterson
Assistants: Joe Varela and Patrick Roseman
Illustrators: John Devine and Dawn Lewis

Acknowledgments

Many of the articles and excerpts in this manual are found in the mission anthology *Perspectives on the World Christian Movement: A Reader* (revised edition), edited by Ralph Winter and Steven Hawthorne and published by William Carey Library. We are heavily indebted to the editors of this anthology for their encouragement in the production of this course. We would especially like to thank Dr. Ralph Winter for his inspiration and genius as the originator of this course, and we recognize his tireless efforts on behalf of the unreached peoples of the world. A special note of appreciation also goes to the *Perspectives* course office in Pasadena, California, which has cooperated fully in the re-edition process, in the hope of greater compatibility with their popular extension course.

My heartfelt thanks go to my assistant editors, Meg Crossman and Dr. Stephen T. Hoke. Meg's advocacy and use of the *World Mission* manuals in the Arizona *Perspectives* courses provided a wealth of insights for improving the material. Her contributions are reflected primarily in the first two volumes. Steve Hoke, veteran missions lecturer, was of invaluable help in improving the third volume. His knowledge, insights, and ready assistance are very much appreciated. Most of the credit for the technical production of this work goes to Susan Peterson. Her long hours of formatting, proofreading, indexing, and producing the figures and tables speak eloquently for themselves. We gratefully acknowledge Joe Varela and Pat Roseman, who assisted Susan in these tasks. We have kept many of John Devine's and Dawn Lewis's illustrations from the first edition. Thank you all for your marvelous help. May it advance the expansion of God's kingdom to the ends of the earth.

Jonathan Lewis, Editor
January 1994

Other Course Materials by the Editor

- *World Mission Leader's Guide*. An aid to those who want to organize and conduct a study group utilizing these manuals. It includes suggestions for promotion and organization of the course, as well as sample answers to each of the questions in the texts. An appendix gives useful helps on group dynamics. Available from William Carey Library.

- *Misión Mundial: Un Análisis del Movimiento Cristiano Mundial* (3 volumes).

- *Guia para el tutor del grupo de estudio de: Misión Mundial* (3 volumes).

- *Video de Misión Mundial* (3 videos, 5 hours total).

  The Second Edition of the Spanish manuals, accompanying leader's guide, and the lecture videos are available from Unilit, 1360 N.W. 88th Ave., Miami, FL 33172.

  Please contact the publisher for other language editions under production.

- *Working Your Way to the Nations: A Guide to Effective Tentmaking*. A 12-lesson course for use by local churches in guiding the preparation of cross-cultural "tentmaking" missionaries. Available from William Carey Library. Editions of this strategic course in Korean, Spanish, and Portuguese are under production.

PART 1

THE BIBLICAL / HISTORICAL FOUNDATION

89994

Preface to the Second Edition

We live in a rapidly changing world. These changes affect the way the advancing World Christian Movement perceives its mandate and carries out its task. The Second Edition of *World Mission* has tried to analyze these trends and incorporate their discussion into the text. Two Thirds World missions, reaching rapidly expanding cities, mission to the world's poor and destitute, the 10/40 window, strategic partnerships, church/mission tension—these and other current issues are woven into the discussion of the biblical, historical, strategic, and cross-cultural foundation of missions, improving and strengthening these basic themes.

The editors have worked closely with the *Perspectives* office at the U.S. Center for World Mission in Pasadena, California, to assure that these manuals are suited for students participating in their extension courses. Questions have been improved, and the research assignment has been redesigned to enhance the application of the end-product. Useful indexes and an appendix have also been added.

Organization and Use of This Manual

World Mission: An Analysis of the World Christian Movement is a manual that can be used by study groups in a formal or informal educational setting. The manual is in three parts, each being a separate unit.

- **Part One, The Biblical/Historical Foundation**, examines the roots of world mission, including its origin and its development through the ages.

- **Part Two, The Strategic Dimension**, defines the remaining mission task and the strategies necessary to reach the unreached.

- **Part Three, Cross-Cultural Considerations**, explores the challenge of cross-cultural communication of the gospel.

Each of the 15 chapters of this manual is divided into three study units. Each unit develops a distinct concept and relates it to the material studied in preceding units. Questions interspersed throughout the text direct the reader's attention to key points and stimulate reflection on the readings.

Each chapter ends with two sections of questions. The first section, **Integrative Assignment**, is designed to help the reader assimilate the material studied. The questions invite the student to do further research and encourage the development of the student's abilities to communicate what is learned. Study groups should use these questions for group discussion. In Part Two of the manual, an "Unreached Peoples" research project is incorporated into the Integrative Assignment. This fascinating project will require extra time and effort from the student.

The second section of questions, **Questions for Reflection**, asks for a response to personal and spiritual issues raised by the readings. We recommend that each student enter his or her thoughts either in the workbook or in a personal diary. We also suggest that a devotional time be provided during each group session to share these comments.

CHAPTER 1

God's Purpose and Plan

"For God so loved the world ..." (John 3:16)

The message of John 3:16 is simple enough for a child to understand, yet so profound that theologians will continue to probe its implications throughout time. Though most of us have individually experienced the salvation God offers through His Son, have we really begun to fathom the Father's love for lost mankind? What does "God so loved the world" really mean?

Since the beginning, God has been at work to fulfill His purposes. He created man to be like Him, placed him in a perfect environment, and enjoyed his fellowship. Man chose to frustrate God's good plan by rebelling against Him and His command. By that rebellion, the sentence of death came upon all men.

God could have justly destroyed mankind at that time. Instead, He chose to bless him by offering redemption and the right to become His children to as many of Adam's descendants as would accept it. In addition, He directed those who received redemption to accept the responsibility of joining Him in extending that redemption to others. This plan of blessing and responsibility constitutes God's world mission.

We begin our study by examining our primary source for what we know about God's mission: the Bible. Using that source, we then explore God's purpose in the creation and attempt to answer the question: What is God really trying to do? As we continue to examine the biblical record, we discover that to accomplish His purpose, God has implemented a plan in which His people are intended to play a significant role. Understanding this plan may give you a whole new perspective on the Bible.

I. Mission, the Basis for the Bible

Most Christians believe that a basis for worldwide mission can be found in isolated parts of the Bible, such as the "Great Commission" passages. In actuality, mission is much more fundamental to all of Scripture. God's worldwide purpose is, in fact, the basis for the entire biblical revelation.

Figure 1-1. The Bible Is Missions!

Simply stated, if God had not purposed to redeem mankind, there probably would have been no need for Him to reveal Himself through the biblical record. In fact, apart from God's redemptive mission, there would have been no chosen nation to trace throughout the Old Testament, no Messiah to expect, and no crucifixion or resurrection to proclaim. The abbreviated record would need only to have included the creation, man's fall, and his subsequent condemnation to death and eternal judgment.

Thank God, He did purpose to redeem mankind! Since He desires our participation in sharing this good news, He gave us a clear account of what He has done and what He yet intends to do. The Bible is the story of God's mission—why and how a loving God is redeeming lost humanity.

As we examine the Bible in this light, we see that redeeming people is at the center of God's concern. We also see that taking the gospel forth is not just a good and right activity. It is a call to partnership with the living God to bring about the glorious fulfillment of Revelation 11:15: "The kingdoms of this world are become the kingdoms of our Lord, and of His Christ; and He shall reign forever and ever."

The Bible: The Mission Manual

God's redemptive mission is the central theme of the Bible. Not only does God's loving purpose radiate from every book, but the Bible is also God's manual on how to accomplish that purpose. In the following article, John Stott helps us understand this dynamic interrelationship. Read the article and carefully answer the study questions that follow each section.

❏ *The Bible in World Evangelization* *

John R. W. Stott **

Without the Bible world evangelization would be not only impossible but actually inconceivable. It is the Bible that lays upon us the responsibility to evangelize the world, gives us a gospel to proclaim, tells us how to proclaim it, and promises us that it is God's power for salvation to every believer. It is, moreover, an observable fact of history, both past and contemporary, that the degree of the church's commitment to world evangelization is commensurate with the degree of its conviction about the authority of the Bible. Whenever Christians lose their confidence in the Bible, they also lose their zeal for evangelism. Conversely, whenever they are convinced about the Bible, then they are determined about evangelism.

* Stott, J. R. W. (1992). The Bible in world evangelization. In R. D. Winter & S. C. Hawthorne (Eds.), *Perspectives on the world Christian movement: A reader* (rev. ed.) (pp. A3-A9). Pasadena: William Carey Library.

** John R. W. Stott is Rector Emeritus of All Souls Church in London, President of Christian Impact, and an Extra Chaplain to Queen Elizabeth II. For 25 years (1952-1977) he led university missions on five continents. He still travels widely, especially in the non-Western world, as a lecturer and speaker. Formerly he addressed five Urbana Student Missions Conventions. His many books include *Basic Christianity, Christian Mission in the Modern World, The Cross of Christ,* and *The Spirit, the Church and the World.*

Let me develop four reasons why the Bible is indispensable to world evangelization.

Mandate for world evangelization

First, the Bible gives us the mandate for world evangelization. We certainly need one. Two phenomena are everywhere on the increase. One is religious fanaticism and the other, religious pluralism. The fanatic displays the kind of irrational zeal which (if it could) would use force to compel belief and eradicate disbelief. Religious pluralism encourages the opposite tendency.

Whenever the spirit of religious fanaticism or of its opposite, religious indifferentism, prevails, world evangelization is bitterly resented. Fanatics refuse to countenance the rival evangelism represents, and pluralists deny its exclusive claims. The Christian evangelist is regarded as making an unwarrantable intrusion into other people's private affairs.

In the face of this opposition we need to be clear about the mandate the Bible gives us. It is not just the Great Commission (important as that is) but the entire biblical revelation. Let me rehearse it briefly.

There is but one living and true God, the Creator of the universe, the Lord of the nations, and the God of the spirits of all flesh. Some 4,000 years ago He called Abraham and made a covenant with him, promising not only to bless him but also through his posterity to bless all the families of the earth (Gen. 12:1-4). This biblical text is one of the foundation stones of the Christian mission. For Abraham's descendants (through whom all nations are being blessed) are Christ and the people of Christ. If by faith we belong to Christ, we are Abraham's spiritual children and have a responsibility to all mankind. So, too, the Old Testament prophets foretold how God would make His Christ the heir and the light of the nations (Ps. 2:8; Isa. 42:6; 49:6).

When Jesus came, He endorsed these promises. True, during His own earthly ministry He was restricted "to the lost sheep of the house of Israel" (Matt. 10:6; 15:24), but He prophesied that many would "come from east and west, and from north and south," and would "sit at table with Abraham, Isaac, and Jacob in the kingdom of heaven" (Matt. 8:11; Luke 13:29). Further, after His resurrection and in anticipation of His ascension, He made the tremendous claim that "all authority in heaven and on earth" had been given to Him (Matt. 28:18). It was in consequence of His universal authority that He commanded His followers to make all nations His disciples, baptizing them into His new community and teaching them all His teaching (Matt. 28:19).

And this, when the Holy Spirit of truth and power had come upon them, the early Christians proceeded to do. They became the witnesses of Jesus, even to the ends of the earth (Acts 1:8). Moreover, they did it "for the sake of His name" (Rom. 1:5; 3 John 7). They knew that God had superexalted Jesus, enthroning Him at His right hand and bestowing upon Him the highest rank, in order that every tongue should confess His Lordship. They longed that Jesus should receive the honor due to His name.

> *The church of God is a multinational missionary community, under orders to evangelize until Christ returns.*

Besides, one day He would return in glory, to save, to judge, and to reign. So what was to fill the gap between His two comings? The worldwide mission of the church! Not till the gospel had reached the end of the world, He said, would the end of history come (cf. Matt. 24:14; 28:20; Acts 1:8). The two ends would coincide.

Our mandate for world evangelization, therefore, is the whole Bible. It is to be found in the creation of God (because of which all human beings are responsible to Him), in the character of God (as outgoing, loving, compassionate, not willing that any should perish, desiring that all should come to repentance), in the promises of God (that all nations will be blessed through Abraham's seed and will become the Messiah's inheritance), in the Christ of God (now exalted with universal authority, to receive universal acclaim), in the Spirit of God (who convicts of sin, witnesses to Christ, and impels the church to evangelize), and in the church of God (which is a multinational, missionary community, under orders to evangelize until Christ returns).

This global dimension of the Christian mission is irresistible. Individual Christians and local churches not committed to world evangelization are contradicting (either through blindness or through disobedience) an essential part of their God-given identity.

The biblical mandate for world evangelization cannot be escaped.

> *The Biblical Mandate: The non-negotiable responsibility binding on all those who receive the benefits of God's covenant with Abraham, to share those same benefits with the other families (nations) of the earth.*

1. According to Stott, what direct correlation exists between the church's commitment to world evangelization and her conviction about the authority of the Bible?

_____

_____

_____

2. On what grounds does Stott demonstrate that the mandate for world evangelization is "the whole Bible"?

_____

_____

_____

Now read Stott's comments concerning the biblical message for mission.

Message for world evangelization

Secondly, the Bible gives us the message for world evangelization. The Lausanne Covenant* defined evangelism in terms of the evangel [the gospel]. Paragraph Four begins: "To evangelize is to spread the good news that Jesus Christ died for our sins and was raised from the dead according to the Scriptures, and that as the reigning Lord He now offers the forgiveness of sins and the liberating gift of the Spirit to all who repent and believe."

Our message comes out of the Bible. As we turn to the Bible for our message, however, we are immediately confronted with a dilemma. On the one hand the message is given to us. We are not left to invent it; it has been entrusted to us as a precious "deposit," which we, like faithful stewards, are both to guard and to dispense to God's household (1 Tim. 6:20; 2 Tim. 1:12-14; 2 Cor. 4:1-2). On the other hand, it has not been given to us as a single, neat, mathemati-

---

* The Lausanne Covenant is a declaration of commitment to world evangelization drawn up by participants in the Congress on World Evangelization held in Lausanne, Switzerland, July 1974.

cal formula, but rather in a rich diversity of formulations, in which different images or metaphors are used.

So there is only one gospel, on which all the apostles agreed (1 Cor. 15:11), and Paul could call down the curse of God upon anybody — including himself — who preached a "different" gospel from the original apostolic gospel of God's grace (Gal. 1:6-8). Yet the apostles expressed this one gospel in various ways—now sacrificial (the shedding and sprinkling of Christ's blood), now messianic (the breaking in of God's promised rule), now legal (the Judge pronouncing the unrighteous righteous), now personal (the Father reconciling His wayward children), now salvific (the heavenly Liberator coming to rescue the helpless), now cosmic (the universal Lord claiming universal dominion); and this is only a selection.

The gospel is thus seen to be one, yet diverse. It is "given," yet culturally adapted to its audience. Once we grasp this, we shall be saved from making two opposite mistakes.

The first I will call "total fluidity." I recently heard an English church leader declare that there is no such thing as the gospel until we enter the situation in which we are to witness. We take nothing with us into the situation, he said; we discover the gospel only when we have arrived there. Now I am in full agreement with the need to be sensitive to each

situation, but if this was the point which the leader in question was wanting to make, he grossly overstated it. There is such a thing as a revealed or given gospel, which we have no liberty to falsify.

The opposite mistake I will call "total rigidity." In this case the evangelist behaves as if God had given a series of precise formulas that we have to repeat more or less word for word, and certain images that we must invariably employ. This leads to bondage to either words or images or both. Some evangelists lapse into the use of stale jargon, while others feel obliged on every occasion to mention "the blood of Christ" or "justification by faith" or "the kingdom of God" or some other image.

Between these two extremes there is a third and better way. It combines commitment to the fact of revelation with commitment to the task of contextualization. It accepts that only the biblical formulations of the gospel are permanently normative and that every attempt to proclaim the gospel in modern idiom must justify itself as an authentic expression of the biblical gospel.

But if it refuses to jettison the biblical formulations, it also refuses to recite them in a wooden and unimaginative way. On the contrary, we have to engage in the continuous struggle (by prayer, study, and discussion) to relate the given gospel to the given situation. Since it comes from God we must

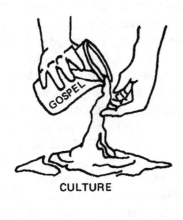

CULTURE

TOTAL FLUIDITY

GOSPEL

CULTURE

TOTAL RIGIDITY

Figure 1-2. Two Opposite Mistakes in Presenting the Gospel

guard it; since it is intended for modern men and women we must interpret it. We have to combine fidelity (constantly studying the biblical text) with sensitivity (constantly studying the contemporary scene). Only then can we hope with faithfulness and relevance to relate the Word to the world, the gospel to the context, Scripture to culture.

3. *In discussing the message of the Bible, Stott points out that there is only one gospel, but there are many formulations, images, and metaphors which are used in communicating it. What are the two dangers he mentions?*

_____

_____

4. *What two attitudes should we combine to avoid these deadly extremes?*

_____

_____

Read Stott's comments regarding the model for world evangelization.

Model for world evangelization

Thirdly, the Bible gives us the model for world evangelization. In addition to a message (what we are to say) we need a model (how we are to say it). The Bible supplies this too: for the Bible does not just contain the gospel; it is the gospel. Through the Bible God is Himself actually evangelizing, that is, communicating the good news to the world. You will recall Paul's statement about Genesis 12:3 that "the Scripture … preached the gospel beforehand to Abraham" (Gal. 3:8, RSV). All Scripture preaches the gospel; God evangelizes through it.

If, then, Scripture is itself divine evangelization, it stands to reason that we can learn how to preach the gospel by considering how God has done it. He has given us in the process of biblical inspiration a beautiful evangelistic model.

What strikes us immediately is the greatness of God's condescension. He had sublime truth to reveal about Himself and His Christ, His mercy and His justice, and His full salvation. And He chose to make this disclosure through the vocabulary and grammar of human language, through human beings, human images, and human cultures.

Yet through this lowly medium of human words and images, God was speaking of His own word. Our evangelical doctrine of the inspiration of Scripture emphasizes its *double authorship* [italics added]. Men spoke and God spoke. Men spoke from God (2 Pet. 1:21), and God spoke through men (Heb. 1:1). The words spoken and written were equally His and theirs. He decided what He wanted to say yet did not smother their human personalities. They used their faculties freely yet did not distort the divine message. Christians want to assert something similar about the incarnation, the climax of the self-communicating God. "The Word became flesh" (John 1:14). That is, God's eternal Word, who from eternity was with God and was God, the agent through whom the universe was created, became a human being, with all the particularity of a first-century Palestinian Jew. He became little, weak, poor, and vulnerable. He experienced pain and hunger and exposed Himself to temptation. All this was included in the "flesh," the human being He became. Yet when He became one of us, He did not cease to be Himself. He remained forever the eternal Word or Son of God.

REFUSAL TO IDENTIFY

TOTAL LOSS OF IDENTITY AND SURRENDER OF VALUES

Figure 1-3. Two Errors in Identifying

Essentially the same principle is illustrated in both the inspiration of the Scripture and the incarnation of the Son. The Word became flesh. The divine was communicated through the human. He identified with us, though without surrendering His own identity. And this principle of "identification without loss of identity" is the model for all evangelism, especially cross-cultural evangelism.

Some of us refuse to identify with the people we claim to be serving. We remain ourselves and do not become like them. We stay aloof. We hold on desperately to our own cultural practices with fierce tenacity, but we treat the cultural inheritance of the land of our adoption without the respect it deserves. We thus practice a double kind of cultural imperialism, imposing our own culture on others and despising theirs. But this was not the way of Christ, who emptied Himself of His glory and humbled Himself to serve.

Other cross-cultural messengers of the gospel make the opposite mistake. So determined are they to identify with the people to whom they go that they surrender even their Christian standards and values. But again this was not Christ's way, since in becoming human He remained truly divine. The Lausanne Covenant expressed the principle in these words: "Christ's evangelists must humbly seek to empty themselves of all but their personal authenticity, in order to become the servants of others" (para. 10).

We have to wrestle with the reasons why people reject the gospel and in particular give due weight to the cultural factors. Some people reject the gospel not because they perceive it to be false, but because they perceive it to be alien.

Dr. Rene Padilla was criticized at Lausanne [the 1974 Congress on World Evangelization] for saying that the gospel some European and North American missionaries have exported was a "culture Christianity," a Christian message that is distorted by the materialistic, consumer culture of the West. It was hurtful to us to hear him say this, but of course he was quite right. All of us need to subject our gospel to more critical scrutiny, and in a cross-cultural situation, visiting evangelists need humbly to seek the help of local Christians in order to discern the cultural distortions of their message.

Others reject the gospel because they perceive it to be a threat to their own culture. Of course Christ challenges every culture. Whenever we present the gospel to Hindus or Buddhists, Jews or Muslims, secularists or Marxists, Jesus Christ confronts them with His demand to dislodge whatever has thus far secured their allegiance and replace it with Himself. He is Lord of every person and every culture. That threat, that confrontation, cannot be avoided. But does the gospel we proclaim present people with other threats that are unnecessary—because it calls for the abolition of harmless customs, or appears destructive of national art, architecture, music, and festivals, or because we who share it are culture-proud and culture-blind? To sum up, when God spoke to us in Scripture He used human language, and when He spoke to us in Christ He assumed human flesh. In order to reveal Himself, He both emptied and humbled Himself. That is the model of evangelism which the Bible supplies. There is self-emptying and self-humbling in all authentic evangelism; without it we contradict the gospel and misrepresent the Christ we proclaim.

> **Two reasons people reject the gospel even when they want to believe:**
>
> 1. **It appears to be alien to their culture.**
> 2. **It seems to be a threat to their culture.**

5. *In this section, Stott again points out two extremes which can cause us to fail as messengers of the gospel. Explain these extremes in your own words.*

_____

_____

_____

_____

6. *In what ways did Christ portray a balanced model for cross-cultural witness?*

_____

_____

_____

_____

Read this final section of Stott's article.

Power for world evangelization

Fourthly, the Bible gives us the power for world evangelization. It is hardly necessary for me to emphasize our need for power, for we know how feeble our human resources are in comparison with the magnitude of the task. We also know how armor-plated are the defenses of the human heart. Worse still, we know the personal reality, malevolence, and might of the devil and of the demonic forces at his command.

Sophisticated people may ridicule our belief and caricature it, too, in order to make their ridicule more plausible. But we evangelical Christians are naive enough to believe what Jesus and His apostles taught. To us it is a fact of great solemnity that, in John's expression, "the whole world is in the power of the evil one" (1 John 5:19). For until they are liberated by Jesus Christ and transferred into His kingdom, all men and women are the slaves of

Satan. Moreover, we see his power in the contemporary world—in the darkness of idolatry and of the fear of spirits, in superstition and fatalism, in devotion to gods which are no gods, in the selfish materialism of the West, in the spread of atheistic communism, in the proliferation of irrational cults, in violence and aggression, and in the widespread declension from absolute standards of goodness and truth. These things are the work of him who is called in Scripture a liar, a deceiver, a slanderer, and a murderer.

Preaching the gospel is the God-appointed means by which the prince of darkness is defeated and the light comes streaming into people's hearts.

So Christian conversion and regeneration remain miracles of God's grace. They are the culmination of a power struggle between Christ and Satan or (in vivid apocalyptic imagery) between the Lamb and the Dragon. The plundering of the strong man's palace is possible only because he has been bound by the One who is stronger still and who by His death and resurrection disarmed and discarded the principalities and powers of evil (Matt. 12:27-29; Luke 11:20-22; Col. 2:15).

How then shall we enter into Christ's victory and overthrow the devil's power? Let Luther answer our question: *ein wortlein will ihn fallen* ("one little word will knock him down"). There is power in the Word of God and in the preaching of the gospel. Perhaps the most dramatic expression of this in the New Testament is to be found in 2 Corinthians 4. Paul portrays "the god of this world" as having "blinded the minds of the unbelievers, to keep them from seeing the light of the gospel of the glory of Christ ..." (v. 4).

If human minds are blinded, how then can they ever see? Only by the creative Word of God. For it is the God who said, "Let light shine out of darkness," who has shone in our hearts to "give the light of the knowledge of the glory of God in the face of Christ" (v. 6). The apostle thus likens the unregenerate heart to the dark primeval chaos and attributes regeneration to the divine fiat, "Let there be light."

If then Satan blinds people's minds, and God shines into people's hearts, what can we hope to contribute to this encounter? Would it not be more modest for us to retire from the field of conflict and leave them to fight it out? No, this is not the conclusion Paul reaches. On the contrary, in between verses 4 and 6, which describe the activities of God and Satan, verse 5 describes the work of the evangelist: "We preach... Jesus Christ as Lord." Since the light which the devil wants to prevent people from seeing and which God shines into them is the gospel, we had better preach it! Preaching the gospel, far from being unnecessary, is indispensable. It is the God-appointed means by which the prince of darkness is defeated and the light comes streaming into people's hearts. There is power in God's gospel—His power for salvation (Rom. 1:16).

We may be very weak. I sometimes wish we were weaker. Faced with the forces of evil, we are often tempted to put on a show of Christian strength and engage in a little evangelical saber rattling. But it is in our weakness that Christ's strength is made perfect, and it is words of human weakness that the Spirit endorses with His power. So it is when we are weak that we are strong (1 Cor. 2:1-5; 2 Cor. 12:9-10).

Let it loose in the world!

Let us not consume all our energies arguing about the Word of God; let's start using it. It will prove its divine origin by its divine power. Let's let it loose in the world! If only every Christian missionary and evangelist proclaimed the biblical gospel with faithfulness and sensitivity, and every Christian preacher were a faithful expositor of God's Word! Then God would display His saving power.

Without the Bible world evangelization is impossible. For without the Bible we have no gospel to take to the nations, no warrant to take it to them, no idea of how to set about the task, and no hope of any success. It is the Bible that gives us the mandate, the message, the model, and the power we need for world evangelization. So let's seek to repossess it by diligent study and meditation. Let's heed its summons, grasp its message, follow its directions, and trust its power. Let's lift up our voices and make it known.

7. According to Stott, what kind of power is needed for world evangelization?

_____

_____

_____

8. What role does Stott feel the Word of God should play in our witness?

_____

_____

_____

In the first part of this lesson, we have seen that mission is the reason God gave the Bible and that the Bible is our manual for mission. In this next part, we want to examine why God is involved in mission in the first place.

II. God's Purpose

What is God's purpose for His creation? What is He really trying to do? The following article by Stanley Ellisen delves into these questions by articulating two problems God is faced with and what He is doing about them. Read the following article and answer the study questions at the end.

❑ *Everyone's Question: What Is God Trying to Do?* *

Stanley A. Ellisen **

God's eternal kingdom

The Bible describes God as an eternal King: "The Lord is King forever" (Ps. 10:16). It also declares that He is sovereign over all things (Ps. 103:19). Being infinite, He is everywhere. So, at every time and place, in all the vast reaches of His universe, God has been in full control. He has never compromised this supreme prerogative of His Godhood. To do so would make Him less than God. It is essential to recognize His undiminished sovereignty if we are to have a proper view of His kingdom. His work of creation, with all the apparent risks involved, was the work of His sovereignty.

Primeval rebellion

In the operation of His kingdom God rules by the principle of delegated authority. He organized the angels as a hierarchy, assigning levels of responsibility and spheres of service. To act as His supreme lieutenant in directing this kingdom, God endowed one specific archangel with striking beauty, wisdom, and power (Ezek. 28:12-17; Jude 9). He

* Ellisen, S. A. (1992). Everyone's question: What is God trying to do? In R. D. Winter & S. C. Hawthorne (Eds.), *Perspectives on the world Christian movement: A reader* (rev. ed.) (pp. A19-A24). Pasadena: William Carey Library.

** Stanley A. Ellisen is Professor of Biblical Literature and Chairman of the Division of Biblical Studies at Western Conservative Baptist Seminary in Portland, Oregon. The author of five books and numerous articles, Ellisen has also served in a number of pastorates in the Pacific Northwest and Southwest.

named him Lucifer and gave him a throne from which to rule (Isa. 14:12-14). This angel ruled as God's prime minister par excellence. How long this harmonious arrangement continued in the distant past is not recorded.

Endowed with freedom of choice, the crucial test of any creature was allegiance to the will of God. That crucial test came for Lucifer when he shifted his gaze to himself and his God-given features of splendor. Dazzled by his own greatness, he asserted independence and presumed himself to be "like the Most High" (Isa. 14:14). In that moment of decision he thrust himself outside the stabilizing axis of God's will and began the swirling catapult into the oblivion of a godless being. His decision was final and never repented of.

Lucifer, however, was not alone in this choice. He evidently had a following of one-third of the angels of heaven (Rev. 12:4-7), which also suggests the great allurement of his leadership. With this crowd of rebels he formed a kingdom of his own, a counterfeit kingdom of darkness. His name was changed to Satan ("adversary"), in keeping with his behavior. If God is sovereign, why didn't He immediately destroy this arch rebel? Why didn't He have a mass execution for the whole horde of disobedient angels? Or at least, why didn't He lock them up forever in the abyss of hell?

> *So deep is God's sovereignty that He is able to make the wrath of men to praise Him and all His enemies to serve Him.*

The answer is that God does have such a plan, but He is temporarily using these rebels to accomplish another purpose. In the outworking of His program, God was not locked into a one-track plan but was able to flex with the punches, so to speak. So deep is His sovereignty that He is able to make the wrath of men to praise Him and all His enemies to serve Him (Ps. 76:10). The devastating irony of it for His enemies is that they end up serving Him in spite of themselves. Some of the fallen angels He chained until judgment; others He has allowed a limited liberty until His further purpose is accomplished.

The central fact to observe is that God did allow the formation of a kingdom of darkness. This kingdom was formed through voluntary forces led by Satan, not through God's creation, as such. It thus became an opposite pole to God's kingdom of light and an alluring option for all moral creatures in their exercise of moral freedom. It is a counterfeit kingdom running concurrently with the true kingdom of righteousness. Very often it seems to be dominant, not only coercing men and women but winning them. This is partly because of its modus operandi. Contrary to many naive opinions, the devil is not a red monster with a pitchfork, but often a do-gooder. His goal in life is to counterfeit the works of God. This has been his prized ambition ever since he went into business for himself. His first recorded intention ended with the words, "I will be like the Most High" (Isa. 14:14). This counterfeiting effort is his most effective ploy, for the more closely he can imitate God's work, the less likely will men be inclined to seek God or pursue His will.

God's earthly kingdom inaugurated

After the fall of Satan, God began another creation: man. He likewise endowed this being with freedom of choice, dangerous though this second venture appears. Freedom of choice was essential to human personality, if man and woman were to be made in the image of God. God's grand design is to reproduce Himself in human personalities, especially His traits of love and holiness. And these divine characteristics can grow only in the soil of moral freedom. Fellowship involves moral choice.

By this freedom God sought to establish man and woman in a wholesome relationship to His sovereignty. He sought to relate to them by love, not coercion. The bond of love is infinitely stronger than that of muscle. With this in mind He made Adam and Eve partners in His rule. As an initial test they were forbidden to eat of the "tree of the knowledge of good and evil" (Gen. 2:17). They were given a choice of compliance or disobedience, clear and simple. The tree was not put there as a teaser or trap, but as an inevitable test. It gave the couple a choice as to whether they would be loyal to God or submit to enticing alternatives presented by the serpent. Had they turned from his evil suggestion to firm commitment to God, they might have eaten of the "tree of life" and been eternally confirmed in righteousness (Gen. 3:24; Rev. 22:2). But they each disobeyed the direct command of God, and the fall of the race took place.

By this deliberate action they declared their independence from the will of God and their affiliation with Satan's kingdom of darkness. The cause of this disaster was not the tree; nor was it the serpent or the devil behind the serpent (Rev. 12:9). These provided only an occasion for two individuals to express their freedom of choice with respect to the will of God. The cause of disaster was in their decision. In this test of allegiance they failed and fell, along with the previously fallen host of angels.

To all outward appearance, this second fall of God's creation seemed to dash God's high hopes of extending His kingdom in moral agents. Man was given cosmic responsibilities to have dominion over the earth—but he could not be trusted with a piece of fruit. Was the divine gift of free choice too risky? Would this endowment be the suicidal undoing of the whole race? It certainly seemed to be counterproductive to God's purpose, for sin appeared to be coming up the victor.

The two problems summarized

The dilemma at this point may be summarized as two problems which God acquired in the creative process. One was the fact that His trusted lieutenant, Lucifer, defected and started a counterkingdom, stealing also the allegiance of a large contingent of the angels. The second was that man, made in God's image, also defected and fell into a state of sin and personal disintegration. Thus God's kingdom was dissected and partially usurped.

The question is often raised as to why God bothered with a salvage operation. Why not destroy everything and start over? Of course this was not within His sovereign plan, nor would it have been a real solution to the deep challenge the double rebellion posed. God not only rose to the insidious challenge of sin, but His great heart of grace initiated an operation that would marvelously redeem sinners. In this plan He addressed Himself to two problems: (1) how to reclaim His usurped kingdom, and (2) how to provide redemption for mankind. The solution God sought could not deal with both problems separately; He thus devised a plan whereby the victory over the counterfeit kingdom would provide salvation for mankind. It could not be achieved by a mere display of divine muscle; the answer was not to crack the whip. Cataclysmic and inclusive judgment would be postponed. It would require action with the depth and power of His greatest attribute: love.

Ellisen's article begins by affirming God's eternal sovereignty. God has allowed Satan, and later man, to contest that sovereignty. Nevertheless, this rebellion has posed a twofold "problem" for God.

9. Summarize the major aspects of God's twofold "problem."

_____

_____

10. What is the crucial test of any creature's allegiance to God?

_____

_____

Now read the last part of the article dealing with God's kingdom and redemptive programs.

God's kingdom and redemptive programs

When Adam and Eve first sinned, God began His judgment with the serpent (Gen. 3:14, 15). In this judgment He also gave the proto-evangel,* announcing His redemptive purpose for men. To the serpent He said, "And I will put enmity between you and the woman, and between your seed and her seed; He shall bruise you on the head, and you shall bruise him on the heel."

This message was obviously for man as well as Satan, perhaps more so. In it God prophesied that, following a two-way enmity, two bruisings or crushings would take place. The serpent's head would be crushed by the woman's seed, and the heel of the woman's seed would be crushed by the serpent. The two figures in this conflict are later declared to be Christ, who was the seed born of a woman (Gal. 4:4), and Satan, called "the serpent of old" (Rev. 20:2).

By analyzing these two crushings we get a thumbnail sketch of God's program with respect to Satan and man. The first statement, "He shall bruise you on the head," was a prophecy that Christ would destroy the devil. Christ Himself spoke of His binding Satan, the "strong man" of this world system, and casting him out (Matt. 12:29; John 12:31). Christ's death on the cross provided the ground for Satan's final destruction, for "he who builds the scaffold finally hangs thereon." And with his final judgment, the counterfeit kingdom of his making will also be destroyed. This, of course, has not yet taken place, but will occur after Christ's millennial reign. This whole process by which God reclaims His authority in all realms and forever stops all rebellion can be thought of as God's "kingdom program."

The second crushing announced in Genesis 3:15 is the heel-crushing of the seed of the woman by the serpent. This devilish assault was fulfilled on the cross, where Satan was the driving force behind the crucifixion of Christ. The heel-crushing suggests the temporary nature of Christ's death in contrast to the head-crushing of the serpent. Christ's death on the cross then became the ground for God's redemptive program, the program by which He provided salvation for men.

Thus, in this proto-evangel in Eden, God introduced in outline form His twofold program for His kingdom and man's redemption. He would ultimately reclaim His total kingdom by destroying Satan and Satan's kingdom and would redeem believing men in the process by the death of Christ.

11. Why is Genesis 3:15 (the proto-evangel) significant to our understanding of God's purpose and plan?

_____

_____

_____

God's twofold program unfolds

The rest of the Old Testament pictures the progressive development of this twofold purpose of God in the earth. The Lord chose two men of faith through whom He inaugurated these programs and set them in motion. The first was Abraham, who lived about 2000 B.C. With him God made a covenant, promising among other things a seed that would bless all nations. This seed Paul identified as Christ, and the

* The proto-evangel is a preparation for the fuller message to come, as recorded in Genesis 3:15. It is the first biblical reference to the gospel message.

blessing which was to come through Him he identified as redemption or justification (Gal. 3:6-16). Abraham's seed would bring redemption to men, fulfilling the redemptive program.

To fulfill His kingdom purpose, God chose David out of the same line about 1000 B.C. and made a covenant about a kingdom and a royal seed (2 Sam. 7:12-16). This seed of David eventually would rule over the house of Israel forever. Besides ruling over Israel, it was later revealed that this anointed One would extend His rule over the whole world (Amos 9:12; Zech. 14:9). Through the seed of David, God would fulfill His kingdom program by destroying the rebels and governing the world in righteousness.

Two typical sons

It is interesting to note also that each of these two men was given a son who typified the seed he was promised. Abraham's son, Isaac, typified Christ in His redemptive function, being offered on Mount Moriah as a living sacrifice. David's son, Solomon, typified Christ in His royalty, being a king of glory and splendor. These two sons strikingly typified that seed of Abraham and of David who was looked for with such anticipation throughout the rest of the Old Testament period. In this light, it is no wonder that the Spirit of God begins the New Testament by introducing its central figure as "the son of David, the son of Abraham" (Matt. 1:1).

Two typical animals

The Old Testament also portrays the redemptive and kingdom functions of Christ by two symbolic animals. The sacrificial lamb typified Him in His redemptive work as the "Lamb of God who takes away the sin of the world" (John 1:29). It portrayed Him as the Lord's servant who was led "like a lamb... to slaughter" (Isa. 53:7).

The other animal typifying Christ in the Old Testament is the lion (Gen. 49:9, 10). John, in Revelation 5:5, refers to this Old Testament metaphor when he describes Christ as the "Lion... from the tribe of Judah." As the king of the beasts, the lion represents kingly authority. The point is that out of the tribe of Judah would come a Ruler who would rule Israel and the world.

The two programs related

Although these two functions of Christ are inextricably related throughout the Bible, they are distinct in their purposes. The kingdom purpose is primarily for God, having to do with His reclaiming what was lost from His kingdom. The redemptive purpose relates primarily to man, providing the basis of his salvation. Though the kingdom purpose is broader, extending to the whole spiritual realm, it could not be accomplished without the redemptive program for man. Notice how John relates the two in his prophetic vision of Revelation 5. After seeing Christ as the Lion and Lamb, he hears the angelic throng loudly acclaim: "Worthy is the Lamb that was slain to receive power and riches and wisdom and might and honor and glory and blessing" (Rev. 5:12). He will have shown not only His right but His worthiness to rule as God's Lion, having been slain as God's Lamb. Before He moves in to destroy the kingdom of darkness with wrath, He had to walk the fires of judgment to salvage sinners, laying down His life as a lamb. These two roles then are inter-

Figure 1-4. God's Twofold Program

woven, but they reach in two directions and demonstrate two qualities of God's nature.

This reclaimed kingdom Christ will finally present back to the Father (1 Cor. 15:24). That presentation will constitute the fulfillment of His twofold commission from the Father in His role as the seed of the woman. And, of supreme importance, the process by which He will have reclaimed that kingdom will be through His redemptive love, not His coercive might. This redemptive grace is the genius of His twofold program, and it will also constitute the basis of His eternal fellowship with men. That divine-human fellowship will not be based on fear or force, but on love.

12. *The author outlines God's twofold program to deal with each aspect of His "problem." Through which two men of the Old Testament does He begin each part of the solution?*

_____

_____

13. *In what ways do their two sons typify the two aspects of the program?*

_____

_____

14. *How do two specific animals portray the redemptive and kingly functions of Jesus Christ?*

_____

_____

15. *What event will constitute the fulfillment of God's twofold program?*

_____

In counteracting the problem of rebellious mankind under the power of a satanic counterkingdom, God's redemptive and ruling purposes are intertwined.

- God aims to reestablish His rightful reign over all creation.

- God aims to reconcile people to Himself through Christ's death and the resurrection.

These two central purposes are the reason for His people's mission: that God's holy and loving rule would be extended throughout the earth, and people from every nation would be restored to fellowship with Him.

God's purposes on earth can be summarized:

1. To redeem a people from every people.
2. To rule a kingdom over all other kingdoms.

III. God's Plan

Immediately after Adam's and Eve's willful rebellion in the Garden of Eden, God committed Himself to a redemptive plan. How did man respond to God's initial overtures to reestablish their former relationship? Let us examine the emerging pattern found in Genesis 3-11 that has repeated itself throughout redemptive history.

Satan tempted Eve with the same temptation to which he fell prey. He wanted to be equal with God (Isa. 14:14), and that is what he promised Eve if she tasted of the forbidden fruit (Gen. 3:5). This desire to cast off God's Lordship has been at the root of man's sin problem from the very beginning.

In spite of this ingrained attitude of rebellion, God has always shown mercy and offered reconciliation. When Adam and Eve sinned and their eyes were opened to their nakedness, the Lord's first act was one of tender mercy: He provided garments of skin for them (Gen. 3:21) and removed their shame. Although they had to suffer the consequences of their sin and were expelled from the Garden, God continued to communicate with them and demonstrate loving concern for them.

The human race as a whole was not interested in accepting the restoration of God's sovereignty. With the multiplication of men came the multiplication of violence and wickedness. Genesis 6:5 records of man that "every intent of the thoughts of his heart was only evil continually." The Lord was deeply grieved by this conduct. Mankind again paid the consequences of sin, and the race was almost destroyed by a great flood. Yet God showed mercy by saving one righteous man, Noah, and his family and by giving them a new start. When Noah and his family descended from the ark, God reestablished His command to them to "be fruitful and multiply, and fill the earth" (Gen. 9:1).

Although guaranteed by covenant that God would never destroy the earth again by flood (Gen. 9:11), Noah's descendants were unwilling to trust in His faithfulness. They determined to protect themselves, building a great tower to escape any future flood. This action was also an attempt on their part to actively disobey God's command to go forth and fill the earth (Gen. 9:1, 7). The people wanted to make a name for themselves and resisted God's plan (Gen. 11:4).

God dealt firmly with this willful disobedience by confusing the people's language at Babel (Gen. 11:7-9). Unable to communicate with each other, mankind's rebellious attempt at unified self-sufficiency was frustrated. The nations were scattered, thus fulfilling God's intention to have them populate the entire world. From this initial dispersion arose the tremendous variety of ethnic groups, cultures, and languages that are found today.

Genesis 10:32 summarizes the situation, saying, "These are the families of the sons of Noah, ... and out of these the nations were separated on the earth after the flood." Scholars agree that Genesis 10 is one of the most complete listing of the nations that existed at the time. In typical Hebrew style of stating outcomes and then explaining how they came about, this list of 70 nations (the outcome) precedes the story of Babel (the event), which explains why they were divided. Immediately after the rebellion of Genesis 10 and 11, God begins the foundation of a new strategy: He will build a particular nation (through Abraham) to reach all the other nations.

When Jacob and his children relocated to Egypt, there were 70 members recorded in his family. It is as if God underlined His intent to reach all 70 nations. See Figure 1-5 for a listing of the many nations with which God's people had the opportunity to interact throughout their history.

PEOPLE GROUPS IN CONTACT WITH THE PEOPLE OF GOD, 2000 B.C. TO 3 B.C.	
PATRIARCHS *Genesis, Job*	Chaldeans, People of Ebla, People of Haran, Egyptians (Gen. 12); Canaanites, Perizzites (Gen. 13); Rephaites, Zuzites, Emites, Horites, Amalekites, Amorites (Gen. 14); Kenites, Kenizzites, Kadmonites, Hittites, Girgashites, Jebusites (Gen. 15); Moabites, Ammonites (Gen. 19); Philistines (Gerar, Gen. 20); Asshurites, Letushites, Leummites, Midianites, Ishmaelites, Arameans (Gen. 25); Hivites, Edomites (Gen. 36); Adullamites (Gen. 38)
SOJOURN IN EGYPT/ EXODUS *Exodus, Leviticus, Numbers, Deuteronomy, Joshua*	Midianites, Egyptians, Canaanites, Hittites, Amorites, Perizzites, Hivites, Jebusites (Ex. 3); Amalekites, Nephilim (Num. 13); Ammonites (Num. 21); Moabites (Num. 22)
JUDGES *Judges, Ruth, 1 Samuel*	Canaanites, Perizzites, Jebusites, Amorites, Sidonians, Hivites, Philistines (Phoenicians), Hittites, Jebusites, Amalekites, Moabites, Ammonites, Midianites, Abiezrites (Jud. 8); Maonites (Jud. 10); Egyptians
KINGS *2 Samuel, 1 & 2 Kings, 1 & 2 Chronicles, Psalms, Proverbs, Ecclesiastes, Song of Solomon, Isaiah, Jeremiah, Lamentations*	Philistines, Amalekites, Ammonites, Arameans, Philistines, Edomites, Moabites, Hittites, Gibeonites, Amorites, Hararites (2 Sam. 23); Egyptians, Phoenicians (Tyre and Sidon), Assyrians, Chaldeans, Sabeans (Queen of Sheba's people group)
BABYLONIAN EXILE *2 Kings, Ezra, Nehemiah, Esther, Daniel, Hosea through Malachi*	Assyrians, Babylonians, Chaldeans, Medes, Persians, Egyptians, Phoenicians, Moabites, Philistines
INTERTESTAMENTAL	Seleucids, Egyptians, Assyrians, Persians, Greeks, Romans, Berbers?, Celts?, Goths?

Figure 1-5

The Breadth of God's Purpose

While it is clear from Scripture that God desires that all men come into a right relationship with Him, it is apparent that not all men will do so. What is our responsibility in this matter? Many have asked, "What about those who have never heard?" In the following article, Robertson McQuilkin discusses the implications of these serious questions.

❑ *Lost* *

Robertson McQuilkin **

Have you ever experienced the terror of being lost—in some trackless mountain wilderness, perhaps, or in the labyrinth of a great, strange city? Hope of finding your way out fades and fear begins to seep in. You have likely seen that fear of lostness on the tear-streaked face of a child frantically screaming or quietly sobbing because he is separated from his parent in a huge shopping center. Lost.

Three of four people have never heard with understanding the way to life in Christ and, even more tragic, half the people of the world cannot hear because there is no one near enough to tell them.

Equally terrifying and more common is the feeling of being hopelessly entangled or trapped in a frustrating personal condition or circumstance: alcoholism, cancer, divorce. Incredibly alone! Lost.

The Bible uses the word "lost" to describe an even more terrible condition. Those who are away from the Father's house and haven't found the way back to Him are "lost." Jesus saw the crowds of people surging about Him as sheep without a shepherd, helpless and hopeless, and He was deeply moved.

Worse than being trapped and not knowing the way out is to be lost and not even know it, for then one does not look for salvation, recognize it when it comes, nor accept it when it is offered. That's being lost.

How many are lost in our world? We are told there are 200 million evangelicals.*** Some of these are lost, no doubt, but at least that many people believe Jesus is the only way of salvation and that through faith in Him one is forgiven and made a member of God's family. Surely some who are not evangelical have saving faith. So let us double the number to a hypothetical 400 million. Those who remain number more than four billion people or nine of every ten on earth. These are the lost—longing for salvation but not finding it, or trusting some other way to find meaning and hope.

The tragedy of this century of exploding population is that three of four people have never heard with understanding the way to life in Christ and, even more tragic, half the people of the world cannot hear because there is no one near enough to tell them. As we approach the end of the second millennium A.D., one of every two on planet earth lives in a tribe or culture or language group that has no evangelizing church at all. If someone does not go in from the outside, they have no way of knowing about Jesus.

But are these people in the "dark half of the world" really lost? What of those who have never had a chance, who have never heard—are *any* of them lost? Are *all* of them lost?

Universalism

Throughout church history there have been those who teach that none will finally be lost. The old universalism taught that all ultimately will be saved because God is good. Not much was heard of this position from the days of Origen in the third century until the 19th century when it was revived, especially by the Universalist Church. Simultaneously with the founding of the Universalist Church, which was honest enough to be up front about it and call itself by that name, the teaching began to spread in many mainline denominations.

There are problems with this position. Philosophically, such a teaching undermines belief in the aton-

---

* McQuilkin, R. (1984). *The great omission* (pp. 39-53). Grand Rapids: Baker Book House.

** Robertson McQuilkin was formerly the President and is now Chancellor at Columbia Biblical Seminary and Graduate School of Missions in Columbia, South Carolina. He is the author of several books, including *Understanding and Applying the Bible* and *The Great Omission*.

*** Ralph Winter places this estimate at 500 to 700 million.

ing death of Christ. For if all sin will ultimately be overlooked by a gracious deity, Christ never should have died. It was not only unnecessary, it was surely the greatest error in history, if not actually criminal on the part of God for allowing it to happen. Universalism, therefore, philosophically demands a view of the death of Christ as having some purpose other than as an atonement for sin.

Another problem the Universalists faced is that Scripture consistently teaches a division after death between those who are acceptable to God and those who are not. This teaching and that concerning the atonement are so strong in the Bible that Universalists did not accept the authority of Scripture. Thus the marriage between the Universalist Church and the Unitarian Church was quite natural.

The New Universalism

A New Universalism arose in the 20th century which took the Bible more seriously. It was Trinitarian. Christ did die for sinners, and *all* will ultimately be saved on the basis of Christ's provision.

Karl Barth and many of his neo-orthodox disciples took such a position. All will be saved because God is all-powerful. His purposes will be accomplished. And He purposes redemption.

There were philosophical and biblical problems with this position also. Philosophically, if all will be saved eventually, for whatever reason, preaching the gospel is not really necessary. Why did Christ make this the primary mission of the church if all will ultimately find acceptance with God with or without the gospel? The more serious problem is biblical: Christ clearly taught of an eternal hell of a great gulf between the saved and the lost (Luke 16:19-31). In fact, He clearly taught that the majority are on the broad road that leads to destruction (Matt. 7:13-14).

The Wider Hope Theory

Because Universalism cannot be reconciled with biblical data, there were those who promoted what was called a "Wider Hope." Not all will be saved, but many who have not heard of Christ will be saved because God is just and will not condemn the sincere seeker after truth. The problem is that if sincerity saves in religion, it is the only realm in which it saves. For example, it does not save in engineering. The architect who designed the magnificent John Hancock Building in Boston was sincere. The builder was sincere. The glassmaker was sincere. The owner, especially, was sincere. But when the giant sheets of glass began to fall on the streets below, sincerity did not atone for error. Neither does sincerity save in chemistry. We do not say, "If you drink arsenic, sincerely believing it to be Coca-Cola, according to your faith be it unto you." Sincerity does not alter reality. We shall consider the question of God's justice later.

The New Wider Hope Theory

The 19th century doctrine of the Wider Hope has been superseded by what I have called the "New Wider Hope." According to this teaching, those who live by the light they have may be saved on the merits of Christ's death through general revelation. Or, at least, they will be given a chance at death or after death. This is a more conservative version of the New Universalism. Richard Quebedeaux identifies this position as held by some "younger evangelicals," the New Left. A practical problem is that preaching the gospel seems almost criminal, for it brings with it greater condemnation for those who reject it, whereas they conceivably could have been saved through general revelation had they not heard the gospel. In any event, it certainly seems less urgent to proclaim the way of salvation to those who may well be saved without that knowledge. A mutation of this view is the idea that only those who reject the gospel will be lost. This viewpoint is not widespread because it makes bad news of the Good News! If people are lost only if they hear and reject, it is far better not to hear and be saved. On this view it would be better to destroy the message than to proclaim it!

16. *What common fault does the author find with the historical universalist positions he mentions?*

Only one way? Only one name?

For one committed to the authority of Scripture, our debate concerning the reasonableness of each position must yield to the authority of Scripture. What does Scripture teach concerning the eternal spiritual condition of those who have not heard the gospel?

> For God so loved the world that He gave His one and only Son that whoever believes in Him shall not perish but have eternal life. For God did not send His Son into the world to condemn the world, but to save the world through Him. Whoever believes in Him is not condemned, but whoever does not believe stands condemned already because he has not believed in the name of God's one and only Son.... Whoever believes in the Son has eternal life, but whoever rejects the Son will not see life, for God's wrath remains on him (John 3:16-18, 36).

Scripture teaches clearly that there are those who perish and those who do not. Notice that it is those who believe on *Christ*—not simply those who, through their encounter with creation and their own innate moral judgment, believe in a righteous Creator—who receive eternal life. God's intent is to "save the world through Him [Christ]" (3:17). The word "through" speaks of agency: it is by means of Jesus Christ that a person gains eternal life.

The passage does not deny other agencies, however. The Japanese proverb assures us that many roads lead up famed Mount Fuji, but they all reach the top. This is the Japanese way of expressing the viewpoint that all religions will have a good outcome. But Jesus Christ Himself said, "No one comes to the Father except through Me" (John 14:6). In other words, Jesus Christ is the *only* agency of salvation.

The New Wider Hope would affirm this. Salvation is by Jesus Christ alone. But, it would hold, that does not mean Jesus Christ must be known by a person for that person to be saved.

Jesus assures us that people will be judged because they have not believed on the name (John 3:18). Peter is even more explicit in telling us that there is no salvation in any other name given among men (Acts 4:12). Surely it is no accident that the name is so prominent in the Bible, especially in teaching on saving faith. Peter did not say, "in no other person." When a person is named, the identity is settled and ambiguity is done away. Peter does not make room for us to call on the Ground of Being or the great "all." You will be saved, he tells us, if you call on and believe in the name of Jesus of Nazareth, the Messiah. John, Jesus, and Peter are not the only ones with this emphasis. Paul also speaks to the issue:

> ... "Everyone who calls on the name of the Lord will be saved." How, then, can they call on the one they have not believed in? And how can they believe in the one of whom they have not heard? And how can they hear without someone preaching to them? And how can they preach unless they are sent? As it is written, "How beautiful are the feet of those who bring good news!" (Rom. 10:13-15).

The ones who call on the name are the ones who will be saved. But what of those who have not heard so they cannot call? Paul does not assure us that those who have not heard may simply believe on whatever they have heard. Rather, "faith comes from hearing the message, and the message is heard through the word of Christ" (Rom. 10:17).

Scripture is very clear that there are two kinds of people, both in life and in death: the saved and the lost. It is also very clear on the way of salvation. But still, for those who truly care, questions may remain: Is God loving, powerful, fair, just?

Is God loving? Yes, God is good and that is why men are lost. In love He created a being in His own image, not a robot programmed to respond as the Maker designed. In creating such a being to freely love and be loved, God risked the possibility of such a being rejecting His love in favor of independence or even self-love. Humankind did, in fact, choose this op-tion. Still true to His character, God provided a way back even though the cost was terrible. But the way back must not violate the image of God in man, must not force an obedient response. Rather, the God of love chooses to wait lovingly for the response of love. Those who wish to reject Him may do so.

17. According to McQuilkin, what does Scripture say a person has to know and do in order to be saved?

_____

_____

_____

God's judgment based on man's response to light received

But is it fair and just for God to condemn those who have not had an opportunity to respond to His offer of grace? The Bible does not teach that God will judge a person for rejecting Christ if he has not heard of Christ. In fact, the Bible teaches clearly that God's judgment is based on a person's response to the truth he has received.

God's judgment is based on a person's response to the truth he has received.

That servant who knows his master's will and does not get ready or does not do what his master wants will be beaten with many blows. But the one who does not know and does things deserving punishment will be beaten with few blows. From everyone who has been given much, much will be demanded; and from the one who has been entrusted with much, much more will be asked (Luke 12:47-48).

When you enter a town and are welcomed, eat what is set before you. Heal the sick who are there and tell them, "The kingdom of God is near you." But when you enter a town and are not welcomed, go into its streets and say, "Even the dust of your town that sticks to our feet we wipe off against you. Yet be sure of this: The kingdom of God is near." I tell you, it will be more bearable on that day for Sodom than for that town. Woe to you, Korazin! Woe to you, Bethsaida! For if the miracles that were performed in you had been performed in Tyre and Sidon, they would have repented long ago, sitting in sackcloth and ashes. But it will be more bearable for Tyre and Sidon at the judgment than for you. And you, Capernaum, will you be lifted up to the skies? No, you will go down to the depths. He who listens to you listens to Me; he who rejects you rejects Me; but he who rejects Me rejects Him who sent Me (Luke 10:8-16).

Judgment is against a person in proportion to his rejection of moral light. All have sinned; no one is innocent. Therefore, all stand condemned. But not all have the same measure of condemnation, for not all have sinned against equal amounts of light. God does not condemn a person who has not heard of Christ for rejecting Him, but rather for rejecting the light he does have.

Not all respond to the light they have by seeking to follow that light. But God's response to those who seek to obey the truth they have is the provision of more truth. To him who responds, more light will be given:

The disciples came to him and asked, "Why do you speak to the people in parables?" He replied, "The knowledge of the secrets of the kingdom of heaven has been given to you, but not to them. Whoever has will be given more, and he will have an abundance. Whoever does not have, even what he has will be taken from him. That is is why I speak to them in parables: Though seeing, they do not see; though hearing, they do not hear or understand. In them is fulfilled the prophecy of Isaiah: 'You will be ever hearing but never understanding; you will be ever seeing but never perceiving. For this people's heart has become calloused; they hardly hear with their ears, and they have closed their eyes. Otherwise they might see with their eyes, hear with their ears, understand with their hearts, and turn, and I would heal them.' But blessed are your eyes because they see, and your ears because they hear" (Matt. 13:10-16).

He said to them, "Do you bring in a lamp to put it under a bowl or a bed? Instead, don't you put it on its stand? For whatever is hidden is meant to be disclosed, and whatever is concealed is meant to be brought out into the open. If anyone has ears to hear, let him hear."

"Consider carefully what you hear," He continued. "With the measure you use, it will be measured to you—and even more. Whoever has will be given more; whoever does not have, even what he has will be taken from him" (Mark 4:21-25).

This repeated promise of additional light to those who obey the light they have is a basic and very important biblical truth concerning God's justice and judgment.

This repeated promise of additional light to those who obey the light they have is a basic and very important biblical truth concerning God's justice and judgment. Cornelius, the Roman officer, responded to the light he had with prayer and good deeds. God did not leave him in ignorance and simply accept him on the basis of his response to the initial light he had received. God sent Peter to him with additional truth (Acts 10). To him who had, more was given. Since this is revealed as God's way of dealing with men, we can be very sure that every person has received adequate light to which he may respond. God's existence and His power are made clearly evident to all people through creation (Rom. 1:18-21) and through each person's innate moral judgment or conscience (Rom. 2:14, 15). To the one who responds obediently, God will send additional light.

Of course, His method for sending this light is a human messenger. Paul makes clear in his letter to the church at Rome (10:14, 15) that the solution to the terrible lost condition of men is the preacher who is sent, the "beautiful feet" of him who goes. Ultimately, then, the problem is not with God's righteousness, but with ours.

In conclusion: Our responsibility

But suppose no one goes? Will God send some angel or some other special revelation? On this, Scripture is silent and, I believe, for good reason. Even if God did have such an alternative plan, were He to reveal that to us, we who have proved so irresponsible and disobedient would no doubt cease altogether obedience to the Great Commission.

But the question will not go away. How does one respond in a Japanese village when a new convert inquires, "What about my ancestors?" My response is simple: I am not the judge. "Will not the Judge of all the earth do right?" (Gen. 18:25). Abraham was pleading with God for the salvation of innocent people who did not deserve to be condemned and destroyed along with the guilty. He was appealing to God's justice, and God responded with grace more than Abraham dared ask. This crucial question recorded in the first book of the Bible is answered in the last: "Yes, Lord God Almighty, true and just are your judgments" (Rev. 16:7). We are not called as judge—either of God, whose ways we do not fully know, nor of man, whose destiny we are not called upon to settle. Rather, we are commissioned as His representatives to find the lost, declare amnesty to the captive, release the prisoner.

We may not be able to prove from Scripture with absolute certainty that no soul since Pentecost has ever been saved by extraordinary means without the knowledge of Christ. But neither can we prove from Scripture that a single soul has been so saved. If there is an alternative, God has not told us of it. If God in His revelation felt it mandatory not to proffer such a hope, how much more should we refrain from such theorizing. It may or may not be morally right for me to think there may be another way and to hope there is some other escape. But for me to propose it to other believers, to discuss it as a possibility, is certainly dangerous, if not immoral. It is almost as wrong as writing out such a hope so that those who are under the judgment of God may read it, take hope, and die. So long as the truth revealed to us identifies only one way of escape, this is what we must live by and proclaim.

The lost condition of human beings breaks the Father's heart. What does it do to ours?

Consider the analogy of a security guard charged with the safety of residents on the 10th floor of a nursing home. He knows the floor plan posted in a prominent place, and it is his responsibility in case of fire to get the residents to the fire escape which has been clearly marked. Should a fire break out and lives be put in jeopardy, it would be his responsibility to get those people to the fire escape. If he discusses with the patients or with a colleague the possibility of some other unmarked fire escape or recalls to them the news report he read of someone who had jumped from the 10th floor of a building and survived, he could surely be charged with criminal negligence. He must live and labor in obedience to the facts that are certain and not delay to act. He must not lead people astray on the basis of conjecture or logical deduction from limited information.

When all has been said that can be said on this issue, the greatest remaining mystery is not the character of God nor the destiny of lost people. The greatest mystery is why those who are charged with rescuing the lost have spent two thousand years doing other things, good things, perhaps, but have failed to send and be sent until all have heard the liberating word of life in Christ Jesus. The lost condition of human beings breaks the Father's heart. What does it do to ours?

In a dream I found myself on an island—Sheep Island. Across the island sheep were scattered and lost. Soon I learned that a forest fire was sweeping across from the opposite side. It seemed that all were doomed to destruction unless there were some way of escape. Although there were many unofficial maps, I had a copy of the official map and there discovered that indeed there is a bridge to the mainland, a narrow bridge, built, it was said, at incredible cost.

My job, I was told, would be to get the sheep across that bridge. I discovered many shepherds herding the sheep who were found and seeking to corral those who were within easy access to the bridge. But most of the sheep were far off and the shepherds seeking them few. The sheep near the fire knew they were in trouble and were frightened; those at a distance were peacefully grazing, enjoying life.

I noticed two shepherds near the bridge whispering to one another and laughing. I moved near them to hear the cause of joy in such a dismal setting. "Perhaps the chasm is narrow somewhere, and at least the strong sheep have opportunity to save themselves," said one. "Maybe the current is gentle and the stream shallow. Then the courageous, at least, can make it across." The other responded, "That may well be. In fact, wouldn't it be great if this proves to be no island at all? Perhaps it is just a peninsula and great multitudes of sheep are already safe. Surely the owner would have provided some alternative route." And so they relaxed and went about other business.

In my mind I began to ponder their theories: Why would the owner have gone to such great expense to build a bridge, especially since it is a narrow bridge, and many of the sheep refuse to cross it even when they find it? In fact, if there is a better way by which many will be saved more easily, building the bridge is a terrible blunder. And if this isn't an island, after all, what is to keep the fire from sweeping right across into the mainland and destroying everything? As I pondered these things I heard a quiet voice behind me saying, "There is a better reason than the logic of it, my friend. Logic alone could lead you either way. Look at your map."

There on the map, by the bridge, I saw a quotation from the first undershepherd, Peter: "For neither is there salvation in any other, for there is no other way from the island to the mainland whereby a sheep may be saved." And then I discerned, carved on the old rugged bridge itself, "I am the bridge. No sheep escapes to safety but by me."

In a world in which nine of every ten people are lost, three of four have never heard the way out, and one of every two cannot hear, the church sleeps on. "How come?" Could it be we think there must be some other way? Or perhaps we don't really care that much.

18. *What relationship is likely to exist between a person's conviction about the lostness of man without Christ and his or her conviction about mission work?*

_____

_____

_____

As McQuilkin notes, we can't always have everything figured out. If God's redemptive purpose is to include more than those who call on His name for salvation, He hasn't chosen to reveal that to us. In the meantime, let's focus on what we do know about His plan and our role in it.

Summary

If God had not intended to redeem mankind and reestablish His loving rule, then He would have had no reason to give us His revelation, the Bible. Mission is the basis of the Bible, and the Bible is our manual for understanding God's mission. It reveals God's mandate, message, and model for mission, as well as His power for its fulfillment.

We begin our search for understanding God's ultimate purpose by examining events surrounding the dawn of creation. Satan's and man's rebellions posed a twofold "problem" for God. Instead of destroying everyone, He determined to provide a means to redeem mankind and reestablish His sovereignty.

While God desires that all men be saved, there is no biblical evidence to support the assumption that they *will* be saved apart from God's redemptive provision. Only through "hearing of the Word" can men come to a knowledge of the "narrow way."

Integrative Assignment

The questions in the Integrative Assignment in each chapter are designed to help you synthesize the material that has been presented. Since some questions may require fairly lengthy answers, we have not provided space in this workbook for you to write but suggest instead that you use your own paper for these assignments.

1. *Why are God's redemptive mission and the Bible indispensable to each other? Make an outline of the points you would use in proving this assertion to a somewhat skeptical audience.*

2. *Many unbelievers are confused by the problem of evil. They ask, "If God is the God of love, how can He permit evil in the world?" From your present understanding of God's purpose and Satan's and man's rebellion, how would you explain the presence of evil in the world and what God is doing about it?*

3. *Universalism is a subtle and often unchallenged belief in the church. Have you settled this issue in your own mind? From the evidence presented by McQuilkin and your own reflection, state your position and outline your supporting arguments.*

Questions for Reflection

The Questions for Reflection are intended for your own reflection and meditation. You will not be asked to turn in your answers, although you may want to share some of your impressions with others from time to time. Be honest with yourself and with the Lord. You will find that this simple exercise will do much to help you measure progress on your spiritual journey.

1. *Reread Genesis 1-12. What has impressed you most in this study regarding the purpose and plan of God for the ages?*

_____

_____

_____

_____

_____

_____

_____

_____

_____

_____

_____

2. The rebellious nature of man's heart was demonstrated repeatedly in Genesis 1-11. Is it still a problem today? Examine your own heart over Psalm 51.

_____

_____

_____

_____

_____

_____

_____

_____

_____

_____

3. As believers, none of us is exempt from serving our King in His great cause. How does He expect you to serve? Set apart a daily time to study His Word and to seek His will. Record your thoughts and impressions.

_____

_____

_____

_____

_____

_____

_____

_____

_____

_____

_____

CHAPTER 2

Israel, the Covenant People

*"And I will establish My covenant between Me and you
and your descendants after you throughout their generations
for an everlasting covenant ..." (Gen. 17:7)*

The first chapter of our study traced mankind's rebellion from Adam's and Eve's initial sin, through the conditions which brought about the flood, and on to the third great failure at Babel. By rejecting God's dominion and choosing a life of self-exaltation and self-rule, the human race placed itself under Satan's chaotic control. In spite of mankind's rebellious heart, God in His mercy chose to begin a salvage operation outlined briefly in the proto-evangel given to Adam in Genesis 3:15.

God initiated His plan by approaching a man named Abram in Ur of the Chaldees (presently Iraq). The Lord made a proposal to Abram, which has become known as the "Abrahamic Covenant" (Gen. 12:1-3). This covenant was not a narrowing of His concern to one man or one people, but the creation of a nation for a worldwide mission: to communicate His redemptive message to all the other nations. God would no longer deal with people in a general way but would aim at reaching them nation by nation.

Much of the Old Testament is the account of how the Hebrew people came into being, their response to the opportunities God gave them to fulfill their covenant obligations, and the consequences of their actions. The Old Testament can be better understood by keeping these three points in mind:

1. *Obligation* – Israel was created with the expectation that she would be a blessing to all other nations.

2. *Opportunity* – Israel was given the means and the opportunities to fulfill her charge to be a blessing.

3. *Response* – Israel failed to respond voluntarily to her part of the covenant. God continually reminded Israel of her obligation and used her to touch the nations regardless of her disobedience.

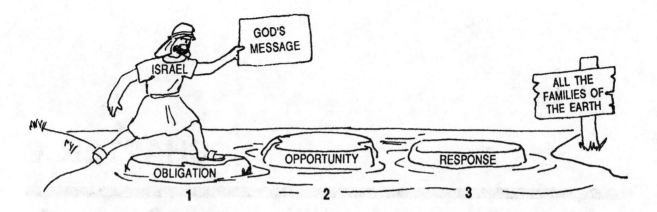

When viewed from this perspective, all of the events in the Old Testament take on new significance. Instead of simply presenting the Old Testament as a series of historical and cultural events in the life of a struggling people whom God chose for His own reasons, this outline shows purpose and planning behind each incident. Familiar Old Testament accounts take on new meaning when read with God's mission to the nations in mind. You will need your Bible alongside you to explore this study.

I. The Abrahamic Covenant

Throughout the ages, God's relationship with the human race has been expressed in various covenants found in the Bible. These contracts with Adam, Noah, Abraham, Moses, and David have provided clear expressions of God's intended relationship with His people. In our study of world mission, the Abrahamic Covenant is of particular significance. In the following article, John Stott gives an in-depth explanation of the importance of the Abrahamic Covenant to the entire missionary enterprise.

❑ *The Living God Is a Missionary God* *

John R. W. Stott

Millions of people in today's world are extremely hostile to the Christian missionary enterprise. They regard it as politically disruptive (because it loosens the cement which binds the national culture) and religiously narrow minded (because it makes exclusive claims for Jesus), while those who are involved in it are thought to suffer from an arrogant imperialism.

And the attempt to convert people to Christ is rejected as an unpardonable interference in their private lives. "My religion is my own affair," they say. "Mind your own business, and leave me alone to mind mine."

It is essential, therefore, for Christians to understand the grounds on which the Christian mission rests. Only then shall we be able to persevere in the missionary task, with courage and humility, in spite of the world's misunderstanding and opposition. More precisely, biblical Christians need biblical incentives. For we believe the Bible to be the reve-

* Stott, J. R. W. (1992). The living God is a missionary God. In R. D. Winter & S. C. Hawthorne (Eds.), *Perspectives on the world Christian movement: A reader* (rev. ed.) (pp. A10-A18). Pasadena: William Carey Library.

lation of God and of His will. So we ask: Has He revealed in Scripture that "mission" is His will for His people? Only then shall we be satisfied. For then it becomes a matter of obeying God, whatever others may think or say. Here we shall focus on the Old Testament, though the entire Bible is rich in evidence for the missionary purpose of God.

The call of Abraham

Our story begins about four thousand years ago with a man called Abraham, or more accurately, Abram as he was called at that time. Here is the account of God's call to Abraham.

> The Lord had said to Abram, "Leave your country, your people, and your father's household and go to the land I will show you. I will make you into a great nation and I will bless you; I will make your name great, and you will be a blessing. I will bless those who bless you, and whoever curses you I will curse; and all peoples on earth will be blessed through you." So Abram left, as the Lord had told him; and Lot went with him. Abram was seventy-five years old when he set out from Haran (Gen. 12:1-4).

God made a promise (a composite promise, as we shall see) to Abraham. And an understanding of that promise is indispensable to an understanding of the Bible and of the Christian mission. These are perhaps the most unifying verses in the Bible; the whole of God's purpose is encapsulated here.

By way of introduction, we shall need to consider the setting of God's promise, the context in which it came to be given. Then we shall divide the rest of our study into two. First, *the promise* (exactly what it was that God said He would do) and second—at greater length—*its fulfillment* (how God has kept and will keep His promise). We start, however, with the setting.

Genesis 12 begins: "Now the Lord said to Abram." It sounds abrupt for an opening of a new chapter. We are prompted to ask: "Who is this 'Lord' who spoke to Abraham?" and "Who is this 'Abraham' to whom He spoke?" They are not introduced into the text out of the blue. A great deal lies behind these words. They are a key which opens up the whole of Scripture. The previous eleven chapters lead up to them; the rest of the Bible follows and fulfills them.

What, then, is the background to this text? It is this. "The Lord" who chose and called Abraham is the same Lord who in the beginning created the heavens and the earth, and who climaxed His creative work by making man and woman unique creatures in His own likeness. In other words, we should never allow ourselves to forget that the Bible begins with the universe, not with the planet earth; then with the earth, not with Palestine; then with Adam the father of the human race, not with Abraham the father of the chosen race. Since, then, God is the Creator of the universe, the earth, and all mankind, we must never demote Him to the status of a tribal deity or petty godling like Chemosh the god of the Moabites, or Milcom (or Molech) the god of the Ammonites, or Baal the male deity, or Ashtoreth the female deity, of the Canaanites. Nor must we suppose that God chose Abraham and his descendants because He had lost interest in other peoples or given them up. Election is not a synonym for elitism. On the contrary, as we shall soon see, God chose one man and his family in order, through them, to bless *all* the families of the earth.

> *Genesis 12:1-4 are perhaps the most unifying verses in the Bible; the whole of God's purpose is encapsulated here.*

We are bound, therefore, to be deeply offended when Christianity is relegated to one chapter in a book on the world's religions as if it were one option among many, or when people speak of "the Christian God" as if there were others! No, there is only one living and true God, who has revealed Himself fully and finally in His only Son Jesus Christ. Monotheism lies at the basis of mission. As Paul wrote to Timothy, "There is one God, and there is one mediator between God and men, the man Christ Jesus" (1 Tim. 2:5).

The Genesis record moves on from the creation of all things by the one God and of human beings in His likeness, to our rebellion against our own Creator and to God's judgment upon His rebel creatures—a judgment which is relieved, however, by

His first gospel promise that one day the woman's seed would "bruise," indeed "crush," the serpent's head (3:15).

The following eight chapters (Genesis 4-11) describe the devastating results of the Fall in terms of the progressive alienation of human beings from God and from our fellow human beings. This was the setting in which God's call and promise came to Abraham. All around was moral deterioration, darkness, and dispersal. Society was steadily disintegrating. Yet God the Creator did not abandon the human beings He had made in His own likeness (Gen. 9:6). Out of the prevailing godlessness He called one man and his family, and promised to bless not only them but through them the whole world. The scattering would not proceed unchecked; a grand process of ingathering would now begin.

---

1. Why is it so important to establish the identity of the Lord who spoke to Abraham?

Stott continues by describing God's promise to Abraham, followed by the stages of the fulfillment of that promise.

The promise

What then was the promise which God made to Abraham? It was a composite promise consisting of several parts.

First, it was the promise of *a posterity*. He was to go from his kindred and his father's house, and in exchange for the loss of his family God would make of him "a great nation." Later, in order to indicate this, God changed his name from "Abram" ("exalted father") to "Abraham" ("father of a multitude") because, He said to him, "I have made you the father of a multitude of nations" (17:5).

Second, it was the promise of *a land*. God's call seems to have come to him in two stages, first in Ur of the Chaldees while his father was still alive (11:31; 15:7) and then in Haran after his father had died (11:32; 12:1). At all events he was to leave his own land, and in return God would show him another country.

Third, it was the promise of *a blessing*. Five times the words *bless* and *blessing* occur in 12:2-3. The blessing God promised Abraham would spill over upon all mankind.

A posterity, a land, and a blessing. Each of these promises is elaborated in the chapters that follow Abraham's call.

First, *the land*. After Abraham had generously allowed his nephew Lot to choose where he wanted to settle (he selected the fertile Jordan valley), God said to Abraham: "Lift up your eyes, and look from the place where you are, northward and southward and eastward and westward; for all the land which you see I will give to you and to your descendants for ever" (13:14-15).

Second, *the posterity*. A bit later God gave Abraham another visual aid, telling him to look now not to the earth but to the sky. On a clear, dark night He took him outside his tent and said to him, "Look toward heaven and number the stars." What a ludicrous command! Perhaps Abraham started, "1, 2, 3, 5, 10, 20, 30…," but he must soon have given up. It was an impossible task. Then God said to him: "So shall your descendants be." And we read: "He believed the Lord." Although he was probably by now in his eighties, and although he and Sarah were still childless, he yet believed God's promise, and God "reckoned it to him as righteousness." That is, because he trusted God, God accepted him as righteous in His sight.

Third, *the blessing*. "I will bless you." Already God has accepted Abraham as righteous or (to borrow the New Testament expression) has "justified him by faith." No greater blessing is conceivable. It is the foundation blessing of the covenant of grace, which a few years later God went on to elaborate to Abraham: "I will establish my covenant between me and you and your descendants after you... for an everlasting covenant, to be God to you and to your

descendants after you... and I will be their God" (17:7-8). And He gave them circumcision as the outward and visible sign of His gracious covenant or pledge to be their God. It is the first time in Scripture that we hear the covenant formula which is repeated many times later: "I will be their God and they shall be my people."

A land, a posterity, a blessing. "But what has all that to do with mission?" you may be asking with impatience. My answer is, "Everything! Be patient a little longer and you will see." Let us turn now from the promise to the fulfillment.

2. Describe in your own words what God promised Abraham.

_____

_____

_____

The fulfillment

The whole question of the fulfillment of Old Testament prophecy is a difficult one in which there is often misunderstanding and not a little disagreement. Of particular importance is the principle, with which I think all of us will agree, that the New Testament writers themselves understood Old Testament prophecy to have not a *single* but usually a *triple* fulfillment—past, present, and future. The past fulfillment was an immediate or historical fulfillment in the life of the nation of Israel. The present is an intermediate or gospel fulfillment in Christ and His church. The future will be an ultimate or eschatological fulfillment in the new heaven and the new earth.

1. Immediate fulfillment

God's promise to Abraham received an immediate historical fulfillment in his physical descendants, the people of Israel.

God's promise to Abraham of a numerous, indeed of an innumerable, posterity was confirmed to his son Isaac (26:4, "as the stars of heaven") and his grandson Jacob (32:12, "as the sand of the sea"). Gradually the promise began to come literally true.

Perhaps we could pick out some of the stages in this development.

The first concerns the years of slavery in Egypt, of which it is written, "The descendants of Israel were fruitful and increased greatly; they multiplied and grew exceedingly strong; so that the land was filled with them" (Ex. 1:7; cf. Acts 7:17). The next stage I will mention came several hundred years later when King Solomon called Israel "a great people that cannot be numbered or counted for multitude" (1 Kings 3:8). A third stage was some three hundred fifty years after Solomon; Jeremiah warned Israel of impending judgment and captivity, and then added this divine promise of restoration: "As the host of heaven cannot be numbered and the sands of the sea cannot be measured, so I will multiply the descendants of David my servant" (Jer. 33:22).

So much for Abraham's posterity; what about the land? Again we note with worship and gratitude God's faithfulness to His promise. For it was in remembrance of His promise to Abraham, Isaac, and Jacob that He first rescued His people from their Egyptian slavery and gave them the territory which came on that account to be called "the promised land" (Ex. 2:24; 3:6; 32:13), and then restored them to it some seven hundred years later after their captivity in Babylon. Nevertheless, neither Abraham nor his physical descendants fully inherited the land. As Hebrews 11 puts it, they "died in faith *not having received what was promised.*" Instead, as "strangers and exiles on the earth" they "looked forward to the city which has foundations, whose builder and maker is God" (see Heb. 11:8-16, 39-40).

God kept His promises about the posterity and the land, at least in part. Now what about the blessing? Well, at Sinai God confirmed and clarified His covenant with Abraham, and pledged Himself to be Israel's God (for example, Ex. 19:3-6). And throughout the rest of the Old Testament God went on blessing the obedient while the disobedient fell under His judgment.

Perhaps the most dramatic example comes at the beginning of Hosea's prophecy, in which Hosea is told to give his three children names which describe God's awful and progressive judgment on Israel. His firstborn (a boy) he called "Jezreel," meaning "God will scatter." Next came a daughter, "Loruhamah," meaning "not pitied," for God said He would no longer pity or forgive His people. Lastly he had another son, "Lo-ammi," meaning "not my people," for God said they were not now His people. What terrible names for the chosen people of God! They sound like a devastating contradiction of God's eternal promise to Abraham.

But God does not stop there. For beyond the coming judgment there would be a restoration, which is described in words which once more echo the promise to Abraham: "Yet the number of the people of Israel shall be like the sand of the sea, which can be neither measured nor numbered" (Hos. 1:10). And then the judgments implicit in the names of Hosea's children would be reversed. There would be a gathering instead of a scattering ("Jezreel" is ambiguous and can imply either), "not pitied" would be pitied, and "not my people" would become "sons of the living God" (1:10–2:1).

The wonderful thing is that the Apostles Paul and Peter both quote these verses from Hosea. They see their fulfillment not just in a further multiplication of Israel but in the inclusion of the Gentiles in the community of Jesus: "Once you were no people but now you are God's people; once you had not received mercy but now you have received mercy" (1 Pet. 2:9-10; cf. Rom. 9:25-26).

This New Testament perspective is essential as we read the Old Testament prophecies. For what we miss in the Old Testament is any clear explanation of just *how* God's promised blessing would overflow from Abraham and his descendants to "all families of the earth." Although Israel is described as "a light to lighten the nations," and has a mission to "bring forth justice to the nations" (Isa. 42:1-4, 6; 49:6), we do not actually see this happening. It is only in the Lord Jesus Himself that these prophecies are fulfilled, for only in His day are the nations actually included in the redeemed community. To this we now turn.

3. *How did God's promises of a posterity, a land, and a blessing set the stage for His plans for all nations?*

_____

_____

_____

2. Intermediate fulfillment

God's promise to Abraham receives an intermediate or gospel fulfillment in Christ and His church.

Almost the first word of the whole New Testament is the word "Abraham." For Matthew's Gospel begins, "The book of the genealogy of Jesus Christ, the son of David, the son of Abraham. Abraham was the father of Isaac...." So it is right back to Abraham that Matthew traces the beginning not just of the genealogy but of the gospel of Jesus Christ. He knows that what he is recording is the fulfillment of God's ancient promises to Abraham some two thousand years previously (see also Luke 1:45-55, 67-75).

Part of God's covenant with Abraham promised an overspill of blessing to all the nations of the earth.

Yet from the start Matthew recognizes that it isn't just *physical* descent from Abraham which qualifies people to inherit the promises, but a kind of *spiritual* descent, namely, repentance and faith in the coming Messiah. This was John the Baptist's message to crowds who flocked to hear him: "Do not presume to say to yourselves, 'We have Abraham as our father'; for I tell you, God is able from these stones to raise up children to Abraham" (Matt. 3:9; Luke 3:8; cf. John 8:33-40). The implications of his words would have shocked his hearers since "it was the current belief that no descendant of Abraham could be lost." *

And God has raised up children to Abraham, if not from stones, then from an equally unlikely source, namely, the Gentiles! So Matthew, although the most Jewish of all four Gospel writers, later records Jesus as having said, "I tell you, many will come from east and west and sit at table with Abraham, Isaac, and Jacob in the kingdom of heaven, while the sons of the kingdom will be thrown into the outer darkness" (8:11-12; cf. Luke 13:28-29).

It is hard for us to grasp how shocking, how completely topsy-turvy, these words would have sounded to the Jewish hearers of John the Baptist and Jesus. *They* were the descendants of Abraham; so *they* had a title to the promises which God made to Abraham. Who then were these outsiders who were to share in the promises, even apparently usurp them, while they themselves would be disqualified? They were indignant. They had quite forgotten that part of God's covenant with Abraham promised an overspill of blessing to *all* the nations of the earth. Now the Jews had to learn that it was in relation to Jesus the Messiah, who was Himself seed of Abraham, that all the nations would be blessed.

The Apostle Peter seems at least to have begun to grasp this in his second sermon, just after Pentecost. In it he addressed a Jewish crowd with the words: "You are heirs... of the covenant God made with your fathers. He said to Abraham, 'Through your offspring all peoples on earth will be blessed.' When God raised up His servant [Jesus], He sent Him first to you to bless you by turning each of you from your wicked ways" (Acts 3:25-26). It is a very notable statement because he interprets the blessing in the moral terms of repentance and righteousness and because, if Jesus was sent "first" to the Jews, He was presumably sent next to the Gentiles, whose "families of the earth" had been "far off" (cf. Acts 2:39) but were now to share in the blessing.

It was given to the Apostle Paul, however, to bring this wonderful theme to its full development. For he was called and appointed to be the apostle to the Gentiles, and to him was revealed God's eternal but hitherto secret purpose to make Jews and the Gentiles "fellow heirs, members of the same body, and partakers of the promise in Christ Jesus through the gospel" (Eph. 3:6).

Negatively, Paul declares with great boldness, "Not all who are descended from Israel belong to Israel, and not all are children of Abraham because they are his descendants" (Rom. 9:6-7).

---

* Jeremias, J. (1948). *Jesus' promise to the nations* (p. 48). SCM Press.

Who then are the true descendants of Abraham, the true beneficiaries of God's promises to him? Paul does not leave us in any doubt. They are believers in Christ of whatever race. In Romans 4 he points out that Abraham not only received justification by faith but also received this blessing *before he had been circumcised*. Therefore Abraham is the father of all those who, whether circumcised or uncircumcised (that is, Jews or Gentiles), "follow the example of [his] faith" (Rom. 4:9-12). If we "share the faith of Abraham," then "he is the father of us all, as it is written, 'I have made you the father of many nations'" (vv. 16-17). Thus neither physical descent from Abraham, nor physical circumcision as a Jew, makes a person a true child of Abraham, but rather faith. Abraham's real descendants are believers in Jesus Christ, whether racially they happen to be Jews or Gentiles.

What then is the "land" which Abraham's descendants inherit? The letter to the Hebrews refers to a "rest" which God's people enter now by faith (Heb. 4:3). And in a most remarkable expression Paul refers to "the promise to Abraham and his descendants, that they should *inherit the world*" (Rom. 4:13). One can only assume he means the same thing as when to the Corinthians he writes that in Christ

"all things are yours, whether Paul or Apollos or Cephas or the world or life or death or the present or the future, all are yours" (1 Cor. 3:21-23). Christians by God's wonderful grace are joint heirs with Christ of the universe.

Somewhat similar teaching, both about the nature of the promised blessing and about its beneficiaries, is given by Paul in Galatians 3. He first repeats how Abraham was justified by faith, and then continues: "So you see that it is men of faith who are the sons of Abraham" and who therefore "are blessed with Abraham who had faith" (vv. 6-9). What then is the blessing with which all the nations were to be blessed (v. 8)? In a word, it is the blessing of salvation. We were under the curse of the law, but Christ has redeemed us from it by becoming a curse in our place, in order "that in Christ Jesus the blessing of Abraham might come upon the Gentiles, that we might receive the promise of the Spirit through faith" (vv. 10-14). Christ bore our curse that we might inherit Abraham's blessing, the blessing of justification (v. 8) and of the indwelling Holy Spirit (v. 14). Paul sums it up in the last verse of the chapter (v. 29): "If you are Christ's, then you are Abraham's offspring, heirs according to promise."

---

4. *How do the New Testament writers interpret and apply the three elements of the Abrahamic Covenant?*

But we have not quite finished yet. There is a third stage of fulfillment still to come.

3. Ultimate fulfillment

God's promise to Abraham will receive an ultimate or eschatological fulfillment in the final destiny of all the redeemed.

In the book of Revelation there is one more reference to God's promise to Abraham (7:9ff). John sees in a vision "a great multitude which no man could number." It is an international throng, drawn "from

every nation, from all tribes and peoples and tongues." And they are "standing before the throne," the symbol of God's kingly reign. That is, His kingdom has finally come, and they are enjoying all the blessings of His gracious rule. He shelters them with His presence. Their wilderness days of hunger, thirst, and scorching heat are over. They have entered the promised land at last, described now not as "a land flowing with milk and honey" but as a land irrigated from "springs of living water" which never dry up. But how did they come to inherit these blessings? Partly because they have "come out of great tribulation" (evidently a reference to the Christian life with all its trials and sufferings), but mostly because "they have washed their robes and made them white in the blood of the Lamb," that is, they have been cleansed from sin and clothed with righteousness through the merits of the death of Jesus Christ alone. "*Therefore* are they before the throne of God."

Speaking personally, I find it extremely moving to glimpse this final fulfillment in a future eternity of that ancient promise of God to Abraham. All the essential elements of the promise may be detected.

For here are the spiritual descendants of Abraham, a "great multitude which no man could number," as countless as the sand on the seashore and as the stars in the night sky. Here too are "all the families of the earth" being blessed, for the numberless multitude is composed of people from every nation. Here also is the promised land, namely, all the rich blessings which flow from God's gracious rule. And here above all is Jesus Christ, the seed of Abraham, who shed His blood for our redemption and who bestows His blessings on all those who call on Him to be saved.

5. *How does the book of Revelation show Abraham's blessing passed on to all the nations of the earth?*

_____

_____

_____

Stott summarizes his conclusions below.

Conclusion

Let me try to summarize what we learn about God from His promise to Abraham and its fulfillment.

First, He is the God of history. History is not a random flow of events. For God is working out in time a plan which He conceived in a past eternity and will consummate in a future eternity. In this historical process Jesus Christ as the seed of Abraham is the key figure. Let's rejoice that if we are Christ's disciples we are Abraham's descendants. We belong to His spiritual lineage. If we have received the blessings of justification by faith, acceptance with God, and of the indwelling Spirit, then we are beneficiaries today of a promise made to Abraham four thousand years ago.

Second, He is the God of the covenant. That is, God is gracious enough to make promises, and He always keeps the promises He makes. He is a God of steadfast love and faithfulness. Mind you, He does not always fulfill His promises immediately. Abraham and Sarah "died in faith *not* having received what

was promised, but having seen it and greeted it from afar" (Heb. 11:13). That is, although Isaac was born to them in fulfillment of the promise, their seed was not yet numerous, nor was the land given to them, nor were the nations blessed. All God's promises come true, but they are inherited "through faith *and patience*" (Heb. 6:12). We have to be content to wait for God's time.

Third, He is the God of blessing. "I will bless you," He said to Abraham (Gen. 12:2). "God… sent Him [Jesus] to you first, to bless you," echoed Peter (Acts 3:26). God's attitude to His people is positive, constructive, enriching. Judgment is His "strange work" (Isa. 28:21). His principal and characteristic work is to bless people with salvation.

Fourth, He is the God of mercy. I have always derived much comfort from the statement of Revelation 7:9 that the company of the redeemed in heaven will be "a great multitude which no man could number." I do not profess to know how this can be, since Christians have always seemed to be a rather small minority. But Scripture states it for our comfort. Although no biblical Christian can be a universalist (believing that all mankind will ultimately be saved), since Scripture teaches the awful reality and eternity of hell, yet a biblical Christian can—even must—assert that the redeemed will somehow be an international throng so immense as to be countless. For God's promise is going to be fulfilled, and Abraham's seed is going to be as innumerable as the dust of the earth, the stars of the sky, and the sand on the seashore.

Fifth, He is the God of mission. The nations are not gathered in automatically. If God has promised to bless "all the families of the earth," He has promised to do so "through Abraham's seed" (Gen. 12:3; 22:18). Now we are Abraham's seed by faith, and the earth's families will be blessed only if we go to them with the gospel. That is God's plain purpose.

I pray that these words, "all the families of the earth," may be written on our hearts. It is this expression more than any other which reveals the living God of the Bible to be a missionary God. It is this expression too which condemns all our petty parochialism and narrow nationalism, our racial pride (whether white or black), our condescending paternalism and arrogant imperialism. How dare we adopt a hostile or scornful or even indifferent attitude to any person of another color or culture if our God is the God of "all the families of the earth"? We need to become global Christians with a global vision, for we have a global God.

So may God help us never to forget His four-thousand-year-old promise to Abraham: "By you and your descendants *all* the nations of the earth shall be blessed."

---

6. **What does God expect of Abram beyond simply enjoying the blessings He promised?**

_____

_____

7. **What did Abram have to do to accept the covenant relationship?**

_____

_____

The Hebrew word for covenant is a term used in ancient times to signify the formal agreement by which one man bound himself to another as his vassal. In such an agreement, both parties had obligations to fulfill. The vassal was to be totally loyal to his overlord, performing military and other duties in exchange for protection and other benefits. Don Richardson has used the popular term "top line" to express the benefits offered by God in the covenant and "bottom line" to denote the obligations incurred by Abram. Then as now, the effectiveness of such an agreement depends on the faithfulness with which the members uphold their parts. When one of the parties does not carry out his or her obligation, force may be needed to get the unfaithful member to comply.

8. **Why does the covenant with Abraham carry mandate force?**

_____

_____

II. The Covenant Is Established

At various times in Abraham's life, God reiterated the covenant terms to him, expanding Abraham's understanding of what his benefits and responsibilities involved.

9. *Read Genesis 13:14 and 15:5. What significance can be attached to the Lord's use of "stars" and "dust" to describe Abraham's offspring in these verses?*

_____

_____

_____

10. *What missions significance is there in God's changing Abram's name to Abraham in Genesis 17?*

_____

_____

That Abraham was beginning to capture an "all nations" perspective is evident by his actions in Genesis 18:16-33. When the Lord revealed to him that He was about to destroy Sodom and Gomorrah, Abraham became an advocate for these ungodly people and interceded on their behalf.

11. *What does this passage suggest about our own role in reaching the nations?*

_____

_____

The final reiteration of the covenant terms to Abraham occurred when Abraham was given the ultimate test of his faith in Genesis 22:1-19. His obedience, expressed by his willingness to sacrifice Isaac, secured the blessing for all the nations (v. 18). Because he believed God, he reconfirmed his covenant commitment and became the "father of all them that believe" (Rom. 4:11). Abraham was confident that God would uphold His end of the contract. It was that faith in God's faithfulness that "was reckoned to him as righteousness" (Gen. 15:6; James 2:23).

Understanding the Abrahamic Covenant is key to understanding the basic dynamic which governs the participation of God's people in the fulfillment of His eternal purpose. God does bless His people, but He also expects obedience in return. The Abrahamic Covenant also makes clear God's intention to carry out His mission purpose through His children. He blesses them in order that they may be His agents of blessing to the world.

Characteristically, God revealed His plans little by little. To reinforce His directive, He continued to speak to Abraham, to Abraham's immediate offspring, Isaac and Jacob, and to Israel about all this plan entailed. Every renewal of the covenant specified "the nations of the earth" who were to become

GOD BLESSED ABRAHAM

...THAT ALL THE NATIONS OF THE EARTH MIGHT BE BLESSED

recipients of the blessing. How these physical descendants of Abraham responded to their covenant obligations is the theme of the rest of the Old Testament.

Isaac, Abraham's "covenant" son, had the terms of the covenant set forth for him by God in Genesis 26. Likewise, Jacob, Isaac's son and the inheritor of the birthright and the blessing, had the terms of the same covenant given to him by God at Bethel in Genesis 28. From this time on, God called Himself the God of Abraham, Isaac, and Jacob, thus identifying Himself as the God who covenanted with these patriarchs of the nation. Throughout this entire period, God was faithfully at work fulfilling His part of the agreement. He greatly blessed Abraham, Isaac, and Jacob, giving them a land, wealth, fame, and a powerful family. Even the 400-year sojourn in Egypt contained many blessings. The Israelites were initially settled in the choice region of Goshen, where they also enjoyed the protection of Pharaoh's armies. Their women were noted both for their fertility and for their vigor in childbearing. In spite of the Israelites' eventual enslavement, Jacob's handful of 70 multiplied into a nation of millions in the fertile Nile Valley.

The Exodus

The book of Exodus recounts the marvelous ways God worked in delivering the nation of Israel from bondage in Egypt. At every step, God's mighty hand was evident. In all history, no slave people has ever been delivered as they were. In the process, God made His name known among the nations (Ex. 7:5; 9:13-17; 15:15). Three months after this miraculous deliverance, we find Israel camped in the wilderness at the foot of Mount Sinai. Read God's "Eagles' Wings" message to them in Exodus 19:3-6.

12. *God upheld His part of the covenant in delivering Israel. What did He desire of Israel in response to all He had done?*

_____

_____

_____

God's plan was that His message be both visible and portable. That's why He entrusted it to His people. The nation of Israel was to be a "royal priesthood."

13. What is the function of a priest? How does this relate to Israel's role to the nations?

_____

_____

_____

The term "special possession" (Ex. 19:5) can also be translated as "special treasure." The King James Bible uses the phrase "peculiar people" in this verse. Walter Kaiser has noted:

> The old English word "peculiar" came from the Latin word which meant valuables or any kind of moveable goods which were not, in contrast to real estate, attached to the land, such as jewels, stocks, or bonds. The fact was that Israel was to be God's Son, His people, His firstborn (Ex. 4:22), and now His special treasure. The emphasis here is on the *portability* of that message and the fact that God has placed such high value in *people*. This is exactly as Malachi 3:17 describes us: "jewels." *

As God's "special treasure," those selected to receive His blessing, the Israelites were to embody God's grace. They were also to be set apart as a "holy nation" in the way they lived. They were not to pursue the vanities which consumed the Gentile nations but were to be pure, totally separated from the moral pollution of their neighbors. Thus, the Lord would be their God and they would be His people.

Both the Exodus from Egypt and the subsequent conquest of Canaan served to establish this identity of separation by godliness. Through these events, God also sanctified His name, showing His goodness and holiness in contrast to the immoral, capricious, violent, and cruel gods of the surrounding Canaanite nations.

Holiness is often portrayed as a posture of passivity. Yet God's holiness and His defense of it in many of the bloody passages of the conquest can only be explained through the scriptural theme of *antagonism*. Johannes Verkuyl discusses this theme in the following excerpt.

---

* Kaiser, W. C., Jr. (1992). Israel's missionary call. In R. D. Winter & S. C. Hawthorne (Eds.), *Perspectives on the world Christian movement: A reader* (rev. ed.) (p. A29). Pasadena: William Carey Library.

2-14 The Biblical / Historical Foundation

❏ *The Motif of Antagonism* *

Johannes Verkuyl **

The whole Old Testament (and the New Testament as well) is filled with descriptions of how Yahweh-Adonai, the covenant God of Israel, is waging war against those forces which try to thwart and subvert His plans for His creation. He battles against those false gods which human beings have fashioned from the created world, idolized, and used for their own purposes. Think, for example, of the Baals and the Ashtaroth, whose worshippers elevated nature, the tribe, the state, and the nation to a divine status. God fights against magic and astrology which, according to Deuteronomy, bend the line between God and His creation. He contends against every form of social injustice and pulls off every cloak under which it seeks to hide (see Amos and Jeremiah, for example).

The whole of the Old Testament burns with a feverish desire to defeat these opposing powers. There are grand visions of that coming kingdom where every relationship is properly restored and when the whole of creation—people, animals, plants, and every other creature—will perfectly accord with God's intentions for it (see Isaiah 2, Micah 4, and Isaiah 65). The Old Testament longs for this kingdom's final revealing and categorically states its promise that Yahweh shall indeed finally overcome. This too is a highly significant theme for missionary participation. To participate in mission is quite impossible unless one also wages war against every form of opposition to God's intentions wherever it be found, whether in churches, the world of the nations, or one's own life.

The Old Testament ties the antagonistic motif closely with the doxological theme: the glory of Yahweh-Adonai shall be revealed among all peoples. Then every human being shall come to know Him as He really is, the "gracious and merciful God, slow to get angry, full of kindness, and always willing to turn back from meting out disaster" (Jon. 4:1-2).

14. How are "holiness" and "antagonism" a part of God's mission mandate?

_____

_____

_____

The Covenant Continues

The basic terms of the covenant God established with Abraham were continually referred to by the Israelites. In fact, they are restated, in one form or another, in over 50 passages and verses of the Old Testament. One of the clearest of these passages is Psalm 67. Known as the "Our Father" of the Old Testament, this psalm was probably sung at the yearly thanksgiving feast of Pentecost.

---

* Verkuyl, J. (1978). *Contemporary missiology: An introduction* (D. Cooper, Ed. and Trans.) (pp. 95-96). Grand Rapids: Eerdmans.

** Johannes Verkuyl was formerly Professor and Head of the Department of Missiology and Evangelism at the Free University of Amsterdam. He is now retired.

15. *Read Psalm 67. Verses 1-2 and 6-7 demonstrate that the psalmist had a clear understanding of why God blesses Israel. State this reason in your own words.*

_____

_____

_____

16. *What will God do for the nations in verses 3-5? What will their response be?*

_____

_____

_____

In this psalm God's justice is extolled. He is acknowledged as the rightful ruler of the nations. He blesses Israel in order that all the nations may come to recognize His sovereignty. God fulfills His promise, and Israel recognizes her obligation. How fitting that the words should find such tremendous prophetic fulfillment on the first day of Pentecost of the Christian era (Acts 2)!

The Opportunity

That Israel had an obligation to minister to the nations is clear. As a kingdom of priests, the Jews had the role of mediator between God and the nations. How were they to go about fulfilling this function? What kinds of opportunities were they to seek? Were they to actively "evangelize" the nations around them, or should they sit back and wait for the nations to come to them?

Two Forces

In the fulfillment of Israel's obligation, two forces were at work. The first of these was an attractive force, symbolized first by the tabernacle and then by the temple in Jerusalem. These buildings were the places where God's name dwelt. They were holy places, the heart of Israel's religious ceremony and practice. Yet they were not intended just to serve Israel. When Solomon dedicated the temple, it was clear to him that the temple had a wider purpose.

17. *Read 1 Kings 8:41-43, 54-61. How was the temple to serve in reaching the nations?*

_____

_____

_____

18. Now read 1 Kings 10:1-9. What attracted the Queen of Sheba to Israel, and what was her reaction to what she experienced there?

_____

_____

The Bible records several other foreigners who were attracted to Israel because of the evidence of God's blessing, including Ruth, a Moabite woman, and Naaman the Syrian. Hundreds of other unrecorded accounts are evidenced by the fact that on the day of Pentecost there were devout men from "every nation under heaven" (Acts 2:5) staying in Jerusalem. God's plan to reach the nations, however, included much more than a passive attraction.

A second force in operation was an active, expansive force which operated to send God's message beyond the borders of Israel. Some examples of Israelites who were used to proclaim God's message to other nations include captives such as Joseph and exiles such as Daniel and Esther. Or consider the prophet Jonah, who was commanded to preach repentance to Nineveh. Jeremiah was appointed as a "prophet to the nations," and it is speculated that he or other messengers may have traveled widely in delivering his many oracles. Nor did God use only the great in this role of bearing His message. It was a little Israelite slave girl who announced His healing power to Naaman, the mighty but leprous captain of the Syrian army.

Some might argue that these cases are exceptions and would point out that many of these people were captives or otherwise ministered against their wills. However, volunteerism has never been the deciding factor in furthering God's mission. God will use His people to spread His message, whether they are willing agents or not. Israel's tragic history would have been considerably different if she had been a willing instrument of God's redemptive plan. She was not. God used captivity and exile both to judge Israel's disobedience and to extend her witness beyond her borders.

These two dynamic forces are also present today. On a global scale, many are attracted to "Christian" nations because of the evidence of God's blessing through material wealth and stability. In communities, congregations where God's power and grace are evident also draw people. On a personal level, godly character attracts those who want to possess those same qualities. Yet the gospel will not be spread to all nations simply through passive attraction. There are too many social, cultural, and geographic barriers that need to be crossed for this to happen. God's people must be willing to go to the nations with the good news if they hope to fulfill their covenant obligations.

AN ATTRACTIVE FORCE
"Come to the Blessing"

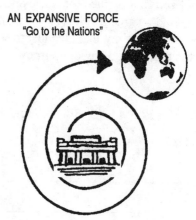
AN EXPANSIVE FORCE
"Go to the Nations"

Figure 2-1. The Two Forces

Israel's Strategic Location

In considering these forces, it is important to note Israel's strategic geographic placement. The land of Israel is located at the juncture of three continents: Asia, Africa, and Europe. Referred to by Ezekiel (38:12) as "the center of the land," it was a major crossroads of the ancient world. This important location afforded God's people many opportunities to expose travelers and traders from many nations to the true God. It was also a well-located base from which emissaries of the one true God could be sent to the nations.

Israel's strategic location presented many redemptive opportunities for God's covenant people. God continues to present opportunities by placing His people in strategic places around the world. The same attractive and expansive forces are still at work today. Together, they provide a dynamic tension for the establishment and propagation of God's kingdom among the peoples of the earth.

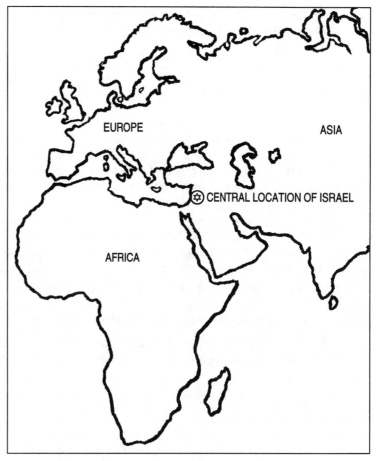

Figure 2-2
Israel's Strategic Location at the Crossroads of
Three Continents: Asia, Africa, and Europe

The Message

The Abrahamic Covenant promised not only that Abraham would be blessed, but that he and his descendants were to bless all nations. The covenant at Sinai specified Israel's role as advocate for the nations and as mobile bearers of the blessing. They knew their obligation and were placed strategically to fulfill their duty. What *was* the message they were to proclaim? They could not yet announce the gospel of repentance through Jesus Christ as we know it today. What were they to tell others?

God's Identity and Character

If the nations were to come under the loving rule of God, they had to know who He was. Almighty YHWH was not just a minor Hebrew deity but the great "I AM" (Ex. 3:13-15), the uncreated Creator of the universe. Each of His many names revealed an aspect of His character. Titles such as Judge of all the earth (Gen. 18:25), Jehovah Jireh ("provider," Gen. 22:14), Jehovah Rapha ("healer," Ex. 15:26), and Jehovah Nissei ("my banner," Ex. 17:15) demonstrated His attributes and relationship to His people.

19. *Read Exodus 34:5-7. How would you explain what this passage tells about the character of God to someone who had never heard of Him?*

_____

_____

_____

As God through His name revealed His character to Israel, He also exalted His name by mighty deeds. He repeatedly demonstrated to the nations His right to be recognized as sovereign of the universe.

God's Saving Power

Not only do the various names applied to God reveal His identity, character, and supremacy, but His name is also the focal point of His power to save. Throughout Scripture we find repeated references to people "calling upon the name of the Lord" and other allusions to the saving power of the name of God.

20. *Study the following texts: Genesis 4:26; 12:8; Psalm 50:15; 55:16; Isaiah 55:6-7; Joel 2:32. What does "calling upon the name of the Lord" really mean?*

_____

_____

_____

New Testament believers often have difficulty understanding how people in Old Testament times were saved. The answer is actually quite straightforward. Many passages in the Bible make it clear that the process of salvation was not significantly different in Old Testament times than it is now. Genuine believers in all ages are saved as they demonstrate belief in the one true God, place their faith in His grace and ability to save them, and submit to His rule in their lives. The New Testament amplifies our knowledge regarding the details of how God intended to accomplish His redemptive plan through Jesus. Old Testament believers, however, had no less confidence than we do that God would make provision for their redemption. Even Job, the protagonist of the oldest book in the Bible, could confidently assert: "I know that my Redeemer lives, and at the last He will take His stand on the earth. Even after my skin is flayed, yet without my flesh I shall see God; whom I myself shall behold, and whom my eyes shall see and not another" (Job 19:25-27).

21. *The concept of "calling on the name of the Lord" is carried over into the New Testament, even after Christ and His redemptive role were fully revealed. Read Romans 10:12-15. What must happen in order for people to be saved in this day and age?*

_____

_____

_____

God's Ultimate Victory

Believers from earliest time have looked forward to the day of God's return to earth and the establishment of His literal, physical kingdom. The prophetic books are filled with dozens of descriptions of that day when God's sovereign rule will be a reality in every corner of the earth. One of the most beautiful of these is given by Micah.

22. Read Micah 4:1-4. How will the nations respond to God's rule?

_____

_____

_____

God's ultimate victory has an "all nations" perspective, as every kingdom of the earth is drawn to His name, His character, and His loving sovereignty.

In word, song, and deed, Israel was to make known to the nations that God is the Sovereign of the universe. Believers throughout the ages have recognized this rule and have submitted to it. From the earliest times, they have been united in the hope of His coming and of the restoration of His kingdom on earth. His kingdom come!

III. Israel's Response

One does not have to be a great Old Testament scholar to see how Israel failed in her responsibility to be God's agent of blessing. She did not perform her basic duty to "do justice, love kindness, and walk humbly with [her] God" (Mic. 6:8). Had she lived a holy life, she would have demonstrated to the world God's identity, character, and saving power. Sadly, at almost every step Israel demonstrated her unfaithfulness to the Lord.

God, however, was faithful and blessed Israel at absolutely every step of her development as a nation. He delivered her from Egypt and nurtured her in the wilderness. He defeated her enemies on every side and allowed her to take possession of the promised land. He gave her the Mosaic Law, a "constitution" which, if followed, guaranteed her health, prosperity, and safety (Deut. 29-30). God intended that He should head up Israel's government Himself and rule through appointed judges. Nevertheless, even during times when God was most actively demonstrating His power on Israel's behalf, the people demonstrated an idolatrous and unbelieving heart.

There were times when, chastened by God's discipline or exuberant with the success He had granted, the Jews would submit to God's will and follow their calling. After a time of enjoying the benefits of their obedience, they would invariably fall prey to a lethal complacency, opening the door to sin and idolatry. Such disobedience ended every period of prosperity. Repentance under dire circumstances would produce deliverance by a patient God, and the cycle would be repeated. Finally, the nation rejected God's rule through the judges in favor of the tyranny of a human king.

Even when the kingdom was established, God's blessing still came. Saul was anointed to be the first king of Israel, but his disobedience cost him the throne. Nevertheless, God did begin to grant Israel deliverance under his rule. Later on, King David was anointed and proved to be a man after God's own heart. Under his reign, the kingdom prospered and expanded its borders. David's son Solomon built upon the accomplishments of his father and ushered the kingdom to its "golden" age. But during the latter part of his reign, his heart turned away from God. Even though there was great wealth evident in Israel during this time, it was acquired through heavy exploitation of the common people (1 Kings 12:4). More significantly, because of the concessions King Solomon made to his pagan wives, he caused the nation to worship false gods (1 Kings 11:1-13).

The account of the kingdom after Solomon's death is one of tragedy and gradual disintegration. Civil strife broke out immediately with the crowning of Solomon's son Rehoboam. This unrest eventually led to civil war and the division of the kingdom. Also, soon after Rehoboam's crowning, the king of Egypt invaded Israel and plundered Jerusalem, thus initiating a long era of oppression and domination of Israel by her neighbors. Although there were brief revivals in Israel's spiritual walk which affected her national fortunes, she never demonstrated real faithfulness to her covenant obligations. In spite of the many warnings her prophets gave her, she insisted on pursuing her own idolatrous way.

God was lovingly persistent with Israel and was more than willing to take her back when she repented. However, she was not responsive to His offers of forgiveness nor to His reproof and discipline. Finally, God was forced to allow His people to be carried into captivity. Exiled from their homeland, they were again placed in a position of servitude.

23. In what significant ways did Israel fail in relation to her covenant obligations to the nations?

_____

_____

_____

God used these circumstances to begin the process of selecting a remnant who would bind themselves to the terms of the covenant that had been made with Abraham. Ezekiel, the great prophet of the Babylonian exile, reviews God's dealings with Israel in Ezekiel 20:30-38. He describes the process God would use to assure Israel's faithfulness as He restored a remnant to their homeland. In verse 33, God declares His intent to enforce His rule on Israel as her rightful King. In the subsequent verses, He outlines a course of disciplinary measures leading up to her restoration as His people. This time, God was not going to allow Israel to run after false gods. Never again was Israel to exhibit an idolatrous lifestyle before the nations.

God was determined to see Israel become faithful not only to Him, but also to His mission purpose. As Isaiah the prophet foretold (Isa. 49:6), the Jews were to become the "servant of the Lord" and a "light to the nations." After the exile, they did begin to proclaim God's name to the nations. Throughout the 400-year intertestamental period, Jews migrated throughout the known world. Wherever they went, they established synagogues and won the allegiance of many Gentiles to the one true God.

24. What was the reason for and the result of the exile?

_____

_____

_____

Israel Sent Involuntarily

God expects His people to glorify His name by the holiness of their lives. He wants them to demonstrate His saving power by the way they trust Him. He also desires a people who will develop a caring heart. He wants to bless the nations through them as agents of their restoration to God. When God's people do not live holy lives or go to the nations freely, He accomplishes His purposes by sending them forth against their will.

There are many Old Testament accounts of Israelites taken captive or exiled to other nations. Many of these accounts relate how God's name was magnified through these captives. Likewise, the Old Testament relates several instances of nations who were drawn to Israel by the evidence of her blessing and who then took those blessings by force. This pattern begins to emerge in the Old Testament and continues throughout Christian history.

25. Read 2 Kings 5:1-14, 2 Kings 17:24-28, and Daniel 1:1-4. Identify the type of mechanism God used in the lives of the people in these passages, whether involuntary or voluntary, coming or going.

_____

_____

_____

Jonah

The book of Jonah is perhaps the clearest Old Testament example of God's specific command to an Israelite to carry His message to a Gentile nation. Through Jonah's response to that mandate, the book also reveals the ethnocentric (having a sense of ethnic superiority) and rebellious nature which characterized God's people. It may also parallel similar attitudes held by His people today.

Turn to the book of Jonah and review it. Then read the following selection by Johannes Verkuyl.

❏ *The Book of Jonah* *

Johannes Verkuyl

The book of Jonah is so significant for understanding the biblical basis of mission, because it treats God's mandate to His people regarding the Gentile peoples, and thus serves as the preparatory step to the missionary mandate of the New Testament. But it is also important for catching a glimpse of the deep resistance this mandate encounters from the very servant Yahweh has chosen to discharge His worldwide work.

> *Jonah reveals the need for a radical conversion of one's natural tendencies and a complete restructuring of one's life to make it serviceable for mission.*

Today there is much talk and writing about "educating the congregation" and "educating personnel" for mission. Jonah is a lesson in educating a person to be a missionary: it reveals the need for a radical conversion of one's natural tendencies and a complete restructuring of his life to make it serviceable for mission.

Background of the book

The title of the book is the personal name of the unwilling prophet, Jonah, and harks back to the days of King Jeroboam II (787-746 B.C.), when a prophet named Jonah ben Amittai was living. It is obvious, however, that this account is intended for reasons quite other than detailing the events of this prophet's life. The author uses this personal name to portray for his readers a missionary who has no heart for the Gentiles and who, like the later Pharisees, cannot tolerate a God who shows them mercy. In the words of the Dutch author Miskotte, "The writer intends to picture a person who is the exact opposite of an apostle."

The author of Jonah warns his readers against this intolerant attitude and sets before each of them the question of whether he or she is willing to be transformed into a servant who works to accomplish the mandates of God.

As the author sees it, Israel has become so preoccupied with herself that she no longer directs her eyes toward the world of the nations. Israel, the recipient of all God's revelation, refuses to set foot in alien territory to tell the other peoples God's message of judgment and liberation. But the message of the book also is addressed to the New Testament congregation which tries various ways of evading her Lord's command to speak His message to the world.

Jonah's crafty evasion efforts represent a lazy and unfaithful church which does not heed her Lord's command. God has to wrestle against Israel's narrow ethnocentrism which tries to restrict His activity to the boundaries of Israel alone and against the church's ecclesiocentric refusal to go out into the world to proclaim God's message and do His work. The writer is bent on convincing his readers that the radius of God's liberating activity is wide enough to cover both Israel and the Gentiles.

It is a miracle that Jonah, with its strong warning against ethnocentrism, ever made its way into the canon of Scripture. It squarely sets forth man's attempt to sabotage God's worldwide plans so that its readers—Israel, the New Testament church, and us—can hear what the Holy Spirit, through the medium of this little book, is trying to tell them.

---

* Verkuyl, J. (1978). *Contemporary missiology: An introduction* (D. Cooper, Ed. and Trans.) (pp. 96-100). Grand Rapids: Eerdmans.

26. *What purpose does the book of Jonah serve in the Old Testament canon?*

A short review of the book's eight scenes

1 The first scene opens with Jonah receiving the command to go to Nineveh. While the Old Testament usually appeals to the other nations to come to Zion, the mountain of God, Jonah, like the disciples of the New Testament (cf. Matt. 28:18-20), is told to go! The Septuagint translation of Jonah uses the word *porettomai* in 1:2-3 and again in 3:2-3, the very same verb used by Jesus in His Great Commission recorded in Matthew 28. Where must Jonah go? To Nineveh, of all places. Nineveh, a very center of totalitarianism, brutality, and warlike attitudes. To Nineveh, notorious for the shameful hounding, vicious torture, and imperialist brazenness it reserved for those who chose to oppose its policies. God wants His servant to warn Nineveh of impending judgment and to call her to repentance. He wants to save Nineveh! But Jonah refuses. He prepares himself, to be sure, but only to flee from the face of God who is Lord over all.

2 In the second scene God responds to Jonah's flight by sending a mighty storm (1:4-16). The wind obeys Yahweh's commands, but the disobedient Jonah sleeps in the bottom of the boat, oblivious of the fact that the storm is directed at him. At times the church, too, sleeps right through the storm of God's judgment passing over the world, assuring

> *At times the church sleeps right through the storm of God's judgment passing over the world, assuring herself that the wind outside has nothing to do with her.*

herself that the wind outside has nothing to do with her. While the crew vainly searches for the storm's cause, Jonah confesses that he worships and fears the God who made both the sea and the dry land, the one God who is above all nations. This God, he claims, is bringing a charge against him, and the only

way to quiet the waters is to throw him into the sea. In this scene the crew represents the Gentiles, a people for whom Jonah is totally unconcerned, and yet who themselves are interested in sparing his life. After a second order from Jonah, they throw him overboard, and the storm ceases. Scarcely able to believe their eyes, the sailors break forth in praise to the God of Jonah. Their obedience surpasses that of the saboteur Jonah: they are more open to God than the very prophet himself.

3 The third scene (1:17) describes a large fish which, at Yahweh's instructions, opens its mouth to swallow Jonah and spew him onto the shore at the appropriate time. Jonah simply cannot escape God's missionary mandate. The God who whipped up the stormy winds and directed the sailors to accomplish His purposes now guides a fish as part of His plan to save Nineveh. Yahweh continues His work of reforming and preparing His missionary to be a fit instrument in His plans.

4 In the fourth scene (2:1-10) Jonah implores God to rescue him from the belly of the fish. He who had no mercy on the Gentiles and refused to acknowledge that God's promises extended to them now appeals for divine mercy, and by quoting lines from various psalms pants after those promises claimed by worshipers in God's temple.

Yahweh reacts, He speaks to the brute beast, and Jonah lands on shore safe and sound. By his very rescue Jonah was unwittingly a witness of God's saving mercy. Though covered with seaweed, Jonah was nonetheless a testimony that God takes no delight in the death of sinners and saboteurs but rather rejoices in their conversion.

5 In the fifth scene (3:1-4) God repeats His order to the man whose very life affirms the truth of what he confessed in the belly of the fish: "Salvation is from Yahweh."

The Septuagint uses the term *kerygma* in 3:1-2ff. That single word summarizes Jonah's mission: he must proclaim that Nineveh, however godless she may be, is still the object of God's concern, and unless she repents, she will be destroyed. His message must be one of threat as well as promise, of judgment as well as gospel.

6 In the sixth scene (3:5-10) Nineveh responds to Jonah's appeal to repent. The proud, despotic king steps down from his royal throne, exchanges his robes for dust and ashes, and enjoins every man and animal to follow his example. What Israel continually refused to do the heathen Gentiles did do: the cruel king of Nineveh stands as anti-type to the disobedient kings of Judah.

The people join the king in repenting. They cease all their devilish work, and the terrifying and coercing engines of political injustice come to a halt. In deep penitence they turn away from idols to serve the God who is Lord of every nation and all creation. All this becomes possible because Yahweh is God. The world of the heathen is a potentially productive mission field for no other reason than this: He alone is God.

The curtain closes on this scene with these amazing words: "God saw what they did, and how they abandoned their wicked ways, and He repented and did not bring upon them the disaster He had threatened."

Yahweh is faithful to His promises. Still today His will for Moscow and Peking, for London and Amsterdam is no less "gracious and full of mercy" than it was for Nineveh. To borrow from Luther, who loved to preach from the book of Jonah, the left hand of God's wrath is replaced by His right hand of blessing and freedom.

---

27. What are the two elements of the message Jonah was to preach to Nineveh?

_____

_____

_____

_____

---

7 The seventh scene (4:1-4) recounts the fact that the greatest hurdle to overcome in discharging the missionary mandate was not the sailors, nor the fish, nor Nineveh's king and citizenry, but rather Jonah himself—the recalcitrant and narrow-minded church. Chapter 4 describes Jonah, who has long since departed the city to find shelter east of the borders. The 40-day period of repentance has passed, but since God has changed His mind about destroying it, the city continues to be nourished by Yahweh's grace and mercy. Jonah is furious that God has extended His mercy beyond the borders of Israel to the Gentiles. He wanted a God cut according to his own pattern: a cold, hard, cruel-natured god with an unbending will set against the heathen. He cannot stand to think of the Gentiles as part of salvation history.

This is Jonah's sin, the sin of a missionary whose heart is not in it. He who once pleaded with God for mercy from the desolate isolation of a fish's belly now is angry that this God shows mercy to the nations. He vents his fury in the form of a prayer found in 4:2, the key text of the whole book: "And he prayed to the Lord, 'This, O Lord, is what I feared when I was in my own country, and to forestall it I tried to escape to Tarshish: I knew that thou art a gracious and compassionate God, long-suffering and ever constant, and always willing to repent of the disaster.'"

Part of the text comes from an ancient Israelite liturgy which every Israelite knew by heart and could rattle off in worship at the temple or synagogue while half asleep (cf. Ex. 34:6; Ps. 86:15;

103:8; 145:8; Neh. 9:17). But Jonah cannot stand to think that this liturgy is true not only for Jerusalem, the location of God's temple, but for other places as well—Nineveh, São Paulo, Nairobi, New York, and Paris.

Why is Jonah really so angry? For no other reason than that God is treating those outside His covenant the same as He is those within. But Jonah's anger in effect is putting him outside the covenant, for he obstinately refuses to acknowledge the covenant's purpose—to bring salvation to the heathen. He had not yet learned that Israel could not presume upon some special favors from God. Both Israel and the Gentiles alike live by the grace which the Creator gives to all of His creatures. So God comes to His prophet, but no longer as a covenant partner; He comes as the Creator and asks His creature: "Do you have a right to be so angry?"

8 In the eighth and last scene (4:5-11) one can see God still working to teach His thick-skulled missionary His lessons. He did not catch the point of the storm, the sailors, the fish, and Nineveh's conversion because he did not want to. Now Yahweh tries one more approach—the miraculous tree. A climbing gourd springs up quickly, offers Jonah protection against the beating sun, but as quickly withers and dies, the victim of an attacking worm. Jonah is peeved.

At that point God again turns to His missionary student, using the tree as His object lesson. The very God who directs the whole course of history, rules the wind and waves, and turned Nineveh's millions to repentance now asks tenderly: "Are you so angry over the gourd? You are sorry about the gourd, though you had nothing to do with growing it, a plant which came up in a night and withered in a night. And should not I be sorry for the great city of Nineveh, with its hundred and twenty thousand who cannot tell their right hand from their left, and cattle without number?" God spares and rescues. Jerusalem's God is Nineveh's as well. Unlike Jonah, He has no "Gentile complex."

And while He never forces any one of us, He tenderly asks us to put our whole heart and soul into the work of mission. God is still interested in transforming obstinate, irritable, depressive, peevish Jonahs into heralds of the good news which brings freedom.

The book ends with an unsettling question which is never answered: God reached His goal with Nineveh, but what about Jonah? No one knows. The questions of Israel and the church and their obedience is still an open one.

The question is one which every generation of Christians must answer for itself. Jacques Ellul closes his book *The Judgment of Jonah* with these words: "The book of Jonah has no conclusion, and the final question of the book has no answer, except from the one who realizes the fullness of the mercy of God and who factually and not just mythically accomplishes the salvation of the world." *

Jonah is father to all those Christians who desire the benefits and blessings of election but refuse its responsibility.

The New Testament church must pay close heed to the message of Jonah's book. Jesus Christ is "One greater than Jonah" (Matt. 12:39-41; Luke 11:29-32). His death on the cross with its awful cry of God-forsakenness and His resurrection with its jubilant shout of victory are signs of Jonah for us, pointing to the profound meaning of His whole life and attesting that God loved the world so much.

If a person draws his lifeblood from the One greater than Jonah and yet declines to spread the good news among others, he in effect is sabotaging the aims of God Himself. Jonah is father to all those Christians who desire the benefits and blessings of election but refuse its responsibility.

Thomas Carlisle's poem "You Jonah" closes with these lines:

---

* Ellul, J. (1971). *The judgment of Jonah* (p. 103). Grand Rapids: Eerdmans.

And Jonah stalked
to his shaded seat
and waited for God
to come around
to his way of thinking.

And God is still waiting
for a host of Jonahs
in their comfortable houses
to come around
to His way of loving.

28. *How does the book of Jonah demonstrate the Old Testament themes of Israel's obligation, opportunity, and response, together with God's persistence in fulfilling His mission purpose?*

_____

_____

_____

_____

29. *What parallels can be drawn between Jonah's attitude and the attitudes which characterize many churches?*

_____

_____

_____

_____

_____

It would be inappropriate to discuss Israel's disobedience and failures without examining ourselves in the same light. Israel was idolatrous, rebellious, and ethnocentric. Could it be that Christians are sometimes guilty of the same sins and failures? Is it possible that we are just as negligent in our attitude toward the nations? God is unchanging and is totally faithful. How often we disappoint Him with our unfaithfulness and disobedience!

Israel's Dispersion

During the events leading up to the demise of Israel as a political entity, the prophets continually challenged Israel's decadence and unfaithfulness to God. They reminded her of her covenant obligations: to proclaim and exemplify God's identity and character. Sometimes they succeeded in turning Israel's eyes back towards God for a short time. Then God blessed Israel, and she fulfilled her role as a positive witness before the nations. Too often, however, she was a negative witness and a stumbling block to the advancement of God's kingdom. God had to judge and discipline her.

Devoid of God's protection and blessing, Israel was consumed by the nations around her. In 722 B.C., the Israelites of the Northern Kingdom were exiled to Assyria, and Assyrians were brought to Israel, where they mixed racially with the Jews to become the Samaritans. During the rule of King Jehoiakim (609-587 B.C.), the Jews were forcibly deported to Babylon. Later, in 587 B.C., Nebuchadnezzar, King of Babylon, destroyed Jerusalem, thus signaling the end of the Kingdom of Judah as a political entity. It wasn't until 536 B.C. that Cyrus issued a decree allowing Jews to begin returning to their land. The Jews were to wait nearly 2,500 years until their national autonomy was restored in 1948.

Through exile and captivity, Israel began fulfilling her duty. Many of the brightest chapters of the Old Testament are the accounts of the faithful witness of Israelites who were forcibly taken to other nations. Through their testimony, God's name was exalted and glorified before the Gentiles. In the fire of tribulation, the best element came forth and was purified. Under these circumstances, the Israelites began to acknowledge the sovereignty of their God. Never again would the remnant that survived the captivity play the harlot by worshiping the gods of the nations. Thus they became the first people to staunchly embrace monotheism (belief in only one omnipotent God).

After the Jews returned to Israel from captivity, God's missionary purpose was carried out through the *Diaspora* (dispersion). During this time, a faithful remnant of Jews who were scattered throughout the Babylonian and Persian Empires spread God's name among the nations. It was during this period that synagogues first appeared. Under the Greek and Roman Empires the dispersion continued. Jews migrated to all of the important commercial and trade centers of the known world, where they prospered and multiplied. Wherever they went, they maintained their culture and established their religious centers. It was these Diaspora Jews whom the apostle Paul invariably contacted as he traveled from city to city during his missionary journeys.

In Matthew 23:15, Christ attests to the fact that some Jews even began to take their obligation seriously enough to begin missionary work. They traveled land and sea to convert Gentiles to the Jewish faith. Johannes Verkuyl comments on this "intertestamental period" in the following paragraph:

> Research into the period of the Jewish Diaspora has uncovered evidence of a Jewish effort to proselytize, which, in turn, definitely stamped later missionary work carried on by the Gentile as well as the Jewish Christians. The Septuagint (the Greek translation of the Old Testament) went through the whole of the civilized world and was explained in the synagogues. Diaspora Judaism's missionary impact was far greater than many realize. What is more, Judaism affected early Christianity, for the Jewish Christians kept close contact with the synagogue communities. The synagogue played a crucial role, for it attracted not only proselytes (Gentiles who adopted the complete range of Jewish beliefs and practices, including circumcision) but also a class it termed "God fearers" (Gentiles who accepted most of Judaism's ethics and some of its culture, but refused circumcision).*

---

* Verkuyl, J. (1978). *Contemporary missiology: An introduction* (D. Cooper, Ed. and Trans.) (p. 101). Grand Rapids: Eerdmans.

30. *During the time of the Diaspora, how was God setting the stage for the rapid spread of Christianity in the first century?*

_____

_____

_____

Summary

After mankind's failure to respond to God through His dealings with the human race in Genesis 1-11, God began to manifest His intention to reclaim His kingdom nation by nation. He chose Abraham and promised to bless him and make of him a great nation. That nation would in turn be an instrument of blessing to all the other nations. The Old Testament can thus be interpreted through understanding the obligation inherent in the Abrahamic Covenant, the opportunities God provided to fulfill the covenant, and Israel's response. The Abrahamic Covenant became the basis by which God's people could understand how God planned to use them in carrying out His redemptive purpose.

The covenant was firmly established with Abraham, Isaac, and Jacob. Later, it was passed on to the nation of Israel. God provided the message through the revelation of His character and through mighty deeds. He also provided the chance to be a witness to the nations by placing Israel in a strategic location. Israel, however, did not take seriously her covenant obligations, and God was forced to judge her.

Since Israel was unwilling to fulfill her obligation among the nations voluntarily, God used persecution and exile to disperse the Jews throughout the earth. Through the 400-year intertestamental period, the world finally began to hear the message Israel was intended to bear. Thousands of "God fearers" around the known world congregated with Jews to acknowledge Jehovah as Lord of the universe, paving the way for the coming of the Messiah.

Integrative Assignment

1. *Using Genesis 12:1-3, Exodus 19:5-6, and Psalm 67 as a basis, prepare a concise outline for a short talk entitled, "God Blesses Us That All the Nations of the Earth Might Be Blessed."*

2. *How do attractive and expansive forces work together for the establishment and expansion of God's kingdom? Illustrate your answer.*

3. *Identify three instances of missionary activity in the Old Testament, beyond those already studied, and explain what mechanism God used to fulfill His purpose through His people, whether involuntary or voluntary, coming or going.*

Questions for Reflection

1. *"Abraham believed God and it was reckoned to him as righteousness" (James 2:23). Our righteousness is also based on our belief that God will do what His Word says He will do. There is a direct relationship between the depth of our understanding of God's Word and our ability to act on it faithfully. Are you committed to knowing God's Word intimately? If you haven't done so already, schedule a daily time for Bible reading. Start by reading and meditating on Psalm 119. Covenant with God to be a faithful student of His Word. Write your commitment below.*

_____

_____

_____

_____

_____

_____

_____

_____

_____

_____

2. *In addition to affecting the establishment of God's kingdom in Old Testament times, attractive and expansive forces also play a part in our lives as individual believers. In what way are you "attractive" to unbelievers? In what ways are you ministering blessing to them?*

_____

_____

_____

_____

_____

_____

_____

_____

_____

_____

3. *Idolatry is not simply the worship of idols. It is anything that captivates our heart and causes our affections to stray from God. Solomon permitted his affections to focus on his wives and concubines, with the result that his relationship with God was severely harmed. What "idols" are the biggest stumbling blocks to believers today? Are your affections placed wholly on God? Read Psalm 42:1. Then write out a verse which reflects your own heart's desire for God.*

_____

_____

_____

_____

_____

_____

_____

_____

_____

_____

CHAPTER 3

The Messiah, His Messengers, and the Message

"…when the fullness of time came, God sent forth His Son, born of a woman …" (Gal. 4:4)

From the earliest Genesis records, God has been at work to redeem a people from every people and to rule a kingdom over all other kingdoms. Through our study of the Abrahamic Covenant and other key passages in the last two chapters, we have come to understand that the Old Testament clearly contains God's command to His people to bless all nations.

Now, as we study the New Testament era in this chapter, we find that God's concern for all nations continues as the central purpose of His dealings with the human race. Initially, we will examine Christ's role as "the Son of Man" and His ministry and teaching to His disciples as He developed in them an "all peoples" perspective. In the second section, we will consider the Great Commission and key events in the book of Acts which spurred the expansion of the gospel. We will also explore the clear relationship between the church and the missionary task. In the final part of this chapter, we want to examine Christ's message, the gospel of the kingdom, analyzing its meaning, its mission, and our motive for sharing it.

I. Jesus, the Messiah for All Peoples

With the coming of Jesus the Messiah, God initiated a special phase of the reestablishment of His kingdom on earth. It was not, however, the kingdom the Jewish leadership hoped for. They were looking for a political dominion; Christ brought a spiritual one. They expected a Messiah who would rally the nation of Israel and overthrow the evil yoke of Roman rule; Christ taught that they should "render to Caesar what is Caesar's" (Matt. 22:21).

Jesus of Nazareth's kingdom message was so radically different from the Jews' expectations that those who did not have "eyes to see or ears to hear" (Matt. 13:13-15) could only respond with unbelief and rejection. Even those Jews who did believe in Jesus found it difficult to disassociate the coming of the Messiah from the establishment of a literal, political kingdom. The disciples' confusion was due in part to Old Testament prophetic passages which speak to the eventual physical rule of Christ on this earth. It was hard for the disciples to understand the nature of the kingdom as Jesus taught and lived it.

1. *Israel's expectations for the coming of the Messiah were wrapped up in deeply ingrained hopes. Read the following passages and describe what these hopes were: Zephaniah 3:14-17, Isaiah 2:2-4, Isaiah 66:13-16.*

_____

_____

_____

_____

2. *Now contrast these expectations with Christ's birth, life, and teachings.*

_____

_____

_____

_____

_____

_____

_____

_____

Jesus' life and teachings were an enigma to those who expected the Messiah to come in power and might. Even for those who accepted Jesus as Christ, the association of His coming with nationalistic hopes had created a sense of extreme ethnocentricity. Jesus' disciples could accept Him as the Messiah for the Jews, but could their master also be a Messiah for all nations?

It takes more than a cursory reading of Scripture to understand how Jesus demonstrated His knowledge of His essentially spiritual, messianic role to all mankind. In the following excerpt, H. Cornell Goerner explains how the title Jesus chose for Himself clearly identified Him with His worldwide mission.

❏ *Jesus and the Gentiles* *

H. Cornell Goerner **

Son of Man

Nothing is more revealing than the personal title which Jesus chose for Himself. We have seen that He did not like the term "Son of David," the popular designation of the Messiah. He realized that He was indeed "the Son of God" referred to in Psalm 2:7, and during His trial before the Sanhedrin, He acknowledged this. But the title which He used throughout His ministry was "Son of Man."

More than 40 times in the Gospels the term is used, always by Jesus referring to Himself. The disciples never used the term, but called Him "Lord," "Master," or "Teacher." For Jesus, the words were almost a substitute for the personal pronoun "I." Again and again He said it: "The Son of Man has nowhere to lay His head" (Matt. 8:20). "The Son of Man has authority on earth to forgive sins" (Matt. 9:6). "The Son of Man is Lord of the Sabbath" (Matt. 12:8). "Then they shall see the Son of Man coming in clouds with great power and glory" (Mark 13:26).

Jesus derived this term from two principal sources: the books of Ezekiel and Daniel. "Son of man" is the distinctive title applied to the prophet Ezekiel by God and occurs 87 times. The Hebrew is *ben Adam*, literally, "son of Adam," or "son of mankind."

3. In what way did the title Jesus chose for Himself demonstrate His identification with all · mankind?

_____

_____

4. Why is it important for us to understand that Jesus' messianic role was global in its perspective?

_____

_____

Goerner goes on to illustrate how this identification with all mankind was expressed in Jesus' ministry.

From the beginning

As we have already seen, the vision of a universal kingdom was integral to the plan of Jesus from the very beginning of His ministry. The fact that one of the wilderness temptations involved "all the king-

---

* Goerner, H. C. (1979). *All nations in God's purpose* (pp. 74-78). Nashville: Broadman Press.

** After teaching missions and comparative religion at Southern Baptist Seminary for more than 20 years, in 1957 H. Cornell Goerner became Secretary for Africa, Europe, and the Near East for the Foreign Mission Board of the Southern Baptist Convention. He retired in 1976 as Secretary for West Africa and now is a pastor of a church in a community near Richmond, Virginia.

doms of the world and their glory" (Matt. 4:8) is conclusive. Jesus did aspire to world dominion. His ambition to rule over the nations was not wrong. The temptation was to take a shortcut to that noble goal: to adopt the methods of the devil. In rejecting Satan's methods, Jesus did not give up His aim of worldwide authority. Rather, He chose the path of suffering and redemption which He found outlined in the Scriptures.

The first sermon at Nazareth demonstrates that His life purpose extended far beyond the nation of Israel. He was not surprised that His own people did not receive His message. "That's the way it has always been," He said. "The prophets have always found greater faith among foreigners than among their own people" (Luke 4:24, author's paraphrase). He then gave an example: "There were many widows in Israel in the days of Elijah… and yet [he] was sent to none of them, but only to Zarephath, in the land of Sidon, to a woman who was a widow" (Luke 4:25-26). His hearers knew the rest of the story told in 1 Kings 17. Received into a Gentile home, Elijah performed the remarkable miracle of replenishing the flour and oil, then later restored the widow's son to life—not a Jewish widow, but a Gentile!

No more dramatic illustration could have been given that the grace of God was not limited to the people of Israel.

Jesus did not stop with Elijah. He rubbed salt into the wounded feelings of His audience with the story of Elisha. For Naaman, the Syrian, was not only a Gentile, but a military leader—captain of the Syrian army which at that very time was at war with Israel and had almost eradicated the hapless little nation (2 Kings 5:1-14). Yet, although there were many lepers in Israel, "none of them was cleansed, but only Naaman the Syrian" (Luke 4:27). No more dramatic illustration could have been given that the grace of God was not limited to the people of Israel and that Gentiles often displayed greater faith than those who were considered "children of the kingdom."

Small wonder that the proud citizens of Nazareth were infuriated at this brash young man, who in-

sulted their nation and called in question their privileged status as God's "chosen people"! But for His miraculous power, they would have hurled Him to His death on the jagged rocks at the foot of a cliff (Luke 4:28-30).

To the Jews first

Jesus did have a deep conviction of a special mission to the Jewish nation. He expressed this so strongly that some have concluded that He envisioned no mission beyond Israel. But careful consideration of all His words and actions reveals that it was a question of strategy. As Paul later expressed it, his mission was "to the Jew first, and also to the Greek" (Rom. 1:16; 2:10).

Jesus' concern for Israel was shown in the instructions to the 12 disciples as He sent them out on their first preaching mission. "Do not go in the way of the Gentiles," He said, "and do not enter any city of the Samaritans; but rather go to the lost sheep of the house of Israel" (Matt. 10:5-6). The reason is obvious. The time was short, and doom was coming to the nation, if there was not speedy repentance. The need was urgent, more so for Israel than for the Gentile nations, whose time of judgment would come later. Indeed, in the very same context is the prediction that the preaching ministry of the disciples would be extended to the Gentiles: "You shall even be brought before governors and kings for My sake, as a testimony to the Gentiles" (v. 18). But they must concentrate upon the Jewish cities first, because their time of opportunity was short (v. 23).

Luke tells of a later preaching mission in which 70 others were sent out two by two (Luke 10:1). Just as the 12 apostles symbolically represent the 12 tribes of Israel, the 70 symbolize the Gentile nations. In Genesis 10, the descendants of Noah are listed, 70 in number. Rabbinical tradition assumed that this was the total number of nations scattered over the earth after the Tower of Babel and repeatedly referred to the 70 Gentile peoples. Jesus may have used this means of symbolizing His long-range purpose. The 12 were sent to warn the tribes of Israel of impending judgment. The 70 were sent later on a training mission in preparation for their ultimate mission to the whole world.

THE 12 – ISRAEL   THE 70 – GENTILE NATIONS

Figure 3-1. Two Symbols of Christ's Mission

5. *What evidence from the New Testament does the author present to demonstrate Jesus' lack of ethnic self-centeredness?*

_____

_____

_____

6. *In what ways was the sending of the 12 disciples first, and later the 70, symbolically significant of Christ's whole mission?*

_____

_____

_____

7. *Why did Jesus give priority to reaching the Jews? Are there other reasons you can think of beyond the author's strategic consideration?*

_____

_____

_____

_____

It is clear from the Old and New Testaments that the gospel was to be heard first by the Jews. Christ understood this, along with His need to fulfill the many prophetic passages regarding His coming within the context of the Jewish nation. It is also clear from Scripture (see John 12:20-26) that the blood of the new covenant had to be poured out first in order that forgiveness could be understood and received by the "many" Gentile nations.

Because of their knowledge of Scripture, the Jews were strategically equipped to grasp the atonement message. They knew the prophetic passages regarding the Messiah. Although they were not receptive, they *knew who Jesus claimed to be.* Had they accepted Him, they were undoubtedly in the best position to communicate this message to all mankind.

Disciples to Apostles

Christ had a clear understanding of His *global* messianic role. His disciples, however, did not necessarily share that understanding. Jesus had to use encounters with Gentiles to begin to give them an "all peoples" perspective. How successful was He in doing this? In the following excerpt, Don Richardson traces the passages in which Jesus encountered these "foreigners" during His ministry and shows how wisely He used these times to challenge His disciples' attitudes.

❏ *A Man for All Peoples* *

Don Richardson **

Millions of Christians know, of course, that Jesus, at the end of His ministry, commanded His disciples to "go and make disciples of all [peoples]" (Matt. 28:19). We respectfully honor this last and most incredible command He gave with an august title— the Great Commission. And yet millions of us deep down in our hearts secretly believe, if our deeds are an accurate barometer of our beliefs (and Scripture says they are), that Jesus really uttered that awesome command without giving His disciples ample warning.

Read cursorily through the four Gospels, and the Great Commission looks like a sort of afterthought paper-clipped onto the end of the main body of Jesus' teachings. It is almost as if our Lord, after divulging everything that was really close to His heart, snapped His fingers and said, "Oh yes, by the way, men, there's one more thing. I want you all to proclaim this message to everyone in the world, regardless of his language and culture. That is, of course, if you have the time and feel disposed."

Did Jesus hit His disciples with the Great Commission cold turkey? Did He just spring it on them at the last minute without fair warning and then slip away to heaven before they had a chance to interact with Him about its feasibility? Did He fail to provide reasonable demonstration on ways to fulfill it?

How often we Christians read the four Gospels without discerning the abundant evidence God has provided for an entirely opposite conclusion! Consider, for example, how compassionately Jesus exploited the following encounters with Gentiles and Samaritans to help His disciples think in cross-cultural terms.

A Roman centurion

On one occasion (Matt. 8:5-13), a Roman centurion, a Gentile, approached Jesus with a request on behalf of his paralyzed servant. Jews, on this occasion, urged Jesus to comply. "This man deserves to have you do this, because he loves our nation and has built our synagogue," they explained.

In fact, walls and pillars of a synagogue built probably by that very centurion still stand 2,000 years later near the north shore of the Sea of Galilee! But notice the implication of the Jews' reasoning. They were saying, in effect, that if the centurion had not thus helped them, neither should Jesus help the

---

* Richardson, D. (1981). *Eternity in their hearts* (pp. 136-139, 149, 152-154, 162-163). Ventura, CA: Regal Books.

** Don Richardson pioneered work for Regions Beyond Missionary Union (RBMU) among the Sawi tribe of Irian Jaya from 1962 to 1977. Author of *Peace Child, Lords of the Earth,* and *Eternity in Their Hearts,* Richardson is now Minister-at-Large for RBMU.

centurion of his pitifully paralyzed servant! How clannish of them! Little wonder Jesus could not help sighing occasionally, "O unbelieving and perverse generation... how long shall I stay with you? How long shall I put up with you?" (Matt. 17:17).

Jesus responded to the centurion, "I will go and heal him."

At that moment the centurion said something quite unexpected: "Lord, I do not deserve to have you come under my roof. But just say the word, and my servant will be healed. For I myself am a man under authority, with soldiers under me.... When Jesus heard this, He was astonished," wrote Matthew. What was so astonishing? Simply this—the centurion's military experience had taught him something about authority. As water always flows downhill, so also authority always flows down an echelon (a chain of command). Whoever submits to authority from a higher level of an echelon is privileged also to wield authority over lower levels. Jesus, the centurion noticed, walked in perfect submission to God: therefore Jesus must have perfect authority over everything below Him on the greatest echelon of all—the cosmos! Ergo! Jesus must possess an infallible ability to command the mere matter of the sick servant's body to adapt itself to a state of health!

Jesus exploited the occasion to teach His disciples that Gentiles have just as great a potential for faith as Jews!

"I tell you the truth," Jesus exclaimed, "I have not found anyone in Israel with such great faith!" As in many other discourses, Jesus exploited the occasion to teach His disciples that Gentiles have just as great a potential for faith as Jews! And they make just as valid objects for the grace of God too!

Determined to maximize the point, Jesus went on to say: "I say to you that many will come from the east and the west [Luke, a Gentile writer, adds in his parallel account: 'and from the north and the south'] and will take their places at the feast with Abraham, Isaac, and Jacob in the kingdom of heaven. But the subjects of the kingdom [this could only mean the Jews as God's chosen people] will be thrown out-

side, into the darkness, where there will be weeping and gnashing of teeth" (Matt. 8:7-12; Luke 13:28, 29).

Feasts are usually called to celebrate. What would you guess that future feast attended by Abraham and a host of Gentile guests will celebrate?

Intimations of the Great Commission to follow could hardly have been clearer! Wait, there is still much more!

A Canaanite woman

Still later, a Canaanite woman from the region of Tyre and Sidon begged Jesus' mercy on behalf of her demon-possessed daughter. Jesus at first feigned indifference. His disciples, glad no doubt to see their Messiah turn a cold shoulder to a bothersome Gentile, concurred at once with what they thought were His true feelings. "Send her away," they argued, "for she keeps crying out after us" (see Matt. 15:21-28).

Little did they know that Jesus was setting them up. "I was sent only to the lost sheep of Israel," He said to the woman. Having already manifested an apparent insensitivity toward the woman, Jesus now manifests an apparent inconsistency also. He has already healed many Gentiles. On what basis does He now reject this one's plea? One can imagine the disciples nodding grimly. Still they did not suspect. Undissuaded, the Canaanite woman actually knelt at Jesus' feet, pleading, "Lord, help me!"

"It is not right to take the children's bread." Then He added the crusher—"and toss it to their dogs!" "Dogs" was a standard epithet Jews reserved for Gentiles, especially Gentiles who tried to intrude upon Jewish religious privacy and privilege. In other words, Jesus now complements His earlier "insensitivity" and "inconsistency" with even worse "cruelty."

Was this really the Savior of the world talking? No doubt His disciples thought His reference quite appropriate for the occasion. But just when their chests were swollen to the full with pride of race, the Canaanite woman must have caught a twinkle in Jesus' eye and realized the truth!

"Yes, Lord," she replied ever so humbly, not to mention subtly, "but even the dogs eat the crumbs that fall from their master's table!" (Matt. 15:21-27; see also Mark 7:26-30).

"Woman, you have great faith!" Jesus glowed. "Your request is granted!" No, He was not being fickle! This was what He intended to do all along. Immediately preceding this event, Jesus had taught His disciples about the difference between real versus figurative uncleanness. This was His way of driving the point home. "And her daughter was healed from that very hour," Matthew records (v. 28).

A Samaritan village

When on a later occasion Jesus and His band approached a certain Samaritan village, the Samaritans refused to welcome Him. James and John, two disciples whom Jesus nicknamed "sons of thunder" for their fiery tempers, were incensed. "Lord," they exclaimed indignantly (stamping their feet), "do you want us to call fire down from heaven to destroy them?"

Jesus turned and rebuked James and John. Some ancient manuscripts add that He said, "You do not know what kind of spirit you are of, for the Son of Man did not come to destroy men's lives, but to save them" (Luke 9:51-55, including footnote).

With those words, Jesus identified Himself as a Savior for Samaritans!

Greeks at Jerusalem

Later on, some Greeks came to a feast at Jerusalem and sought audience with Jesus. Philip and Andrew, two of Jesus' disciples, relayed the request to Jesus who, as usual, exploited the occasion to get another wedge in for the "all peoples" perspective: "But I, when I am lifted up from the earth, will draw all men to myself" (John 12:32). This prophecy foreshadowed the manner of Jesus' death—crucifixion! But it also foretold the effect! All men—not merely in spite of Jesus' humiliation, but because of it—would be drawn to Him as God's anointed deliverer. On the surface this statement could be interpreted to mean that everyone in the world will become a

Christian. Since we know that this is quite unlikely, the statement probably means instead that some of all kinds of men will be drawn to Jesus when they learn that His death atoned for their sins. And that is

---

All men—not merely in spite of Jesus' humiliation, but because of it—would be drawn to Him as God's anointed deliverer.

---

exactly what the Abrahamic Covenant promised—not that all people would be blessed, but that all peoples would be represented in the blessing. Jesus' disciples thus gained still another fair warning of the Great Commission soon to follow!

On the road to Emmaus

Just as the disciples still did not believe Jesus' intimations of Gentile evangelism, so also they never really believed Him when He said He would rise from the dead. But He surprised them on both counts! Three days after His entombment He resurrected! And one of His first encounters after resurrection began in incognito fashion with two of His disciples on a road leading to Emmaus (see Luke 24:13-49). During the opening exchange the two disciples, still not recognizing Jesus, complained: "We had hoped that [Jesus] was the one who was going to redeem Israel" (v. 21); they did not add, "and make Israel a blessing to all peoples." A blind spot in their hearts still effectively obscured that part of the Abrahamic Covenant.

"How foolish you are," Jesus responded, "and how slow of heart to believe all that the prophets have spoken! Did not the Christ have to suffer these things and then enter His glory?" (vv. 25, 26).

Then, beginning with the five "books of Moses and all the Prophets, He explained to them what was said in all the Scriptures concerning Himself."

He had covered much of that ground before, but He went over it again—patiently (v. 27). And this time, the two disciples' hearts burned within them as He opened the Scriptures (see v. 32). Was a wider perspective at last winning its way into their hearts?

Later they recognized Jesus, but at the same moment He vanished from their sight! They retraced their steps at once to Jerusalem, found the Eleven (as the disciples were called for a while after Judas' defection), and recounted their experience. But before they finished talking, Jesus Himself appeared among them, and the Eleven experienced the end of the story for themselves!

As unerringly as a swallow returning to its nest, Jesus returned to the Scriptures and their central theme: "Then He opened their minds so they could understand the Scriptures. He told them, This is what is written: The Christ will suffer and rise from the dead on the third day, and repentance and forgiveness of sins will be preached in His name to all nations [i.e., *ethne*—peoples], beginning at Jerusalem. You are witnesses of these things" (Luke 24:45-48).

8. What attitudes in the disciples was Jesus challenging through His encounters with Gentiles? What similar attitudes may be present in the church today, and how could they be recognized?

_____

_____

_____

Go and make disciples

Notice, however, that He still did not command them to go. That would come a few days later, on a mountain in Galilee where—as far as the disciples were concerned—it all started. And here is the working of the command which the Abrahamic Covenant had already foreshadowed for 2,000 years, and which Jesus for three long years had been preparing His disciples to receive:

> All authority in heaven and earth has been given to me. Therefore go and make disciples of all nations, baptizing them in the name of the Father and of the Son and of the Holy Spirit, and teaching them to obey [note the limitation that follows] everything I have commanded you. And surely I will be with you always, to the very end of the age (Matt. 28:18-20).

It was not an unfair command. The Old Testament foreshadowed it. Jesus' daily teaching anticipated it. His frequent prejudice-free ministry among both

Samaritans and Gentiles had given the disciples a real-life demonstration of how to carry it out. Now He added the promise of His own authority bequeathed and His own presence in company—if they obeyed!

Still later, moments before He ascended back into heaven from the Mount of Olives (near Bethany), He added a further promise: "You will receive power when the Holy Spirit comes on you; and you will be my witnesses...."

Then followed Jesus' famous formula for the exocentric [outward] progression of the gospel: "...in Jerusalem, and in all Judea and Samaria, and to the ends of the earth" (Acts 1:8).

It was Jesus' last command. Without another word, and without waiting for any discussion of the proposal, He ascended into heaven to await His followers' complete obedience to it!

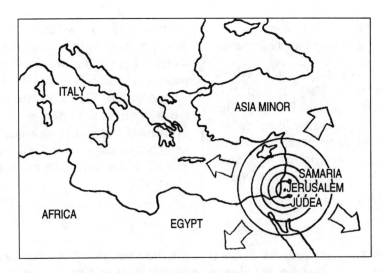

Figure 3-2. Outward Progression of the Gospel

The Great Commission

The most often quoted versions of the Great Commission are found in Matthew 28:18-20 and Mark 16:15-16. In both cases, the objective of the mandate is global in scope. Matthew's account of this universal directive is considered the most complete. In the following excerpt, Johannes Verkuyl elaborates on this passage.

❏ *The Great Commission of Matthew 28* *

Johannes Verkuyl

That only Matthew contains a mandate for engaging in worldwide mission is a popular and stubborn misconception. But there is no doubt about it: the concluding verses of Matthew's Gospel express it the most forthrightly. Not only is the conclusion to Matthew's Gospel extremely powerful compared to the other Gospels and Acts, but the final verses form a climax and present a summary of what was written before. They are the key to understanding the whole book.

In these concluding verses Jesus, the risen Lord, standing atop one of the mountains in Galilee—could it be the same one from which He delivered His Sermon on the Mount (Matt. 5:1)?—proclaims a three-point message to His disciples.

Jesus' authority

He mentions His authority in language reminiscent of Daniel 7:13-14 and of His own words before the Sanhedrin recorded in Matthew 26:64. No area, people, or culture now lies outside the domain of His power and authority. The missionary command which follows is directly connected to this report of the risen Lord's coronation. Having arisen, He now has exalted authority over the whole world. Thus, the mission mandate is not the basis for His enthronement. Rather, the reverse is true: the mandate *follows from* the fact of His authority. However the several recorded missionary mandates may vary, they all in unison proclaim this one truth: a saving and liberating authority proceeds from Him, the

* Verkuyl, J. (1978). *Contemporary missiology: An introduction* (D. Cooper, Ed. and Trans.) (pp. 106-108). Grand Rapids: Eerdmans.

victim who became a victor. He is the crucified Lord who now rules. His power is not that of a despot bent on destruction; instead He uses His power for our healing and liberation and accomplishes these goals by love, reconciliation, and patience.

Jesus' continuing mandate to mission

After His enthronement, the crucified and risen Lord issues His mandate to mission. The time between His resurrection and second coming is not simply an empty interim but rather a period during which the discharge of this command is included in the process of enthronement. Philippians 2:5-11 contains a strong parallel to this truth stated here.

"Go therefore" means "to depart, to leave, to cross boundaries" — sociological boundaries, racial boundaries, cultural boundaries, geographic boundaries.

What does the enthroned Lord command His disciples to do? He says, first of all, "Go therefore." The author chooses the Greek word *poreuthentes,* which means "to depart, to leave, to cross boundaries"—sociological boundaries, racial boundaries, cultural boundaries, geographic boundaries. This point is most important to one who carries on the task of communicating the gospel. It affects work done in his own area as well as in faraway places. The missionary must always be willing and ready to cross boundaries, whether they be at home or away. The word *poreuomai* in this text reminded the early Christian church of a peripatetic Jesus and His disciples who were continually crossing boundaries to reach out to the other person. Jesus also commands His followers to "make disciples of all nations." The author makes the Greek noun *mathetes* into a verb. The verbal form of this word occurs four times in the New Testament (in Matt. 13:52 and 27:57, in Acts 14:21, and here in Matt. 28:20). To become a disciple of Jesus involves sharing with Him His death and resurrection and joining Him on His march to the final disclosure of His messianic kingdom. He commands us to *make* disciples, that is, to move them to surrender to His liberating authority and to volunteer for the march already enroute to a new order of things, namely, His kingdom.

Jesus' promise

When Jesus adds the concluding words of promise, "Lo, I am with you always, even to the close of the age," He is reminding His disciples that He will be present among them in a new manner. The promise holds true for all time. Note in passing how often the word "all" occurs in this text: all power, all peoples, all the commandments, and finally, the word "always."

Christ promises to be with His church during "all of her days." As she discharges her missionary calling, the church must forever be asking, "What kind of day is it today?" for no two days are alike in her history. But however much the days and ages may change as the church carries on her mission in the six continents, one fact never changes: Jesus Christ is urging on His church to complete her missionary calling as He guides her to her final destination. And this missionary movement which emanates from Him will not cease until the end of the world. Thus, even though the methods of carrying it out must be changed continually, the task itself remains the same.

---

9. What is the objective of the Great Commission according to Matthew and Mark?

_____

_____

_____

10. *What is the main verb of Matthew 28:18-20, and how do the other three verbs relate to it?*

_____

_____

_____

II. Messengers for All Peoples

With so clear and inspirational a command as the Great Commission, we can imagine all 11 of the disciples hurrying off to evangelize the world. Unfortunately, Scripture doesn't record this kind of commitment. In the following article, Meg Crossman traces the disciples' disappointing performance.

❏ *The Reluctant Messengers*

Meg Crossman *

Jesus spent the major part of His ministry training leaders. He entrusted His disciples with His message of love and truth—a message He commissioned them to take to all people, nations, tribes, and tongues. In His post-resurrection teaching, He made this focus especially direct and clear. How quickly did the disciples respond?

Traditionally, these early leaders are portrayed to us as dynamic apostles who immediately went forth with the Word to all. The facts, however, are a little different. The apostles certainly shook Jerusalem and their own culture with their proclamation. Were they equally responsive when it came to the call to be a light to the nations? Let us reexamine the book of Acts, looking especially at the cross-cultural facets of the apostles' commission.

Pentecost

The great breakthrough of Pentecost obviously demonstrated God's desire that His message be intelligible to people from all nations. As men from all over the Mediterranean world gathered for the Feast of Pentecost, the Holy Spirit was poured out in an evident and particular way: wind, tongues of fire, and the miraculous ability of the gathered peo-ple to hear the 120 speaking the "wonderful works of God" each in his own native language. Rather than being proclaimed in faultless Hebrew or common Aramaic, the words of praise resounded in languages from all across the Roman world. Could there have been a clearer witness of the Father's intention that all should be able to hear of His love?

Jerusalem and Samaria

The apostles rightly began to proclaim the message in Jerusalem, both by words of power and by deeds of holiness. Mighty miracles supported and confirmed their claims. Many heard and responded. The church grew in depth and in numbers. God was glorified in Jerusalem and Judea. However, at the same time, the book of Acts documents the Jewish church's reticence to make plans for reaching people of other races and cultures.

Surely it could be expected that some action would be taken to reach at least the nearby people of Samaria. After all, the Samaritans had even been specifically named in Jesus' directive of Acts 1:8. No such initiative, however, appears to have been intended. It was not until persecution arose after the martyrdom of Stephen that scattered believers (but

* Meg Crossman is a Perspectives coordinator in Tempe, Arizona, and supervises several additional courses in the area. She has lived in Egypt and Japan, worked as a short-term missionary in China, and serves on the board of directors of Caleb Project.

not the apostles) "went everywhere preaching the word" (Acts 8:4).

Interestingly, it was a Greek believer, Philip, who took the message to Samaria. Perhaps the prejudice of the native-born Jews against their half-breed cousins next door was too great to allow living concern to arise quickly for Samaria's salvation. After a number of Samaritans had been converted, the apostles sent Peter and John to investigate the work and pray for the new believers (Acts 8:14ff). Curiously, having set their seal on the Samaritan conversions, Peter and John did not seem to make plans to set up a regular ministry outpost in Samaria. Instead, they preached, prayed, and *returned to Jerusalem* (Acts 8:25).

As if to encourage Philip that he was moving in the right direction, the Spirit of the Lord immediately entrusted him with an even more culturally distant task. Instead of alerting someone still in Jerusalem (and physically much nearer), the angel of the Lord sent open-hearted Philip down to Gaza for the sake of an Ethiopian official who was also a eunuch (forbidden to enter a Jewish congregation by Deuteronomy 23:1). Philip's fruitful ministry resulted in the Ethiopian's conversion. Philip then found himself in the town of Azotus. He went right on preaching up the coast to Caesarea, where the Roman procurators resided.

Joppa

Meanwhile, Peter, traveling around the country, ministered to converted Jews in Joppa (Acts 10). Yet a thrice-repeated vision was necessary to prepare Peter's heart to even consider going to Gentiles, who were actually *asking for a witness*. If the issue was simply giving witness to the household of the centurion Cornelius, surely there was Philip, already arrived in Caesarea, upon whom the Lord could have called. It seems clear, however, that this incident was necessary for the church leadership to become convinced of God's inexorable world-embracing purpose.

In spite of Peter's vision, the instantaneous response of the gathered Gentiles and the miraculous attestation of the Holy Spirit amazed Peter and his companions. The reluctance with which they admitted Gentiles to baptism is evident. Peter later recounted

his response not as, "How glorious that these people want to know God!" but, "Who was I that I could stand in God's way?" (Acts 11:17).

Peter returned to Jerusalem, needing to convince his fellow believers that he had not erred. In the only part of Acts which is repeated almost word for word, he recounted the entire incident (perhaps because the Holy Spirit wanted to emphasize this vital lesson by repetition). Apostolic response was not, "Praise God! Let's go tell other nations!" Instead, Luke recorded that they "held their peace" and said, "Well then, God has granted to the Gentiles also the repentance that leads to life" (Acts 11:18).

Some may object that this assessment of apostolic reluctance to spread the gospel is too harsh. After all, the apostles were attending to a new and struggling community with limited resources. There were many needs at home. Perhaps they did not feel an individual "call" to go to other nations. They may have felt the need to stay in Jerusalem since the city's destruction by Titus was imminent. Many people undoubtedly needed to hear and have the chance to repent before that terrible judgment fell.

Even if all these things were true, the apostles might surely have planned or commissioned others to go. They certainly knew enough about the Pharisaic bands who witnessed throughout the Roman Empire to realize that specific plans had to be made and people sent forth if purposeful missionary work was to be accomplished. No evidence emerges that these things took place.

A new breed of apostle

In Acts 9, God's desire to see His message taken to the nations was manifested in an unlikely candidate: Saul of Tarsus, an adamant persecutor of the church. The person least likely to be won at all was selected for this trans-national task: "He is a chosen vessel unto Me, to bear My name before the Gentiles, kings, and the children of Israel. For I will show him how great things he must suffer for My name's sake" (Acts 9:15-16). Saul's call to the nations was confirmed by Ananias, the man sent to pray for Paul: "The God of our fathers has appointed you to know His will... for you will be a witness for Him to all men..." (Acts 22:14-15).

Meanwhile, some of the scattered lay people hadn't realized that they needed to be careful to whom they spoke. In Acts 11:19-21 (perhaps 30 years after the outpouring at Pentecost), they couldn't resist telling the good news to Greeks in Antioch. Incredibly, a great harvest occurred. Again this called for apostolic investigation, and Barnabas was sent to undertake it. Having met and befriended Saul in Jerusalem shortly after Saul's conversion, Barnabas saw a perfect place to use the gifts of this new "apostle." Saul, born and raised in a Gentile city, understood the Greek mind and culture. He also knew the Scriptures intimately, having studied in Gamaliel's school in Jerusalem. Isn't it interesting that this very "Gentile" church in Antioch would shortly become the first to embrace the vision of actively evangelizing other nations, sending forth Paul and Barnabas in cross-cultural witness!

When Paul began to respond actively to God's directive, "Go! For I will send you far away to the Gentiles" (Acts 22:21), he experienced immediate response not only among the Jews, but also among the "God fearers." "God fearers" were Gentiles who believed in the God of Israel and had attached themselves to the synagogue, but they were unwilling to submit to circumcision or keep the Jewish law. They were delighted with the message of salvation available through faith in Jesus.

What opened the door to Gentiles, however, was one of the biggest stumbling blocks for the Jewish Christians: Paul's willingness to let Gentile Christians keep their "gentileness." As the equivalent of an ecclesiastical lawyer, Paul had the ability to discern and defend the scriptural background for his contention. This controversy raged in the early church until the Council of Jerusalem met to take up the matter, as recorded in Acts 15.

The Council of Jerusalem

Called before the church leaders in Jerusalem, Paul and Barnabas gave a spirited defense of their ministry throughout the Gentile world. They explained their teaching and detailed the confirmation of it by signs and wonders. At last, both Peter and James spoke out in favor of their approach, quoting from Amos regarding God's plan to rebuild the Tabernacle of David, "in order that the rest of mankind may seek the Lord, and all the Gentiles who are called by My name" (Acts 15:16, 17). James concluded that this approach *is* God's desire. These apostolic leaders affirmed the reality that faith in Jesus alone could save Gentiles. They merely asked Gentile believers to refrain from behavior that would be extremely offensive to Jewish culture, so that Jewish believers would not be troubled by fellowshiping with them.

This watershed decision by the Jerusalem Council opened the door for great movements to God among peoples throughout the Roman world. However, it did not signal a new missions thrust from Jerusalem.

Galatia

Interestingly, the letter Paul wrote defending and explaining the freeing of ethnic Christians from conformity to Jewish culture was addressed to the Galatians. This trading people, located near the Black Sea in Turkey, were the ancestors of the Celts (the Latin word for Celt was *Galatoi*). They were a Gentile people who had been thrown into confusion by the preaching of Judaizers, who wanted them to live by Old Testament law.

All cultures were acceptable, but not all apostles were ready to reach out to them.

Not only did Paul not expect Jewish legal requirements from the Galatians, he warned them that trying to add any such thing to their faith would actually bring them under a curse (Gal. 3:10-11)! In this letter, probably written a number of years after the Jerusalem Council, Paul recounted having to rebuke Peter publicly for his unwillingness to stand by the Gentile converts in the presence of brethren from Jerusalem (Gal. 2:11-17). At the same time, he affirmed the right of Jews to have their culture recognized, as he personally circumcised Timothy, a half-Jewish young man joining the mission band (Acts 16:3). In the case of Titus, a Greek believer, however, Paul insisted that he be accepted without that ceremonial initiation (Gal. 2:1-3).

All cultures were acceptable, but not all apostles were ready to reach out to them. Don Richardson, in his discussion of "The Hidden Message of Acts," comments:

How amazing! There were now at least 15 men generally recognized as apostles since Matthias, James the Lord's brother, and Saul and Barnabas joined the original 11. And yet, out of the 15, only two are "commissioned" to evangelize the estimated 900 million Gentiles in the world at that time. The other 13 are convinced that they are all needed to evangelize only about three million Jews, among whom there were already tens of thousands of witnessing believers! Their unashamed willingness to let Paul;ministry ofPaul and Barnabas take on the entire Gentile world boggles my mind.*

As far as can be determined historically, all the apostles, other than James, died far from Jerusalem.

Peter was crucified upside down in Rome. Thomas is believed to have been martyred in India, where the Mar Toma churches still bear his name. Andrew may have gone to Scythia (near the Crimean peninsula in the Black Sea) and others to Ethiopia, parts of North Africa, and Arabia. No document records whether they went forth by choice or were forced to flee by the destruction of Jerusalem in 70 A.D. However, the book of Acts clearly documents the difficulty of many of God's dearest and choicest servants in getting beyond their own ethnocentric walls. Not surprisingly, today's challenge is similar: We must help communities of Christians in every nation to reach beyond their own culture in fulfilling God's desire to extend the gospel to those far different from themselves.

11. What was the core issue discussed at the Council of Jerusalem?

_____

_____

_____

12. Why can this issue be viewed as more important to the expansion of the gospel than the initial outpouring of the Spirit in Acts 2?

_____

_____

_____

Expansion of the Church in Acts

The evidence is clear that the disciples weren't moved out of the "home church" to any significant degree until the destruction of Jerusalem. Nevertheless, Christ's clear "all nations" mandate was carried out *in spite of* the reluctant disciples. The well known passage in Acts 1:8, "And you shall be my witnesses," is not simply a reiteration of the Great Commission; it is a prophetic declaration of the progression of the gospel as recorded in this historic book (see Figure 3-3 on the next page).

---

* Richardson, D. (1981). *Eternity in their hearts* (p. 165). Ventura, CA: Regal Books.

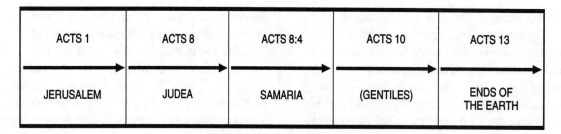

Figure 3-3. The Fulfillment of Acts 1:8

The first phase of this prophetic outline, Jerusalem, was fulfilled by the apostles rather quickly (Acts 1-2). Evidently, it took persecution to move the message out of Jerusalem into Judea and Samaria (Acts 8). No effective witness to Gentiles was extended until Peter, under virtual compulsion, went to the house of Cornelius (Acts 10). Even then, his next stop, once again, was Jerusalem.

It is interesting to note the role Peter had in each of the crucial movements in the progression of the gospel across cultural barriers. In Matthew 16:19, Christ offered the keys of the kingdom to Peter. In Acts 2, Peter's preaching was the "key" which opened the door of the kingdom to the *Jews* assembled for Pentecost in Jerusalem. In Acts 8, he again used that "key" in opening the door of the kingdom to the *Samaritans*, through the laying on of hands and the granting of the gift of the Holy Spirit to these "half-brothers" of the Jews. In Acts 10, Peter again used his "key" to open the door to *Gentiles* in the house of Cornelius. Through these three "key" events, God allowed Peter to participate in the progressive accessing of the gospel first by Jews, then by Samaritans, and lastly by the vast majority of humanity designated in the Bible as "Gentiles."

Paul's Principles and Practice

While Peter opened the door in each of the gospel's major cultural leaps, it was Paul and his apostolic band whom God utilized in the rapid spread of Christianity among the Gentiles of the Mediterranean region. Through this unique missionary team, God provided a model of the most effective means to take the gospel to geographically and culturally distant people. This model, along with Paul's amazing success, has provoked much analysis by missiologists hoping to arrive at major principles which led to Paul's astounding record. The following is a partial listing of the major missions principles which have been identified from Paul's experience and practice.

- *Paul's calling* – Paul had a specific calling to the Gentiles (unreached). He clearly understood his mission (Acts 26) and was willing to pursue it under all circumstances, even when it meant imprisonment and death.

- *Paul's vision* – Paul's principal ambition was to proclaim Christ where no man had gone before. The "regions beyond" were continually beckoning him (Rom. 15:22). This focus needs to be the primary mission vision even today, if the Great Commission is to be completed.

- *Paul's ministry preparation* – Paul was uniquely qualified for mission work. He was from a Gentile city and was born a Roman citizen, which allowed him to travel freely. He had the finest biblical training available and was a member of the scholarly Pharisees. Even with these advantages, the Lord took many years to prepare Paul for service. God's training takes time.

- *Paul's missionary team* – The missionary band was always co-led and involved many other workers, both expatriates and nationals. This principle of "teams" follows Christ's example of sending out two by two.

- *Paul's missionary strategy* – Paul focused on major urban centers from which the gospel could then radiate to the surrounding regions. Once the church was established in such a center, he felt free to move on. He also focused initial efforts on "God fearers," Gentiles who had already indicated receptivity to the message.

13. *As you continue to study the expanding world Christian movement, you will note that the above principles are an integral part of successful strategies throughout missions history. Can you think of others from Paul's ministry?*

_____

_____

_____

_____

_____

Intentional Mission

Chapter 13 of Acts marks the beginning of the third phase of evangelization which Christ predicted in Acts 1:8, "...to the uttermost parts of the earth." The church had been successful in evangelizing Jerusalem. Persecution moved this witness into the rest of Judea and the neighboring region of Samaria. But with the formation of the first Gentile church in Antioch and the clear recognition that the gospel indeed was for everyone, this church began to move in a purposeful manner to send emissaries of the gospel beyond their own geographical and cultural frontiers. The Antioch church was fully involved in the sending of Paul and Barnabas.

14. *Read Acts 13:1-4. Describe in your own words what happened in these verses.*

_____

_____

_____

We are not given much detail concerning the events which may have contributed to the sending of Paul and Barnabas. It is clear, however, that the Holy Spirit had a major role both in calling Paul and Barnabas to the missionary task (v. 2) and in sending them (v. 4). Note that this calling and sending did not bypass the church in Antioch, but that the church was instrumental in the process. The Holy Spirit spoke through the gathered leadership of the assembly and not just to the two men. The Spirit also used the church to commission Paul and Barnabas through the laying on of hands and sending them on their way.

In subsequent passages, we see Paul and Barnabas reporting back to Antioch, "from which they had been commended" (Acts 14:26), and to Jerusalem, from which Barnabas had originally been sent. This reporting demonstrates the organic relationship this apostolic band had to its sending base. Although every evidence suggests that the team operated autonomously in the field, they did maintain a strong link with their sending congregation through the reporting process. The concept of local churches as advanced bases for extending the gospel beyond current frontiers is developed by Arthur Glasser in the following excerpt.

❏ *Church and Mission* *

Arthur F. Glasser **

The most striking illustration of Paul's desire to establish this symbiotic relationship between local church and mobile mission is found in his epistle to the church in Rome. When he wrote this letter, he was midway through his great missionary career: his work in the Eastern Mediterranean had just been completed. Indeed, he could state that "from Jerusalem and as far around as Illyricum" (present day Yugoslavia) he had "fully preached the gospel of Christ" (Rom. 15:19). However, the Western Mediterranean represented unrelieved darkness, with but one point of light: the church in Rome. Apparently, this solitary fact had been on Paul's mind for some years as he agonized in prayer and deliberated about his future ministry (15:22).

So, he took pen in hand and wrote this tremendous epistle. As a "task theologian" he carefully selected certain themes, and developed them to prepare the Roman Christians for his missionary strategy. They had to realize anew (1) the abounding sin of man, with all the world guilty before God (1:18–3:20); (2) the abounding grace of God to sinners, with justification offered to the believing because of Christ's redemptive work (3:21–5:21); (3) the abounding grace of God to Christians, with sanctification made possible through the Holy Spirit's indwelling presence and power (6:1–8:39); (4) the abounding grace of God to the nations, for although Israel had failed through unbelief, God was nonetheless determined to reach them with the gospel through the Church and restore Israel at His return (9:1–11:26); and (5) various practical matters such as the exercise of spiritual gifts (12:1-21), the relation of Church and State (13:1-7), and the importance of love to enable the diversity within the Church effectively to put united heart and conscience to reaching the nations (13:8-15:6).

> **The local congregation needs the mobile team. Church needs mission.**

Only after this extensive review (15:15) does Paul reveal his strategy for the church at Rome: that it was to become a second Antioch, the new base of operations for his mission to Spain and the Western Mediterranean (15:22-24). It would have a significant role, providing Paul with experienced men and undertaking for their financial and prayer support. In other words, this epistle was written to give a strong cluster of house churches in a great pagan city a sense of their missionary responsibility for peoples beyond their borders. Through its participating in the missionary obedience of Paul's apostolic band, the church at Rome would attain a new sense of its role as the "sent people" of God (1:11-15). We conclude: the local congregation needs the mobile team. Church needs mission that the "gospel of the kingdom will be preached throughout the whole world, as a testimony to all nations; and then the end will come" (Matt. 24:14).

---

* Glasser, A. F., Hiebert, P. G., Wagner, C. P., & Winter, R. D. (1976). *Crucial dimensions in world evangelization* (pp. 31-32). Pasadena: William Carey Library.

** Dean Emeritus and Professor Emeritus of the School of World Mission at Fuller Theological Seminary, Arthur F. Glasser served as a missionary in western China with the China Inland Mission (now Overseas Missionary Fellowship) and was also OMF's Home Secretary for North America for 12 years. Glasser is the editor of *Missiology: An International Review*, the official journal of the American Society of Missiology.

15. List at least three ways in which the local church can play a primary role in the missionary task.

_____

_____

_____

_____

16. How is the book of Romans a "missionary" book?

_____

_____

_____

_____

In the following article, Ken Mulholland clearly articulates the importance of the church in maintaining the continuity of the missionary task, not only as the primary *agent* in accomplishing the task, but also as the chief *objective* of missions.

❑ A Church for All Peoples

Kenneth B. Mulholland *

Although intensely personal, the Christian faith is not individualistic. Jesus came not only to save sinners, but also to build His church (Matt. 16:18). He came to establish communities of His followers among every people group on the face of the earth—communities that would reach out to others cross-culturally to share the good news of salvation.

The references to baptism and teaching in the Great Commission passages (e.g., Matt. 28:19) bear witness to the fact that Jesus had "churchness" in mind when He sent His disciples into the world to make other disciples. Commitment to the Messiah implied commitment to the messianic community. As Arthur F. Glasser has put it, "The missionary task is incomplete if it stops short of planting churches." **

The evangelistic sermons recorded in the Acts of the Apostles conclude with a call to repentance, faith, and baptism. When Peter ended his Pentecost sermon, he appealed not just for individual conversion, but also for a public identification with other believers (Acts 2:38). When people came to Christ, they were incorporated into a new and caring community which is both universal and local by the very fact that it includes all God's people in all places and in all times. Yet, while it transcends both space and time, it is also a community which expresses itself visibly and locally through groups of believers gathered into congregations.

In his masterful commentary on the book of Acts, John R. W. Stott describes the marks of the first

---

* Kenneth B. Mulholland is Dean and Professor of Missions at Columbia Biblical Seminary and Graduate School of Missions in Columbia, South Carolina. He and his wife, Ann, previously served for nearly 15 years as missionaries in Central America.

** Glasser, A. F., Hiebert, P. G., Wagner, C. P., & Winter, R. D. (1976). *Crucial dimensions in world evangelization* (p. 6). Pasadena: William Carey Library.

Spirit-filled community that emerged following the Day of Pentecost:

> First, they were related to the apostles (in submission). They were eager to receive the apostles' instructions. A Spirit-filled church is an apostolic church, a New Testament church, anxious to believe and obey what Jesus and His apostles taught. Secondly, they were related to each other (in love). They persevered in the fellowship, supporting each other and relieving the needs of the poor. A Spirit-filled church is a loving, caring, sharing church. Thirdly, they were related to God (in worship). They worshiped Him in the temple and in the home, in the Lord's supper and in the prayers, with joy and with reverence. A Spirit-filled church is a worshiping church. Fourthly, they were related to the world (in outreach). No self-centered, self-contained church (absorbed in its own parochial affairs) can claim to be filled with the Spirit. The Holy Spirit is a missionary Spirit. So a Spirit-filled church is a missionary church.*

The New Testament letters, which are replete with references to "one another," bear witness to the mutual interdependence meant to characterize the life of these early Christian communities. In fact, these letters, most of which are addressed to Christian churches located in the principal cities of the Roman Empire, deal with matters of Christian faith and practice related to the nurture and development of congregational life.

A variety of metaphors illumine not only the relationship between God and His people, but also the mutual interdependence that characterizes God's people. Christians are branches of the same vine, living stones in the same building, sheep in the same flock, children in the same family, organs in the same body.

These congregations are meant to be kingdom communities. Jesus taught His disciples to pray that God's will be done on earth as it is in heaven. The church is a colony of heaven. It is a segment of humanity in which the ground rules are defined by God's will. In a sense, the church is meant to be a pilot project of the kingdom of God, a kingdom outpost, an anticipation of Christ's reign on earth. Thus, the church glorifies God, that is, makes God "look good," by continuing in the world the works of the kingdom which Jesus began. Although the church cannot avoid entirely the organizational and institutional forms of the culture in which it exists, essentially the church is the community of the King.

The goal of missions is to establish within every people group in the world indigenous church movements which are capable of so multiplying congregations that the entire people group is both evangelized and incorporated into the fellowship of the church.

This means that the goal of Christian missions is not limited to mere physical presence among unbelievers nor to the verbal proclamation of the gospel among those who have never heard it. It is not limited to establishing a network of mission stations across a defined geographical area. Neither is it confined to dotting the countryside of a given nation with a series of preaching points or developing Bible study groups in scattered urban neighborhoods. Nor is it restricted to the conversion of individual persons. The goal of missions is to establish within every people group in the world, within every piece of the human mosaic, indigenous church movements which are capable of so multiplying congregations that the entire people group is both evangelized and incorporated into the fellowship of the church.

However, the goal of planting new congregations which are capable of paying their own bills, making their own decisions, and evangelizing their own kind of people is not sufficient. For many years, missionaries believed that when these objectives

---

* Stott, J. R. W. (1990). *The Spirit, the church and the world: The message of Acts* (p. 87). Downers Grove, IL: InterVarsity Press.

had been accomplished, the missionary task was complete. Behind this conviction lay the assumption that only affluent, well-educated Christians were capable of establishing church movements in new cultural and linguistic spheres. The newly established churches in Africa, Asia, and Latin America were too deprived economically and educationally to engage in cross-cultural mission. We now realize that for mission to go full circle, it is necessary for the churches established by missionaries to become sending churches in order to gather the momentum necessary to penetrate each of the world's remaining unreached people groups. Thus, today's existing mission societies relate increasingly not just to the churches which they have brought into being, but to the mission structures which have emerged and are emerging from those churches.

Where there are no churches, there shall be churches. The Apostle Paul captured this central thrust of biblical missions when he testified to the Christians living in Rome: "And I have so made it my aim to preach the gospel, not where Christ was named, lest I should build on another man's foundation" (Rom. 15:20). Cultural boundaries must be crossed. Social barriers must be penetrated. Linguistic obstacles must be bridged. Religious resistance must be overcome. A church movement must be brought into being within each people group. Churches that feel a responsibility themselves to work cross-culturally must be planted. That is the purpose of missions.

17. *What is the central goal of missions?*

_____

_____

_____

III. A Message for All Peoples

Not only did Jesus model His worldwide concern through His ministry, but the gospel He preached was clearly a message for all peoples. The kingdom of God was the central theme of His teaching. His works demonstrated that this kingdom had truly come upon men (Matt. 12:28). Kingdom citizenship was not dependent on ethnicity or national origin. Jesus made it clear that *everyone* could enter that kingdom through the difficult, narrow gate of repentance and faith in God. It was a message appropriate to an "all peoples" perspective, transcending petty nationalistic expectations.

The Gospel of the Kingdom

In order to grasp the true significance of world mission, it is important to understand the dynamic inherent in the gospel of the kingdom. Christians aren't simply exporting "religion" through the missionary enterprise. Neither is their goal to impose cultural norms on the rest of the world or to engage in nationalistic imperialism of any sort. It is critical to understand, however, that missionaries *are* agents of a revolutionary government; they are kingdom envoys and ambassadors for Christ the Lord. In order to understand these concepts, in this section we will examine excerpts from George Eldon Ladd's book, *The Gospel of the Kingdom.*

❏ *The Meaning of the Kingdom of God* *

George Eldon Ladd **

God's kingdom always refers to His reign, His rule, His sovereignty, and not to the realm in which it is exercised. Psalm 103:19, "The Lord has established His throne in the heavens, and His kingdom rules over all." God's kingdom is His universal rule, His sovereignty over all the earth. Psalm 145:11, "They shall speak of the glory of thy kingdom, and tell of thy power." In the parallelism of Hebrew poetry, the two lines express the same truth. God's kingdom is His power. Psalm 145:13, "Thy kingdom is an everlasting kingdom, and thy dominion endures throughout all generations." The *realm* of God's rule is the heaven and earth, but this verse has no reference to the permanence of this realm. It is God's rule which is everlasting. Daniel 2:37, "You, O king, the king of kings, to whom the God of heaven has given the kingdom, the power, and the might, and the glory." Notice the synonyms for kingdom: power, might, glory—all expressions of authority. These terms identify the Kingdom as the "rule" which God has given to the king. Of Belshazzar, it was written, "God has numbered the days of your kingdom and brought it to an end" (Dan. 5:26). It is clear that the realm over which Belshazzar ruled was not destroyed. The Babylonian realm and people were not brought to an end; they were transferred to another ruler. It was the rule of the king which was terminated, and it was the rule which was given to Darius the Mede (Dan. 5:31).

One reference in our Gospels makes this meaning very clear. We read in Luke 19:11-12, "As they heard these things, He proceeded to tell a parable, because He was near to Jerusalem, and because they supposed that the kingdom of God was to appear immediately. He said therefore, 'A nobleman went into a far country to receive a *basileia* and then return.'" The nobleman did not go away to get a realm, an area over which to rule. The realm over which he wanted to reign was at hand. The territory over which he was to rule was this place he left. The problem was that he was no king. He needed authority, the right to rule. He went off to get a "kingdom," i.e., kingship, authority. The Revised Standard Version has therefore translated the word "kingly power."

This very thing had happened some years before the days of our Lord. In the year 40 B.C. political conditions in Palestine had become chaotic. The Romans had subdued the country in 63 B.C., but stability had been slow in coming. Herod the Great finally went to Rome, obtained from the Roman Senate the kingdom, and was declared to be king. He literally went into a far country to receive a kingship, the authority to be king in Judea over the Jews. It may well be that our Lord had this incident in mind in this parable. In any case, it illustrates the fundamental meaning of kingdom.

> **The kingdom of God is His kingship, His rule, His authority.**

The Kingdom of God is His kingship, His rule, His authority. When this is once realized, we can go through the New Testament and find passage after passage where this meaning is evident, where the Kingdom is not a realm or a people, but God's reign. Jesus said that we must "receive the kingdom of God" as little children (Mark 10:15). What is received? The Church? Heaven? What is received is God's rule. In order to enter the future realm of the Kingdom, one must submit himself in perfect trust to God's rule here and now.

We must also "seek first His kingdom and His righteousness" (Matt. 6:33). What is the object of our quest? The Church? Heaven? No; we are to seek

---

* Ladd, G. E. (1959). *The gospel of the kingdom* (pp. 20-21, 55, 127-130, 133-135, 139-140). Grand Rapids: Eerdmans.

** George Eldon Ladd was Professor Emeritus of New Testament Exegesis and Theology at Fuller Theological Seminary in Pasadena, California. He died in 1982 at the age of 71.

God's righteousness—His sway, His rule, His reign in our lives.

When we pray, "Thy kingdom come," are we praying for heaven to come to earth? In a sense we are praying for this; but heaven is an object of desire only because the reign of God is to be more perfectly realized than it is now. Apart from the reign of God, heaven is meaningless. Therefore, what we pray for is, "Thy kingdom come; thy will be done on earth as it is in heaven." This prayer is a petition for God to reign, to manifest His kingly sovereignty and power, to put to flight every enemy of righteousness and of His divine rule, that God alone may be King over all the world.

18. What subtle but important distinction does Ladd point out between the common usage of the word "kingdom" and its biblical usage?

_____

_____

The Nature of the Kingdom

Christ used many parables to illustrate the nature of the kingdom. These stories, woven from the fabric of everyday life, were used to teach new truths which had not yet been revealed about the kingdom. Christ referred to these parables as setting forth the "mystery of the kingdom" (Mark 4:1). This curious term "mystery" was also used by Paul in Romans 16:25-26 to describe the nature of Christ's coming. What was held secret for generations was now revealed. God's kingdom was "at hand," but it did not conform to popular expectations.

It is clear from Old Testament passages that God's kingdom will someday fill the earth. Daniel's prophetic interpretation of Nebuchadnezzar's dream (Dan. 2:31-35) is typical of the prophetic concept of the coming of the kingdom; that is, Christ's reign would shatter all earthly kingdoms and His dominion would be established forever (vv. 44, 45). The coming of the kingdom was seen as one great cataclysmic event, not unlike what believers today expect at Christ's second coming.

The incongruity between this prophetic image and the kingdom Christ brought puzzled even those who most firmly acclaimed Him as Messiah. John the Baptist sent his disciples to inquire if Jesus was the Coming One or if they should look for another (Matt. 11:2-6). John's doubt was produced by the fact that Jesus was not acting according to the Old Testament predictions that John himself had announced. Jesus' answer assured him that indeed, the kingdom had arrived with miracle-working power. But it was not the nation-destroying, justice-producing version of the kingdom that devout Jews awaited.

19. Why is it important to understand the nature of the term "kingdom" if we are to comprehend Christ's global mission?

_____

_____

_____

The kingdom Jesus ushered in was a subtle but powerful prelude to Christ's millennial rule. It is a kingdom which deals with first things first, the destruction of Satan and his perverse dominion over the souls of men. Ladd summarizes it well in the following excerpt.

The mystery of the Kingdom

This is the mystery of the Kingdom, the truth which God now discloses for the first time in redemptive history. God's Kingdom is to work among men in two different stages. The Kingdom is yet to come in the form prophesied by Daniel when every human sovereignty will be displaced by God's sovereignty. The world will yet behold the coming of God's Kingdom with power. But the mystery, the new revelation, is that this very Kingdom of God has now come to work among men, but in an utterly unexpected way. It is not now destroying human rule; it is not now abolishing sin from the earth; it is not now bringing the baptism of fire that John had announced. It has come quietly, unobtrusively, secretly. It can work among men and never be recognized by the crowds. In the spiritual realm, the Kingdom now offers to men the blessings of God's rule, delivering them from the power of Satan and sin. The Kingdom of God is an offer, a gift which may be accepted or rejected. The Kingdom is now here with persuasion rather than with power.

20. What essentially was the new truth Christ revealed about the kingdom?

_____

_____

_____

A Message for All Peoples

In a day in which conversion "formulas" are popular and the gospel of "prosperity" is often proclaimed, it is important to understand what Christ's messengers are to communicate. By understanding the ultimate goal of Christ's mission, we can better understand the message. 1 Corinthians 15:24-28 describes the culmination of Christ's work when at the *end* "...He delivers up the kingdom to the God and Father, when He has abolished all rule and all authority and power." His kingdom work is not completed until "...He has put all His enemies under His feet."

Christ has set out to destroy the enemies of men's souls. He has tackled death, Satan, and sin head on, but His defeat of these three enemies is to be done in stages. His initial victory was won through His death and resurrection. While these events signaled "the beginning of the end," Christ is continuing to wage war against these foes until the final victory is secured.

To understand this concept, we can look to an illustration from history. The most critical European battle of the Second World War was fought on the beaches of Normandy as the Allies gained a needed foothold on the Continent. It was understood by generals on both sides that once this beachhead was established, the destruction of Hitler's armies was inevitable. Yet the final victory did not come for many months, and it was secured only at a cost in human life which was much higher than that experienced before the invasion of Normandy. In the spiritual realm, Christ has won the initial victory. He has invaded enemy territory. The final victory will require time and a great sacrifice of His church in attaining it.

Our message is a liberating one. Christ has defeated death, Satan, and sin. The following three excerpts from Ladd's *Gospel of the Kingdom* will give us a clearer grasp of the powerful message we have to proclaim to the nations.

Victory over death

The Gospel of the Kingdom is the announcement of Christ's conquest over death. We have discovered that while the consummation of this victory is future, when death is finally cast into the lake of fire (Rev. 20:14), Christ has nevertheless already defeated death. Speaking of God's grace, Paul says that it has now been "manifested through the appearing of our Savior Christ Jesus, who abolished death and brought life and immortality to light through the gospel" (2 Tim. 1:10). The word here translated "abolish" does not mean to do away with, but to defeat, to break the power, to put out of action. The same Greek word is used in 1 Corinthians 15:26, "The last enemy to be *destroyed* is death." This word appears also in 1 Corinthians 15:24, "Then comes the end, when He delivers the kingdom to God the Father after *destroying* every rule and every authority and power."

There are therefore two stages in the destruction—the abolition—the defeat of death. Its final destruction awaits the Second Coming of Christ; but by His death and resurrection, Christ has already destroyed death. He has broken its power. Death is still an enemy, but it is a defeated enemy. We are certain of the future victory because of the victory which has already been accomplished. We have an accomplished victory to proclaim.

This is the Good News about the Kingdom of God. How men need this gospel! Everywhere one goes he finds the gaping grave swallowing up the dying.

Tears of loss, of separation, of final departure stain every face. Every table sooner or later has an empty chair, every fireside its vacant place. Death is the great leveler. Wealth or poverty, fame or oblivion, power or futility, success or failure, race, creed, or culture—all our human distinctions mean nothing before the ultimate irresistible sweep of the scythe of death which cuts us all down. And whether the mausoleum is a fabulous Taj Mahal, a massive pyramid, an unmarked forgotten spot of ragged grass, or the unplotted depth of the sea, one fact stands: death reigns.

> *Death is still an enemy, but it is a defeated enemy. We have an accomplished victory to proclaim.*

Apart from the Gospel of the Kingdom, death is the mighty conqueror before whom we are all helpless. We can only beat our fists in utter futility against the unyielding and unresponding tomb. But the Good News is this: death has been defeated; our conqueror has been conquered. In the face of the power of the Kingdom of God in Christ, death was helpless. It could not hold Him, death has been defeated; life and immortality have been brought to light. An empty tomb in Jerusalem is proof of it. This is the Gospel of the Kingdom.

---

21. In your own words, what is the good news regarding death?

_____

_____

_____

Victory over Satan

The enemy of God's Kingdom is Satan; Christ must rule until He has put Satan under His feet. This victory also awaits the Coming of Christ. During the Millennium, Satan is to be bound in a bottomless pit. Only at the end of the Millennium is he to be cast into the lake of fire.

But we have discovered that Christ has already defeated Satan. The victory of God's Kingdom is not only future; a great initial victory has taken place. Christ partook of flesh and blood—He became incarnate—"that through death He might destroy him who has the power of death, that is, the devil, and deliver all those who through fear of death were subject to lifelong bondage" (Heb. 2:14-15). The word translated "destroy" is the same word found in 2 Timothy 1:10 and 1 Corinthians 15:24

and 26. Christ has nullified the power of death; He has also nullified the power of Satan. Satan still goes about like a roaring lion bringing persecution upon God's people (1 Pet. 5:8). He insinuates himself like an angel of light into religious circles (2 Cor. 11:14). But he is a defeated enemy. His power, his domination has been broken. His doom is sure. A decisive, *the* decisive, victory has been won. Christ cast out demons, delivering men from satanic bondage, proving that God's Kingdom delivers men from their enslavement to Satan. It brings them out of darkness into the saving and healing light of the Gospel. This is the Good News about the Kingdom of God. Satan is defeated, and we may be released from demonic fear and from satanic evil and know the glorious liberty of the sons of God.

---

22. How does understanding Satan's defeat affect the way we present the gospel?

_____

_____

_____

Victory over sin

Sin is an enemy of God's Kingdom. Has Christ done anything about sin, or has He merely promised a future deliverance when He brings the Kingdom in glory? We must admit that sin, like death, is abroad in the world. Every newspaper bears an eloquent testimony of the working of sin. Yet sin, like death and Satan, has been defeated. Christ has already appeared to put away sin by the sacrifice of Himself (Heb. 9:26). The power of sin has been broken. "We know this, that our old self was crucified with Him so that the body of sin might be destroyed, and we might no longer be enslaved to sin" (Rom. 6:6). Here a third time is the word "to destroy" or "abolish."

Christ's reign as King has the objective of "abolishing" every enemy (1 Cor. 15:24, 26). This work is indeed future, but it is also past. What our Lord will finish at His Second Coming He has already begun by His death and resurrection. "Death" has been abolished, destroyed (2 Tim. 1:10); Satan has been

destroyed (Heb. 2:14); and in Romans 6:6 the "body of sin" has been abolished, destroyed. The same word of victory, of the destruction of Christ's enemies, is used three times of this threefold victory: over Satan, over death, over sin.

> **Christ's reign as King has the objective of "abolishing" every enemy.**

Therefore, we are to be no longer in bondage to sin (Rom. 6:6). The day of slavery to sin is past. Sin is in the world, but its power is not the same. Men are no longer helpless before it, for its dominion has been broken. The power of the Kingdom of God has invaded This Age, a power which can set men free from their bondage to sin.

The Gospel of the Kingdom is the announcement of what God has done and will do. It is His victory over

His enemies. It is the Good News that Christ is coming again to destroy forever His enemies. It is a gospel of hope. It is also the Good News of what God has already done. He has already broken the power of death, defeated Satan, and overthrown the rule of sin. The Gospel is one of promise but also of experience, and the promise is grounded in experience. What Christ has done guarantees what He will do. This is the Gospel which we must take into all the world.

23. How is our message about sin affected by our understanding of the present and future elements of the kingdom?

_____

_____

_____

The gospel of the kingdom is a powerful message. Christ has defeated the enemies of our souls. His victory means that no one who acknowledges His Lordship needs to remain in slavery to death, Satan, or sin. While in the flesh, we still have struggles. Yet, as we experience His victory now, we are also assured of a future when the final victory is won and the last vestiges of Satanic rule will be destroyed forever.

The Mission and a Motive

In light of the confusion in the minds of the Jews regarding Christ's role as Messiah, it is not surprising to find Jesus' disciples again questioning Him regarding the coming of the kingdom in power during the few days they had with Jesus after His resurrection (Matt. 24:3). Christ's dialogue with them on this subject (vv. 4-14) reveals significant information affecting our view of the remaining task as well. Read the following excerpt from Ladd to see how Jesus dealt with the disciples' question.

When will the Kingdom come?

Perhaps the most important single verse in the Word of God for God's people today is the text for this study: Matthew 24:14.

This verse suggests the subject of this chapter, "When will the Kingdom come?" This of course refers to the manifestation of God's Kingdom in power and glory when the Lord Jesus returns. There is wide interest among God's people as to the time of Christ's return. Will it be soon or late? Many prophetic Bible conferences offer messages which search the Bible and scan the newspapers to understand the prophecies and the signs of the times to try to determine how near to the end we may be. Our text is the clearest statement in God's Word about the time of our Lord's coming. There is no verse which speaks as concisely and distinctly as this verse about the time when the Kingdom will come.

The chapter is introduced by questions of the disciples to the Lord as they looked at the Temple whose destruction Jesus had just announced. "Tell us, when will this be and what shall be the sign of your coming, and of the close of the age?" (Matt. 24:3). The disciples expected This Age to end with the return of Christ in glory. The Kingdom will come with the inauguration of The Age to Come. Here is their question: "When will This Age end? When will you come again and bring the Kingdom?"

Jesus answered their question in some detail. He described first of all the course of This Age down to the time of the end. This evil Age is to last until His return. It will forever be hostile to the Gospel and to God's people. Evil will prevail. Subtle, deceitful influences will seek to turn men away from Christ. False religions, deceptive messiahs will lead many astray. Wars will continue; there will be famines and earthquakes. Persecution and martyrdom will plague the Church. Believers will suffer hatred so long as This Age lasts. Men will stumble and deliver up one another. False prophets will arise, iniquity will abound, the love of many will grow cold.

This is a dark picture, but this is what is to be expected of an age under the world-rulers of this darkness (Eph. 6:12). However, the picture is not one of unrelieved darkness and evil. God has not abandoned This Age to darkness. Jewish apocalyptic writings of New Testament times conceived of an age completely under the control of evil. God had withdrawn from active participation in the affairs of man; salvation belonged only to the future when God's Kingdom would come in glory. The present would witness only sorrow and suffering.

Some Christians have reflected a similar pessimistic attitude. Satan is the "god of This Age"; therefore, God's people can expect nothing but evil and defeat in This Age. The Church is to become thoroughly apostate; civilization is to be utterly corrupted. Christians must fight a losing battle until Christ comes.

The Word of God does indeed teach that there will be an intensification of evil at the end of the Age, for Satan remains the god of This Age. But we must strongly emphasize that God has not abandoned This Age to the evil one. In fact, the Kingdom of God has entered into This evil Age; Satan has been defeated. The Kingdom of God, in Christ, has created the Church, and the Kingdom of God works in the world through the Church to accomplish the divine purposes of extending His kingdom in the world. We are caught up in a great struggle—the conflict of the ages. God's Kingdom works in this world through the power of the Gospel. "And this gospel of the kingdom will be preached throughout the whole world, as a testimony to all nations; and then the end will come."

---

24. *The author suggests that Matthew 24:14 contains a tremendously significant truth for the church today. State in your own words the content of the verse and its implication for the church.*

_____

_____

_____

The gospel of the kingdom is a marvelous message of freedom and power. It is a message which men and women everywhere desperately need to hear and understand. How important is it that the church be involved in discipling the nations? These final two excerpts from Ladd's *Gospel of the Kingdom* show us both the significance of the task and our motive for being involved in it.

The ultimate meaning of history

The Church is "a chosen race, a royal priesthood, a holy nation" (1 Pet. 2:9); and it is in the present mission of the Church, as she carries the Good News of the Kingdom of God unto all the world, that the redemptive purpose of God in history is being worked out.

The ultimate meaning of history between the Ascension of our Lord and His return in glory is found in the extension and working of the Gospel in the world. "This gospel of the kingdom will be preached throughout the whole world, as a testimony to all nations; and then the end will come."

The divine purpose in the nineteen hundred years since our Lord lived on earth is found in the history of the Gospel of the Kingdom. The thread of meaning is woven into the missionary programme of the Church. Some day when we go into the archives of heaven to find a book which expounds the meaning of human history as God sees it, we will not draw out a book depicting "The History of the West" or "The Progress of Civilization" or "The Glory of the British Empire" or "The Growth and Expansion of America." That book will be entitled *The Preparation for and the Extension of the Gospel Among the Nations*. For only here is God's redemptive purpose carried forward.

This is a staggering fact. God has entrusted to people like us, redeemed sinners, the responsibility of carrying out the divine purpose in history. Why has God done it in this way? Is He not taking a great risk that His purpose will fail of accomplishment? It is now over nineteen hundred years, and the goal is not yet achieved. Why did God not do it Himself? Why did

---

God has entrusted to people like us, redeemed sinners, the responsibility of carrying out the divine purpose in history.

He not send hosts of angels whom He could trust to complete the task at once? Why has He committed it to us? We do not try to answer the question except to say that such is God's will. Here are the facts: God has entrusted to us this mission; and unless we do it, it will not get done.

25. In what way is the church's influence on history more significant than the influence of the United Nations or the governments of powerful nations?

_____

_____

_____

A motive for mission

Finally, our text contains a mighty motive. "Then the end will come."

The subject of this chapter is, "When will the Kingdom come?" I am not setting any dates. I do not know when the end will come. And yet I do know this: When the Church has finished her task of evangelizing the world, Christ will come again. The Word of God says it. Why did He not come in A.D. 500? Because the Church had not evangelized the world. Why did He not return in A.D. 1000? Because the Church had not finished her task of worldwide evangelization. Is He coming soon? He is—if we, God's people, are obedient to the command of the Lord to take the Gospel into all the world.

26. Why is the Lord's return such an important motivational factor for the church's involvement in the Great Commission?

_____

_____

_____

"Go ye therefore"

Do you love the Lord's appearing? Then you will bend every effort to take the Gospel into all the world. It troubles me in the light of the clear teaching of God's Word, in the light of our Lord's explicit definition of our task in the Great Commission (Matt. 28:18-20), that we take it so lightly. "All authority in heaven and on earth has been given to Me." This is the Good News of the Kingdom. Christ has wrested authority from Satan. The Kingdom of God has attacked the kingdom of Satan; This Evil Age has been assaulted by The Age to Come in the person of Christ. All authority is now His. He will not display this authority in its final glorious victory until He comes again; but the authority is now His. Satan is defeated and bound; death is conquered; sin is broken. All authority is His. "Go ye therefore." Wherefore? Because all authority, all power is His, and because He is waiting until we have finished our task. His is the Kingdom; He reigns in heaven, and He manifests His reign on earth in and through His church. When we have accomplished our mission, He will return and establish His Kingdom in glory. To us it is given not only to wait for but also to hasten the coming of the day of God (2 Pet. 3:12). This is the mission of the Gospel of the Kingdom, and this is our mission.

Summary

The coming of the Messiah did not fulfill the expectations of devout Jews. Instead of rallying the nation to political fulfillment, Christ identified Himself with the whole of the human race and pursued God's purpose for Himself. Even His disciples had trouble accepting this radically different "kingdom." Although Jesus used every encounter with Gentiles as an opportunity to give His followers an "all peoples" perspective, He did not quickly change their ingrained attitudes. He clearly spelled out the Great Commission to them before His ascension, but the disciples failed to move out of their own cultural comfort zone in taking the gospel to the Gentile nations.

The Holy Spirit, however, was not deterred in moving the good news from the restrictive Jewish environment to the Samaritans and on to the boundless frontiers of the Gentile nations. The book of Acts records this progression and the work of the apostolic bands which God raised up to carry out His missionary mandate. Through obedience to the Great Commission, the church assumes her central role as propagator of other churches to the ends of the earth.

In a day in which different versions of the "gospel" are in circulation, it is important to grasp the original message as Christ and the apostles understood it and preached it. The gospel of the kingdom is still the truth which brings liberation from Satan, sin, and death. Communicating this vital message to each and every people on the face of the earth is the church's explicit mission. The completion of the task prepares the way for the second coming of our Lord in power and glory. Maranatha, come, Lord Jesus!

Integrative Assignment

1. Write a paragraph describing the ways Jesus demonstrated He understood His messianic role to all the peoples of the world.

2. Describe the "ideal" role that the church is to have in the Great Commission. Then correlate this ideal model with what your local church is doing.

3. Prepare an outline for a short talk entitled, "The Liberating Message of the Gospel." Be sure to support each point with Scripture.

Questions for Reflection

1. The key to missions is a mobilized church. Does your church have a mission vision? How can you strengthen the vision that's there? Let God use you to strengthen your church's commitment to world mission through whatever means are available to you. Write your thoughts and action plans below.

_____

_____

_____

_____

_____

_____

_____

2. Christ's disciples aren't the only ones who needed to have their cultural and racial attitudes restructured. Cultural self-centeredness (ethnocentricity) is common to all cultures. In many societies there are dominant cultures which perpetuate social discrimination as a way of protecting their own status position. How are cultural biases expressed in your city? Have these biases been a hindrance to the spread of the gospel? Meditate on Galatians 3:27-29. Pray that the Lord will build a strong "all peoples" outlook in you and your church. Record your thoughts below.

_____

_____

_____

_____

_____

_____

3. *The gospel of the kingdom is a dynamic, liberating force. Many of us, however, live as if this were not a fact. Are you experiencing the victorious message of the kingdom? Meditate on John 8:34-36. Examine your heart before the Lord, and record your thoughts.*

    _____

    _____

    _____

    _____

    _____

    _____

    _____

    _____

    _____

    _____

    _____

CHAPTER 4

Expansion of the World Christian Movement

"And this gospel of the kingdom shall be preached in the whole world ..." (Matt. 24:14)

In the first three chapters of this study, we traced God's mission purpose throughout the Old and New Testaments. We observed how God dealt with mankind in His never-ceasing concern to redeem humanity and restore His kingdom. After Adam's descendants repeatedly failed to acknowledge His loving rule, God chose to raise up a people for Himself through the descendants of Abraham. For the most part, the nation of Israel also failed to serve as a willing agent of God's redemptive purpose. However, by the time of Christ, through exile and dispersion, Israel had been used to extend the knowledge of God's name within the surrounding nations. Thus the stage was set for the coming of the Messiah, God's man for all the peoples.

Christ demonstrated a clear understanding of the worldwide dimensions of His messianic role. He practiced and preached an "all peoples" message. Through encounters with Gentiles, He attempted to confront the narrow, ethnocentric view of the kingdom which His disciples held. His message was accompanied by power to liberate all people everywhere from Satan, sin, and death. He commissioned and sent His disciples to every nation with the gospel of the kingdom, promising to return in glory when the task was finished.

Empowered after Pentecost to carry the good news forth, the disciples worked effectively within their own cultural comfort zone, but they balked at intentional evangelization of the Gentile nations. Through persecution, God scattered His people in such a way that the message did begin to cross cultural boundaries. With the conversion of Cornelius and his household, the fledgling movement was forced to recognize that God's grace had been extended to the Gentiles. Later, at the Jerusalem Council of Acts 15, the church leaders agreed that God's grace did not require converts to accept Jewish customs and culture.

Intentional "missions" began with the Gentile church in Antioch. The Holy Spirit raised up apostolic teams which began to travel the Mediterranean region. They worked effectively to carry the message across cultural boundaries. In spite of persecution and severe opposition, Christianity grew in its scope and influence.

During the first century A.D., Christianity spread throughout much of the Roman Empire and even beyond the borders of that empire. By the time of Christianity's acceptance as the official religion of

Rome in 375 A.D., much of North Africa was evangelized, as well as parts of Asia Minor, the Iberian Peninsula, and Britain. There were communities of believers in Central Asia and even in India. Considering the severe religious and political opposition, geographical barriers, and the restrictive nature of travel, this widespread expansion of the gospel was a remarkable achievement. In this chapter, we will trace the advance of Christianity from this vigorous beginning to the present.

I. Epochs of Mission History

The full story of the advance of the gospel from people to people during the first 1900 years of Christian history is known only by God Himself. Our perceptions are colored by secular, Roman Catholic, and Protestant sources which paint the picture from their particular persuasion. Protestants, for example, espouse the "no saints in the middle" theory, which practically erases the possibility of a vital Christianity between the emergence of the Roman Catholic church in the fourth century and the Protestant Reformation in the 16th. Was God at work through His people during these "dark ages"? If so, how did He move His Great Commission messengers?

In this chapter, Dr. Ralph Winter, missions historian, will explain his view of these and other related issues, tracing the progression of the gospel from Jerusalem to the development of modern missions.

❏ *The Kingdom Strikes Back:*
The Ten Epochs of Redemptive History *

Ralph D. Winter **

Man has virtually erased his own story. Human beings have been pushing and shoving each other so much that they have destroyed well over 90 percent of their own handiwork. Their libraries, their literature, their cities, their works of art are mostly gone. Even what remains from the distant past is riddled with evidences of a strange and pervasive evil that has grotesquely distorted man's potential. This is strange because apparently no other species of life treats its own with such deadly malignant hatred. The oldest skulls bear mute witness that they were bashed in and roasted to deliver their contents as food for still other human beings.

We are not surprised then to find that the explanation for this strangeness comes up in the oldest, detailed, written records—surviving documents that are respected by Jewish, Christian, and Muslim traditions, whose adherents make up more than half of the world's population. These documents, referred to by the Jews as "the Torah," by Christians as the "Books of the Law," and by Muslims as "the Taurat," not only explain the strange source of evil but also

---

* Winter, R. D. (1992). The kingdom strikes back: The ten epochs of redemptive history. In R. D. Winter & S. C. Hawthorne (Eds.), *Perspectives on the world Christian movement: A reader* (rev. ed.) (pp. B3-B21). Pasadena: William Carey Library.

** After serving 10 years as a missionary among Mayan Indians in western Guatemala, Ralph D. Winter spent the next 10 years as a Professor of Missions at the School of World Mission at Fuller Theological Seminary. He is the founder of the U.S. Center for World Mission in Pasadena, California, a cooperative center focused on people groups still lacking a culturally relevant church. Winter has also been instrumental in the formation of the movement called Theological Education by Extension, the William Carey Library publishing house, the American Society of Missiology, the Perspectives Study Program, and the International Society for Frontier Missiology. Since March 1990 he has been the President of the William Carey International University.

describe a counter-campaign and follow that campaign through many centuries.

To be specific, the first 11 chapters of Genesis constitute a trenchant introduction to the whole problem. These pages describe three things: (1) a glorious and "good" original creation; (2) the entrance of a rebellious, evil, superhuman power who is more than a force, actually a personality; and the result; (3) a humanity caught up in that rebellion and brought under the power of that evil.

From Genesis 12 to the end of the Bible, we have a single drama: the entrance into this enemy-occupied territory of the kingdom, the power, and the glory of the living God.

In the whole remainder of the Bible, we have a single drama: the entrance into this enemy-occupied territory of the kingdom, the power, and the glory of the living God. From Genesis 12 to the end of the Bible, and indeed until the end of time, there unfolds the single, coherent drama of "the Kingdom strikes back." In this drama we see the gradual but irresistible power of God reconquering and redeeming His fallen creation through the giving of His own Son at the very center of the 4,000-year period we are now ending.

This counter-attack clearly does not await the appearance of the central Person in the center of the story. Indeed, there would seem to be five identifiable epochs before the appearance of the Christ. While the purpose of this article is mainly to describe the five epochs following His "visitation," in order for those to be seen as part of a single 10-epoch continuum, we will pause to give a few clues about the first five epochs.

The theme that links all 10 epochs is that of the grace of God intervening into history in order to contest the enemy who temporarily is "the god of this world." God's plan for doing this is to reach all peoples by blessing Abraham and Abraham's children by faith. This blessing of God is in effect conditioned upon its being shared with other nations, since those who receive God's blessings are, like Abraham, men of faith who subject themselves to God's will, become part of His kingdom, and represent the extension of His rule throughout the world among all other peoples.

In the first epoch of roughly 400 years, Abraham was chosen and moved to the geographic center of the Afro-Asian land mass. The story of Abraham, Isaac, Jacob, and Joseph is often called the Period of the Patriarchs and displays only small breakthroughs of witness and sharing with the surrounding nations even though the central mandate (Gen. 12:1-3) is repeated twice again to Abraham (18:18; 22:18) and to Isaac (26:4) and Jacob (28:14, 15). Joseph observed to his brothers, "You sold me, but God sent me," and was obviously a great blessing to Egypt. Even the Pharaoh recognized that Joseph was filled with the Holy Spirit. But this was not the intentional missionary obedience God wanted.

As we push on into the next four roughly-400-year periods—(2) the Captivity, (3) the Judges, (4) the Kings, and (5) the second captivity and Diaspora—the promised blessing and the expected mission (to share that blessing with all the nations of the world) often all but disappear from sight. As a result, where possible, God accomplished His will through the voluntary obedience and godliness of His people, but where necessary, He does His will through involuntary means. Joseph, Jonah, the nation as a whole when taken captive represent the category of involuntary missionary outreach intended by God to force the sharing of the blessings. The little girl carried away captive to the house of Naaman the Syrian was able to share her faith. On the other hand, Ruth, Naaman the Syrian, and the Queen of Sheba all came voluntarily, attracted by God's blessings to Israel.

We see in every epoch the active concern of God to forward His mission, with or without the full cooperation of His chosen nation. Thus, when Jesus appears, it is an incriminating "visitation." He comes to His own, and His own receive Him not. He is well received in Nazareth until He refers to God's desire to bless the Gentiles. Then a homicidal outburst of fury betrays the fact that this chosen nation—chosen to receive and to mediate blessings (Ex. 19:5, 6; Ps. 67; Isa. 49:6)—has grossly departed from that. There was indeed a sprinkling of fanatical Bible students who "traversed land and sea to make a single proselyte." But their outreach was not so much to be a blessing to the other nations as it was to sustain and protect the nation Israel. They were not making sure that their converts were circumcised in heart (Jer. 9:24-26; Rom. 2:29).

In effect, under the circumstances, Jesus did not come to give the Great Commission but to take it away. The natural branches were broken off while other "unnatural" branches were grafted in (Rom. 11:13-24). Even so, despite the general reluctance of the chosen missionary nation, many people groups were in fact touched: Canaanites, Egyptians, Philistines (of the ancient Minoan culture), Hittites, the Moabites, the Phoenicians (of Tyre and Sidon), the Assyrians, the Sabeans (of the land of Sheba), the Babylonians, the Persians, the Parthians, the Medes, the Elamites, the Romans.

	TEN EPOCHS	MISSION AGENTS	MECHANISMS
2000 B.C.	1. PATRIARCHS	ABRAHAM	VG
	2. EGYPTIAN CAPTIVITY	JACOB	IG
	3. JUDGES	ISRAEL	I, BA
	4. KINGS	EXILES	I, BA
	5. POST-EXILE	DISPERSED JEWS	IG
	6. ROME	EARLY CHURCH	IG, VG
	7. BARBARIANS	CELTS/MONKS	I, VG
	8. VIKINGS	SLAVES	I, IG
	9. SARACENS	(CRUSADERS), FRIARS	VG
2000 A.D.	10. ENDS OF THE EARTH	MODERN MISSIONS	VG

KEY TO MECHANISMS:
VG   Voluntary Going
IG   Involuntary Going
I   Invasion
BA   Benign Attraction

Figure 4-1. Four Thousand Years of Mission History

And now, as we look into the next 2,000-year period, it is one in which God, on the basis of the intervention of His Son, is making sure that the other nations are both blessed and similarly called "to be a blessing to all the families of the earth." Now, for them, "Unto whomsoever much is given, of him shall much be required." Now the Kingdom strikes back in the realms of the Armenians, the Romans, the Celts, the Franks, the Angles, the Saxons, the Germans, and eventually even those ruthless pagan pirates, the Vikings. All were to be invaded, tamed, and subjugated by the power of the gospel, and expected to share their blessings with still others.

But the next five epochs are not all that different from the first five epochs. Those that are blessed do not seem terribly eager to share those blessings. The Celts are the only nation in the first millennium who give an outstanding missionary response. As we will see, just as in the Old Testament, the coming of blessings brings sober responsibility, dangerous if unfulfilled. And we see repeated again and again God's use of the full range of His four missionary mechanisms.

The coming of blessings brings sober responsibility, dangerous if unfulfilled.

The "visitation" of the Christ was dramatic, full of portent, and strikingly "in due time." Jesus was born a member of a subjugated people. Yet in spite of her bloody imperialism, Rome was truly an instrument in God's hands to prepare the world for His coming. Rome controlled one of the largest empires the world has ever known, forcing the Roman peace upon all sorts of disparate and barbaric peoples. For centuries Roman emperors had been building an extensive communication system, both in the 250,000 miles of marvelous roads which stretched all over the empire, and in the rapid transmission of messages and documents somewhat like the Pony Express on the American frontier. In its conquests, Rome had enveloped at least one civilization far more advanced than her own—Greece—and highly educated artisans and teachers taken as slaves to every major city of the empire taught the Greek language. Greek was understood from England to Palestine. How else could a few gospels and a few letters from St. Paul have had such a widespread impact among so many different ethnic groups in such a short period of time?

Jesus came, lived for 33 years on earth, confronted the wayward, missionary nation, was crucified and buried, rose again, underscored the same commission to all who would respond, and ascended once more to the Father. Today even the most agnostic historian stands amazed that what began in a humble stable in Bethlehem of Palestine, the backwater of the Roman Empire, in less than 300 years had taken control of the Lateran Palace of the emperors of Rome, a gift of Constantine to the church. How did it happen? It is truly an incredible story.

---

1. List some characteristics of the Roman Empire which facilitated the spread of the gospel.

_____

_____

_____

2. What has been the common responsibility of all those who have enjoyed God's blessing throughout the centuries?

_____

_____

_____

3. Why does Winter contend that "Jesus did not come to give the Great Commission but to take it away"?

_____

_____

_____

Being a blessing to all nations is not an option for the people of God. God is determined to see His mission purpose fulfilled and will use His people to carry it out, *one way or another.*

In the next part of this article, Winter pieces together for us the story of the expansion of Christianity from the first century on.

No saints in the middle?

Let us interrupt the story here briefly. We can do well at this point to confront a psychological problem. In church circles today we have fled, or feared, or forgotten these middle centuries. Let us hope evangelicals are not as bad in this respect as the Mormons. They seem to hold to a "BOBO" theory that the Christian faith somehow "blinked out" after the Apostles and "blinked on" again when Joseph Smith dug up the sacred tablets in the 19th century. The result of this kind of BOBO approach is that you have "early" saints and "latter-day" saints, but no saints in the middle. Many Protestants may have roughly the same idea. Such people are not much interested in what happened prior to the Protestant Reformation: they have the vague impression that before Luther and Calvin the church was apostate and whatever there was of real Christianity consisted of a few persecuted individuals here and there. In a series of twenty volumes on "Twenty Centuries of Great Preaching," only half of the first volume is devoted to the first fifteen centuries! In evangelical Sunday schools children are busy as beavers with the story of God's work from Genesis to Revelation, from Adam to the Apostles, and Sunday school publishers may even boast about their "all-Bible curriculum." But this only really means that the children do not get exposed at all to what God did with the Bible between the times of the Apostles and the Reformers, a period which is staggering proof of the uniqueness and power of the Bible! To all such people it is as if there were no saints in the middle.

4. What does Winter mean by the theory of "no saints in the middle"? How has your perception of church history been affected by such a theory?

_____

_____

_____

In the space available, it is possible to trace only the Western part of the story of Christianity—and only its outline at that, but to do that we must recognize certain clear stages that make the whole story fairly easy to grasp. Note the pattern in the chart below.

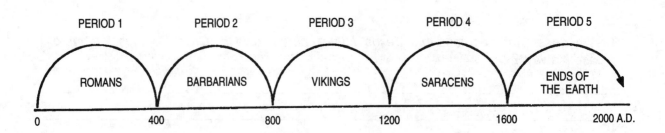

Figure 4-2. Periods of Expansion of Christianity

In Period 1, Rome was won but did not reach out with the gospel to the barbaric Celts and Goths.* Almost as a penalty, the Goths invaded Rome and caved in the whole western part of the empire.

In Period 2, the Goths were added in, and they briefly achieved a new "Holy" Roman Empire. But they also did not effectively reach further north with the gospel.

Thus, in Period 3, again almost as a penalty, the Vikings** invaded the area of these Christianized Celtic and Gothic barbarians, and the Vikings, too, became Christians in the process.

In Period 4, Europe, for the first time united by Christian faith, reached out in a sort of pseudo-mission to the Saracens and pointed further east in the aftermath of the great abortion of the Crusades.***

In Period 5, Europe now reached out to the very ends of the earth. In this period reaching out has been the order of the day, but with highly mixed motives; commercial and spiritual interests have been both a blight and a blessing. Yet, during this period, the entire non-Western world has suddenly been stirred into development. Never before have so few affected so many, and never before has so great a gap resulted between two halves of the world.

What will happen before the year 2000? Will the non-Western world invade Europe and America like the Goths invaded Rome and the Vikings overran Europe? Will the "Third World" turn on us in a new series of barbarian invasions? Will the OPEC nations gradually buy us out and take us over? Clearly we face the reaction of an awakened non-Western world that now suddenly is beyond our control. What will the role of the gospel be? Can we gain any light from these previous cycles of outreach?

5. Based on Figure 4-2, what mechanisms did God use to spread Christianity beyond its established borders during the first four periods that are outlined?

_____

_____

Period 1

After apostolic times, Christianity expanded relentlessly throughout the Greco-Roman world. From a tiny sect in a world full of sects and religions, it blossomed within three centuries to become the official religion under the Roman Emperor Constantine. The blessings inherent in the message spread throughout this cultural basin. Did the Roman church leadership then begin to take this blessing to their neighbors? In the next part of his article, Winter describes how the Roman Empire was conquered by Christianity and how the Empire's response to the Great Commission mandate affected her subsequent history.

---

* The Celts were Indo-Europeans who inhabited much of Europe. The Goths were Germanic people who lived first in the region of the Baltic Sea and later near the Black Sea. They were one of several Barbarian tribes who overthrew the decaying Roman Empire.

** The Vikings were Scandinavian seafaring warriors.

*** Saracens were any persons—Arabs, Turks, or others—who professed the religion of Islam. The Crusades were a series of expeditions from Western Europe to the Eastern Mediterranean, designed to recover the Holy Land from Islam and then retain it in Christian hands. They ultimately failed to accomplish their objectives.

Winning the Romans (0-400 A.D.)

Perhaps the most spectacular triumph of Christianity in history is its conquest of the Roman Empire in roughly 20 decades. We know very little about this period. Our lack of knowledge makes much of it a mystery, and what happened to Christianity sounds impossible, almost unbelievable. Only the early part starts out blazoned in the floodlight of the New Testament epistles themselves. Let's take a glance at that. There we see a Jew named Paul brought up in a Greek city, committed to leadership in the Jewish tradition of his time. Suddenly he was transformed by Christ and saw that the faith of the Jews as fulfilled in Christ did not require Jewish garments but could be clothed in Greek language and customs as well as Semitic. In this one decisive struggle it should have once more been clarified that anyone could be a Christian, be transformed in the inner man by the living Christ—whether Jew, Greek, Barbarian, Scythian, slave, free, male, or female. The Greeks didn't have to become Jews, undergo circumcision, take over the Jewish calendar of festivals or holy days, nor even observe Jewish dietary customs, any more than a woman had to be made into a man to be acceptable to God.

Paul based his work on the radical biblical principle (unaccepted by many Jews to this day) that it is circumcision of the heart that counts (Jer. 9) and that the new believers of a new culture did not have to speak the language, wear the clothes, or follow all

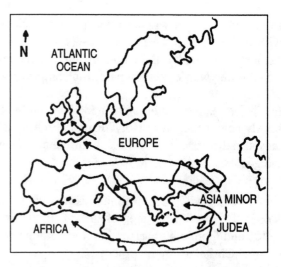

Figure 4-3. Christianization of Roman Empire

the customs of the sending church. This meant that for Greeks, the cultural details of the Jewish law were no longer relevant. Therefore, to the Jews Paul continued as one "under the law of Moses," but to those unfamiliar with the Mosaic Law, he preached the "law of Christ" in such a way that it could be fulfilled dynamically and authentically in their particular circumstances. While to some he appeared to be "without law," he maintained that he was not without law toward God, and indeed, as regards the basic purpose of the Mosaic Law, the believers in the Greek church immediately developed the functional equivalent to it, in their own cultural terms, and they held on to the Old Testament as well.

6. Why was Paul's "radical biblical principle" so critical to the expansion of Christianity into non-Jewish cultures?

_____

_____

_____

We may get the impression that missions in this period benefited very little from deliberately organized effort. But Paul apparently worked within a "missionary team" structure, borrowed from the Pharisees. Paul's sending congregation in Antioch did undertake a definite responsibility. But they sent him off more than they sent him out. Let no one suppose that every new Christian in those days opened his Bible to the Great Commission and dutifully turned over his life to this objective. There is good reason to suppose, for example, that the Christian faith expanded in many areas by the "involuntary-go" mechanism, that is, merely because Christians were dispersed as the result of persecutions. We know that fleeing Arian* Christians had a lot to do with the conversion of the Goths. We have the stories of Ulfilas and Patrick, whose missionary efforts were in each case initiated by the accident of their being taken captive. Furthermore, it is reasonable to suppose that Christianity followed the trade routes of the Roman Empire, and we know that there was a close relationship and correspondence between Christians in Gaul and Asia Minor. Yet we must face the fact that the early Christians of the Roman Empire (as are Christians today) were only rarely both willing and able to take conscious practical steps to fulfill the Great Commission. In view of the amazing results in these early decades, however, we are all the more impressed by the innate power of the gospel itself.

The early Christians (as are Christians today) were only rarely both willing and able to take conscious practical steps to fulfill the Great Commission.

One intriguing possibility of the natural transfer of the gospel within a given social unit is the case of the Celts. Historical studies clarify for us the fact that the province of Galatia in Asia Minor was so called because it was settled by *Galatoi* from Western Europe (who as late as the fourth century still spoke both their original Celtic tongue and also the Greek of that part of the Roman Empire). Whether or not Paul's Galatians were merely Jewish traders living in the province of Galatia or were from the beginning Celtic Galatoi who were attracted to synagogues as "God fearers," we note in any case that Paul's letter to the Galatians is especially wary of anyone pushing over on his readers the mere out-ward customs of the Jewish culture and confusing such customs with essential Christianity. A matter of high missionary interest is the fact that Paul's preaching had tapped into a cultural vein of Celtic humanity that may soon have included friends, relatives, and trade contacts reaching a great distance to the west. Thus Paul's efforts in Galatia may give us one clue to the surprisingly early penetration of the gospel into the main Celtic areas of Europe—a belt running across southern Europe, clear over into Galicia in Spain, Brittany in France, and into the western and northern parts of the British Isles.

There came a time when not only hundreds of thousands of Greek and Roman citizens had become Christians, but Celtic-speaking peoples and Gothic tribespeople as well had developed their own forms of Christianity both within and beyond the borders of the Roman Empire. It is probable that the missionary work behind this came about mainly through unplanned processes involving Christians from the eastern part of the Roman Empire. In any case this achievement certainly cannot readily be credited to Latin-speaking Romans in the West. This is the point we are trying to make. One piece of evidence is the fact that the earliest Irish mission compounds (distinguished from the Western Roman type by a central chapel) followed a ground plan derived from Christian centers in Egypt. And Greek, not Latin, was the language of the early churches in Gaul. Even the first organized mission efforts of John Cassian and Martin of Tours, for example, came from the East by means of commune structures begun in Syria and Egypt. Fortunately, these organized efforts carried with them a strong emphasis on literacy and literature and the studying and copying of biblical manuscripts and ancient Greek classics.

7. *What factors influenced the way the gospel spread in this epoch?*

_____

_____

---

* Arians denied the divinity of Christ and were branded as heretics. They were driven from the Roman Empire by Athanasians, who affirmed the true deity of God the Son.

As amazed pagan leaders looked on, the cumulative impact grew to prominent proportions by 300 A.D. We don't know with any confidence what personal reasons Constantine had in 312 for declaring himself a Christian. We know that his mother in Asia Minor was a Christian and that his father, as a co-regent in Gaul and Britain, did not enforce the Diocletian edicts* against Christians in his area. However, by this time in history the inescapable fact is that there were enough Christians in the Roman Empire to

---

Christianity was the one religion that had no nationalism at its root.

---

make an official reversal of policy toward Christianity not only feasible, but politically wise. According to Professor Lynn White, Jr., at U.C.L.A., one of the great medieval historians of the world today, even if Constantine had not become a Christian, the empire could not have held out against Christianity more than another decade or two! The long development of the Roman Empire had ended the local autonomy of the city-state and created a widespread need for a sense of belonging—he calls it a crisis of identity. Then as now, Christianity was the one religion that had no nationalism at its root. It was not the folk religion of any one tribe. In White's words, it had developed "an unbeatable combination."

Thus, it is the very power of the movement which helps in part to explain why the momentous decision to tolerate Christianity almost inevitably led to its becoming (over 50 years later) the official religion of the empire. Not long after the curtain rises on Christianity as an officially tolerated religion, the head of the Christian community in Rome turns out astonishingly to be the strongest and most trusted man around. Why else would Constantine, when he moved the seat of government to Constantinople, leave his palace (the famous Lateran Palace**) to the people of the Christian community as their "White House" in Rome? Nevertheless, it is simply a matter of record that by 375 A.D. Christianity became the official religion of Rome. For one thing, of course, it couldn't have existed as just another type of tolerated Judaism since it had so much wider an appeal. If it had been merely an ethnic cult, it could not have been even a candidate as an official religion.

More important for us than the fact that Christianity became the official religion is the fact that Western Roman Christianity made no special effort to complete the Great Commission, not in this period. This is not because the Romans were unaware of the vast mission field to the north. Their military and political leaders had had to cope with the Germanic tribespeople for centuries. We shall see how willingly those peoples became Christians.

8. *What political reasons does Winter suggest for the acceptance of Christianity as the official religion of Rome?*

_____

_____

_____

---

* The Emperor Diocletian (284-305 A.D.) was one of the fiercest of the early opponents of Christianity. He issued four edicts against Christianity and carried out full-scale, systematic persecution of Christians during his reign.

** The Lateran Palace is used to this day by the Pope.

9. According to Winter, what is the most important fact to realize, from a missions perspective, concerning the result of the Christianization of Rome?

_____

_____

_____

Throughout the history of its growth and expansion, Christianity has often repeated a similar pattern. The newly introduced gospel message spreads aggressively along relational lines and established social networks. This dynamic flow is stanched, however, when it comes to significant cultural and social barriers. Without special efforts to cross these cultural frontiers, the course of the gospel is halted.

In the case of Rome, the little evangelization that was accomplished among her Barbarian neighbors to the north was through means other than intentional missions by the Roman Christians. Among those who accomplished this work were individuals who were persecuted by the official church as heretics, as in the case of the Arians, who questioned the deity of Christ and were banned from the Empire for this belief. Ulfilas, an Arian who ministered north of the Danube River, reduced the Gothic language to writing and translated the Scriptures for this Barbarian people.

Were the Christianized peoples of northern Europe any better than the Romans in realizing their mission obligation and carrying the good news to their unevangelized neighbors? The following part of Winter's article continues to trace the saga of Christian expansion... and its recession.

II. Barbarians, Vikings, and Saracens

Period 2

Because of repeated hesitation on the part of believers to reach out beyond their culture, God must often use involuntary means to spread the gospel. In this section describing the Christianization of the Barbarians, we see this principle in action.

Winning the Barbarians (400-800 A.D.)

Curiously, as the Barbarian tribespeople became Christianized, they became a greater and greater threat to Rome. Somewhat unintentionally, they wrecked the network of civil government in the West long before they were to try to rebuild it. In fact, the only reason the city of Rome itself was not physically devastated by the invasions, which began in 410, was that the Barbarians were, all things considered, really very respectful of life and property and especially the churches. Why? Because missionary efforts (for which Western Romans could claim little or no credit) had brought the Visigoths, the Ostrogoths, and the Vandals into at

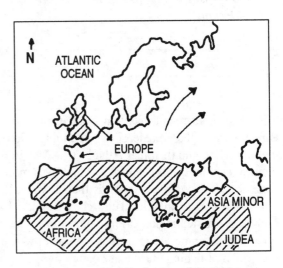

Figure 4-4. Christianization of Barbarians

least a superficial Christian faith. Even secular Romans observed how lucky they were that the invaders held high certain standards of Christian morality.

We are tantalized by the reflection that this much was accomplished by the informal and almost unconscious sharing of the blessings of the gospel. How much better might it have been for the Romans had that brief hundred years of official toleration of Christianity (310-410) prior to the first invasion been devoted to energetic, constructive missionary efforts. Even a little Christianity prevented the Barbarians from that total disregard of civilization which was to be shown by the Vikings in the Third Period. Perhaps a little more Christianity might have prevented the complete collapse of the governmental structure of the Roman Empire in the West. Today, for example, the ability of the new African states to maintain a stable government is to a great extent dependent upon their degree of Christianization (that is, both in knowledge and morality).

In any case, we confront the ominous phenomenon of a partially Christianized Barbarian horde being emboldened and enabled to pour in upon a complacent, officially Christian empire that had failed effectively to reach out to them. This may remind us of our relation to the present-day colossus of China. The Chinese, like the Barbarians north of Rome, have been crucially affected by Christianity. In the past 20 years they have adopted extensively and profoundly a kind of superficial faith which embodies a number of distinctively Christian ingredients—despite the grave distortion of those Christian elements in the Communist milieu. Just as a modicum of Christian faith in some ways strengthened the hand of the Barbarians against the Romans, so the Chinese today are awesomely more dangerous due to the cleansing, integrating, and galvanizing effect

---

> *How much better might it have been for the Romans had that brief hundred years of official toleration of Christianity prior to the first invasion been devoted to energetic, constructive missionary efforts.*

---

of the Communist philosophy and cell structure, which is clearly derived from the West and in many ways specifically from the Christian tradition itself. You can imagine the Barbarians criticizing the softness and degeneracy of the Roman Christians just as the Chinese today denounce the Russians for failing to live up to Communist standards.

Whether or not the Romans had it coming (for failing to reach out), and whether or not the Barbarians were both encouraged and tempered in their conquest by their initial Christian awareness, the indisputable fact is that, while the Romans lost the western half of their empire, the Barbarian world, in a very dramatic sense, gained a Christian faith.

---

10. How were the Barbarians both tempered and encouraged by Christianity in their conquest of Rome?

The immediate result was that right in the city of Rome there appeared at least two "denominations," the one Arian and the other Athanasian. Also in the picture was the Celtic "church," which was more a series of missionary compounds than it was a denomination made up of local churches. Still less like a church was an organization called the Benedictines, which came along later to compete with the Celts in establishing missionary compounds all over Europe. By the time the Vikings appeared on the horizon there were, up through Europe, over 1,000 such mission compounds.

Protestants, and perhaps even modern Catholics, must pause at this point. Our problem in understanding these strange (and much misunderstood) instruments of evangelization is not so much our ignorance of what these people did, as our prejudice that has been developed against monks who lived almost 1,000 years later. It is wholly unfair for us to judge the work of a traveling evangelist like Colomban or Boniface by the stagnation of the wealthy Augustinians in Luther's day—although we must certainly pardon Luther for thinking such thoughts.

It is indisputable that the chief characteristic of these "Jesus People" in this Second Period, whether they were Celtic *peregrini* * or their parallel in Benedictine communes, was the fact that they loved the Bible, that they sang their way through the whole book of Psalms each week as a routine discipline, and that it was they, in any case, who enabled the Kingdom and the power and the glory to be shared with the Anglo-Saxons and the Goths.

It is true that many strange, even bizarre and pagan customs were mixed up as secondary elements in the various forms of Christianity that were active during the period of the Christianization of Europe. The headlong collision and competition between Western Roman and Celtic forms of Christianity undoubtedly eventuated in an enhancement of common biblical elements in their faith. But we must remember the relative chaos introduced by the invasions and therefore not necessarily expect to see, dotting the landscape, the usual parish churches that are familiar in our day.

Under the particular circumstances then (similar to many chaotic corners of the world today), the most durable structure around was the *order*—a fellowship much more highly disciplined and tightly knit than the usual American Protestant congregation today. We must admit, furthermore, that these Christian communities not only were the source of scholarship during the Middle Ages, but they also preserved the technologies of the Roman tradesmen—tanning, dyeing, weaving, metal working, masonry skills, bridge building, etc. Their civil, charitable, and even scientific contribution is, in general, grossly underestimated. Probably the greatest accomplishment of these disciplined Christian

communities is seen in the simple fact that almost our total knowledge of the ancient world is derived from their libraries, whose silent testimony reveals the appreciation they had, even as Christians, of the "pagan" authors of ancient times. In our secular age it is embarrassing to recognize that, had it not been for these highly literate "mission field" Christians who preserved and copied manuscripts (not only of the Bible but of ancient Christian and non-Christian classics as well), we would know no more about the Roman Empire today than we do of the Mayan or Incan Empires or many other empires that have long since almost vanished from sight.

> *Christian communities not only were the source of scholarship during the Middle Ages, but they also preserved the technologies of the Roman tradesmen.*

As a matter of fact, Barbarian Europe was won more by the witness and labors of Celtic and Anglo-Saxon converts than by the efforts of missionaries deriving from Italy or Gaul. This fact was to bear decisively upon the apparently permanent shift of power in Western Europe to the northern Europeans. Even as late as 596, when Rome's first missionary [Augustine] headed north (with great faintheartedness), he crossed the path of the much more daring and widely traveled Irish missionary Colomban, who had worked his way practically to the doorstep of Rome and who was already further from his birthplace than Augustine was planning to go from his. Thus, while Constantinople was considered the "Second Rome" by people who lived in the East, and Moscow was later to become the "Third Rome" to the descendants of the newly Christianized Russians, neither Rome as a city nor the Italian peninsula as a region was ever again to be politically as significant as the chief cities of the daughter nations—Spain, France, Germany, and England.

---

* *Peregrini* were traveling monks sent forth from the Scottish island of Iona. They succeeded in evangelizing much of Britain and Central Europe.

11. *What contributions did the Celts and early monks make to civilization? What efforts did they undertake for the advancement of the Christian movement?*

_____

_____

_____

Toward the end of the Second Period, or at the end of each of these periods, there was a great flourishing of Christianity within the new cultural basin. The rise of a strong man like Charlemagne facilitated communication throughout Western Europe to a degree unknown for 300 years. Under his sponsorship a whole range of issues—social, theological, political—were soberly restudied in the light of the Bible and the writings of earlier Christian leaders in the Roman period. Charlemagne was a second Constantine in certain respects, and his political power was unmatched in Western Europe during a half a millennium. But he was much more of a Christian than Constantine and industriously sponsored far

---

The political force of a colonial power not so much paved the way for Christianity, but as often as not turned people against the faith.

---

more Christian activity. Like Constantine, his official espousal of Christianity produced many Christians who were Christians in name only. There is little doubt that the great missionary Boniface was slain by the Saxons because his patron, Charlemagne (with whose policies he did not at all agree) had brutally suppressed the Saxons on many occasions. Then, as in our own recent past, the political force of a colonial power not so much paved the way for Christianity, but as often as not turned people against the faith. Of interest to missionaries is the fact that the great centers of learning established by Charlemagne were copies and expansions of newly established mission compounds deep in German territory, outposts that were the work of British and Celtic missionaries from sending centers as far away as Iona and Lindisfarne in Britain.

Indeed, the first serious attempt at anything like public education was initiated by this great tribal chieftain, Charlemagne, on the advice and impulse of Anglo-Celtic missionaries and scholars, such as Alcuin, whose projects eventually required the help of thousands of literate Christians from Britain and Ireland to man schools founded on the Continent. It is hard to believe, but Irish teachers of Latin (never a native tongue in Ireland) were eventually needed to teach Latin in Rome, so extensively had the tribal invasions broken down the civilization of the Roman Empire.

The Celtic Christians and their Anglo-Saxon and continental heirs especially treasured the Bible. A sure clue to their chief source of inspiration is the fact that the highest works of art during these "dark" centuries were marvelously "illuminated" biblical manuscripts and devoutly ornamented church buildings; manuscripts of non-Christian classical authors were preserved and copied, but not illuminated. Through the long night of the progressive breakdown of the western part of the Roman Empire, when the tribal migrations reduced almost all of the life in the West to the level of the tribesmen themselves, the two great regenerating ideals were the hope of building anew the glory that was once Rome and the hope of making all subject to the Lord of Glory. The one really high point, when these twin objectives were most nearly achieved, was during Charlemagne's long, vigorous career centered around the year 800. As one recent scholar puts it, "In the long sweep of European history, from the decline of the Roman Empire to the flowering of the Renaissance nearly a thousand years later, his [Charlemagne's] is the sole commanding presence."

No wonder recent scholars call Charlemagne's period the Carolingian Renaissance, and thus discard the concept of "the Dark Ages" for a First Dark Ages early in this period and a Second Dark Ages early in the next period.

Unfortunately, the rebuilt empire (later to be called the Holy Roman Empire) was unable to find the ingredients of a Charlemagne in his successor; moreover, a new threat now posed itself externally. Charlemagne had been eager for his own kind to be made Christian—the Germanic tribes. He offered wise, even spiritual leadership in many affairs but did not throw his weight behind any kind of bold mission outreach to the Scandinavian peoples to the north. What was begun under his son was too little and too late. This fact was to contribute greatly to the undoing of the empire.

---

12. What were Charlemagne's contributions to the spread of Christianity? What was his failure?

_____

_____

_____

Period 3

With the conquest of Rome by the Barbarians from the north, Western civilization suffered a setback which led to what historians have labeled the Dark Ages. Although Rome was in decline, Christianity was making advances throughout Europe. The Barbarians eventually so adopted the Christian faith that they purposefully set out to evangelize the whole of Western Europe. Unfortunately, they failed to cross the cultural barriers and take Christian influence to the Scandinavian north. There, a far more savage people would rise to wreak havoc on their neighbors to the south.

Winning the Vikings (800-1200 A.D.)

No sooner had the consolidation in Western Europe been accomplished under Charlemagne than there appeared a new menace to peace and propriety that was to create a second period of at least semidarkness to last 250 years: the Vikings. These savages further north had not yet been effectively evangelized. While the tribal invaders of Rome, who created the First Dark Ages, were rough forest people who, for the most part, were nevertheless nominally Arian Christians, the Vikings, by contrast, were neither civilized nor Christian. There was another difference: they were men of the sea. This meant that key island sanctuaries for missionary training, like Iona or like the off-shore promontory of Lindisfarne (connected to the land only at low tide), were as vulnerable to attacking seafarers as they had been invulnerable to attackers from the land. Both of these mission centers were sacked more than a dozen times, and their occupants slaughtered or sold off as slaves in middle Europe. It seems unquestionable that the Christians of Charlemagne's empire

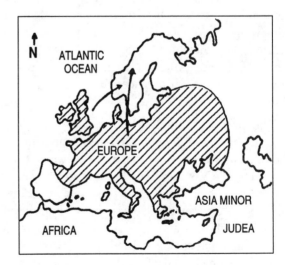

Figure 4-5. Christianization of Vikings

would have fared far better had the Vikings had at least the appreciation of the Christian faith that the earlier Barbarians had when they overran Rome. The very opposite of the Visigoths and Vandals, who spared the churches, the Vikings seemed attracted like magnets to the monastic centers of scholarship and Christian devotion; they took a special delight in burning churches, in putting human life to the sword, and in selling monks into slavery. A contemporary's words give us a graphic impression of their carnage:

> The Northmen cease not to slay and carry into captivity the Christian people, to destroy the churches and to burn the towns. Everywhere, there is nothing but dead bodies—clergy and laymen, nobles and common people, women and children. There is no road or place where the ground is not covered with corpses. We live in distress and anguish before this spectacle of the destruction of the Christian people.*

Once more, when Christians did not reach out to them, pagan peoples came where they were. And once more, the phenomenal power of Christianity manifested itself: the conquerors became conquered by the faith of their captives. Usually it was the monks sold as slaves or the Christian girls forced to be their wives and mistresses which eventually won these savages of the north. In God's eyes, their redemption must have been more important than the harrowing tragedy of this new invasion of barbarian violence and evil which fell upon God's own people whom He loved. (After all, He had not even spared His own Son in order to redeem us!)

In the previous hundred years, Charlemagne's scholars had carefully collected the manuscripts of the ancient world. Now the majority were to be burned by the Vikings. Only because so many copies had been made and scattered so widely did the fruits of the Charlemagnic literary revival survive at all. Once scholars and missionaries had streamed from Ireland across England and onto the Continent, and even out beyond the frontiers of Charlemagne's empire. Thus the Irish volcano which had poured forth a passionate fire of evangelism for three centuries cooled almost to extinction. Viking warriors, newly based in Ireland, followed the paths of the earlier Irish peregrini across England and onto the

Continent, but this time ploughing with them waste and destruction rather than new life and hope.

There were some blessings in this horrifying disguise. Alfred successfully headed up guerrilla resistance and was equally concerned about spiritual as well as physical losses. As a measure of emergency, he let go the ideal of maintaining the Latin tongue as a general pattern for worship and began a Christian library in the vernacular—the Anglo-Saxon. This was a decision of monumental importance which might have been delayed several centuries had the tragedy of the Vikings not provided the necessity which was the mother of invention.

When Christians did not reach out to them, pagan peoples came where they were.

In any case, as Christopher Dawson puts it, the unparalleled devastation of England and the Continent was "not a victory for paganism" (p. 94). The Northmen who landed on the Continent under Rollo became the Christianized Normans, and the Danish who took over a huge section of middle England (along with invaders from Norway who planted their own kind in many other parts of England and Ireland) also were soon to become Christians. The gospel was too powerful. One result was that a new Christian culture spread back into Scandinavia. This stemmed largely from England from which came the first monastic communities and early missionary bishops. What England lost, Scandinavia gained.

It must also be admitted that the Vikings would not have been attracted either to the churches or to the monasteries had not those centers of Christian piety to a great extent succumbed to luxury. The switch from the Irish to the Benedictine pattern of monasticism was an improvement in many respects but apparently allowed greater possibilities for the development of the un-Christian opulence and glitter which attracted the greedy eyes of the Norsemen. Thus another side-benefit of the new invasions was its indirect cleansing and refinement of the Christian movement. Even before the Vikings appeared,

---

* Dawson, C. *Religion and the rise of Western culture*, p. 87.

Benedict of Aniane inspired a rustle of reform here and there. By 910, at Cluny,* a momentous step forward was begun. Among other changes, the authority over a monastic center was shifted away from local politics, and for the first time (as dramatically and extensively) whole networks of "daughter" houses were related to a single, strongly spiritual "mother" house. The Cluny revival, moreover, produced a new reforming attitude toward society as a whole.

The greatest bishop in Rome in the first millennium, Gregory I, was the product of a Benedictine community. So, early in the second millennium, Hildebrand was a product of the Cluny reform. His successors in reform were bolstered greatly by the Cistercian revival which went even further. Working behind the scenes for many years for wholesale reform across the entire church, he finally became Pope Gregory VII for a relatively brief period. But his reforming zeal set the stage for Innocent III, who wielded greater power (and all things considered, greater power for good) than any other Pope before or since. Gregory VII had made a decisive step toward wresting control of the church from secular power—this was the question of "lay investiture." ** It was he who allowed Henry IV to wait for three days out in the snow at Knossis. Innocent III not only carried forward Gregory's reforms, but has the distinction of being the Pope who authorized the first of a whole new series of mission orders—the Friars.

Our First Period ended with a barely Christian Roman Empire and a somewhat Christian emperor—Constantine. Our Second Period ended with a reconstitution of that empire under a Christianized Barbarian, Charlemagne, who was devoutly and vigorously Christian. Our Third Period ends with a Pope, Innocent III, as the strongest man in Europe, made strong by the Cluny, Cistercian, and allied spiritual movements which together are called the Gregorian Reform. The scene was not an enlarged Europe in which no secular ruler could survive without at least tipping his hat to the leaders in the Christian movement. It was not a period in which European Christians had reached out in missions, but they had at least with phenomenal speed grafted in the entire northern area and had also deepened the foundations of Christian scholarship and devotion in the Europe of Charlemagne. The next period would unfold some happy and unhappy surprises. Would Europe now take the initiative in reaching out with the gospel? Would it sink in selfsatisfaction? In some respects it would do both.

13. *What significant principles are to be learned from the invasion by and eventual Christianization of the Vikings?*

---

* Cluny was a town in east central France and the site of a Benedictine abbey.

** Investiture was a controversy over the appointment of clergy by civil or religious authorities.

14. *How did the various orders—Benedictine, Cistercian, etc.—play vital roles in advancing the gospel?*

_____

_____

_____

Period 4

Invasion again played a key role in the expansion of Christianity during the Third Period. Those who did not have the gospel were drawn by the blessings and benefits it wrought in society. However, without the gospel's life-changing message, the invaders sought to obtain the blessings in ways that unleashed devastation. The eventual Christianization of the Vikings and the use of vernacular languages in Christian writings represented great advances for the gospel. Meanwhile, to the southeast, a vigorous new religion had rapidly spread through Arabia, North Africa, the Middle East, and even into Spain, eradicating gains made in previous centuries. How effectively would Christian Europe meet this new threat of Islam?

Winning the Saracens (1200-1600 A.D.)

The Fourth Period began with a spectacular, new evangelistic instrument—the Friars—and it would end with the greatest reformation of all, but was meanwhile already involved for a hundred years in the most massive, tragic misconstrual of Christian mission in all of history. Never before had any nation or group of nations launched as energetic and sustained a campaign into foreign territory as did Europe in the tragic debacle of the Crusades. This was in part the carry-over of the Viking spirit into the Christian church. All of the major Crusades were led by Viking descendants. Yet while the Crusades had many political overtones (they were often a unifying device for faltering rulers), they would not have come about apart from the vigorous sponsorship of the Christian leaders. They were not only an unprecedented blood-letting to the Europeans themselves and a savage wound in the side of the Muslim peoples (a wound which is not at all healed to this day),* but they were a fatal blow to the cause of Christian unity east and west and to the cultural unity of eastern Europe. In the long run, though they held Jerusalem for a hundred years, the Crusaders by

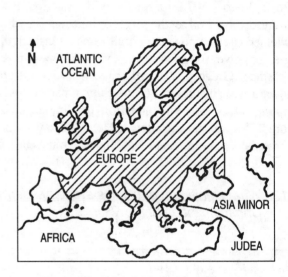

Figure 4-6. Christianization by Crusades

default eventually gave the Byzantine inheritance over to the Ottoman sultans, and far worse, they established a permanent image of brutal, militant Christianity that alienates a large proportion of mankind to this day.

Ironically, the mission of the Crusaders would not have been so successfully negative had it not in-

---

* The horrible atrocities perpetrated by Crusaders against both Jews and Muslims are a major reason both groups are still strongly opposed to the gospel.

volved so high a component of abject Christian commitment. The great lesson of the Crusades is that good will, even sacrificial obedience to God, is no substitute for a clear understanding of His will. It was a devout man, Bernard of Clairvaux, to whom are attributed the words of the hymn "Jesus the Very Thought of Thee," who preached the first crusade. In all this period two Franciscans, Francis of Assisi and Raymond Lull, stand out as the only ones whose insight into God's will led them to substitute the gentle words of the evangel for warfare and violence as the proper means of extending the blessings God committed to Abraham and his children of faith.

At this point we must pause for reflection. We may not succeed, but let us try to see things from God's point of view, treading with caution and tentativeness. We know, for example, that at the end of the First Period, after three centuries of hardship and persecution, just when things were apparently going great, invaders appeared, and chaos and catastrophe ensued. Why? This is the period that could be called the "Constantinian Renaissance"—that is, it was both good and not so good. Just when Christians were translating the Bible into Latin and waxing eloquent in theological debate, when Eusebius was editing a massive collection of previous Christian writings (as the official historian of the government), when heretics were thrown out of the empire (and became, however reluctantly, the only missionaries to the Goths), when Rome finally became officially Christian... then suddenly God brought down the curtain. It was now time for a new cluster of people groups to be confronted with the claims, blessings, and obligations of the expanding Kingdom of Christ.

Similarly, at the end of the Second Period, after three centuries of chaos during which the rampaging Gothic hordes were eventually Christianized, tamed, and civilized, when Bibles and biblical knowledge proliferated as never before, when major biblical/missionary centers were established by the Celtic Christians and their Anglo-Saxon pupils, when, in this Charlemagnic (actually "Carolingian") Renaissance, thousands of public schools led by Christians attempted mass biblical and general literacy, when Charlemagne dared even to attack the endemic use of alcohol, great theologians tussled with theological/political issues, and the Venerable

Bede became Eusebius of this period (indeed, when both Charlemagne and Bede were much more Christian than Constantine and Eusebius), once again invaders appeared and chaos and catastrophe ensued. Why?

Strangely similar, then, is the end of the Third Period. It only took two and a half centuries for the Vikings to capitulate to the "counter-attack of the gospel." The flourishing period was longer than a century and far more extensive than ever before. The Crusades, the cathedrals, the so-called Scholastic theologians, the universities, most importantly the blessed Friars, and even the early part of the Humanistic Renaissance make up this outsized 1050-1350 outburst of a Medieval Renaissance. And then suddenly a new invader appeared, more virulent than ever, and chaos and catastrophe greater than ever occurred. Why?

The great lesson of the Crusades is that good will, even sacrificial obedience to God, is no substitute for a clear understanding of His will.

Was God dissatisfied with incomplete obedience? Were the blessings being kept by those who received them and not sufficiently and determinedly shared with the other nations of the world? The plague that killed one-third of the inhabitants of Europe killed a much higher proportion of the Franciscans (120,000 were laid still in Germany alone). Surely God was not trying to judge their missionary fire. Was He trying to judge the Crusaders, whose atrocities greatly outweighed the Christian devotional elements in their movement? If so, why did He wait so long to do that? And why did He inflict the Christian leadership of Europe so greatly rather than the Crusaders themselves? Why didn't the Crusaders die of the plague?

Perhaps it was that Europe did not sufficiently listen to the saintly Friars; that it was not the Friars that went wrong but the hearers who did not respond. God's judgment upon Europe, then, was to take the gospel away from them, to take away the Friars and their message. Even though to us it seems like it was a judgment upon the messengers rather than upon the resistant hearers, is this not one impression that could be received from the New Testament as well? Jesus Himself came unto His own, and His own received Him not, and Jesus rather than the people was the one who went to the cross. God's judgment may often consist of the removal of the messenger.

In any case, the invasion of the bubonic plague, first in 1346 and every so often during the next decade, brought a greater setback than either the Gothic or the Viking invasions. It first devastated parts of Italy and Spain, then spread west and north to France, England, Holland, Germany, and Scandinavia. By the time it had run its course 40 years later, one-third to one-half of the population of Europe was dead. Especially stricken were the Friars and the truly spiritual leaders. They were the only ones who stayed behind to tend the sick and to bury the dead. Europe was absolutely in ruins. The result? There were three Popes at one point, the humanist elements turned menacingly humanistic, peasant turmoil

> **God's judgment may often consist of the removal of the messenger.**

(often based in justice and even justified by the Bible itself) ended up in orgies and excesses of violence. The poverty, confusion, and lengthy travail led to the new birth of the greatest reform yet seen.

15. Why does Winter suggest invasions and catastrophes repeatedly enveloped Christianity, just when it seemed to be entering stages of stability?

_____

_____

_____

Once more, at the end of one of our periods, a great flourishing took place. Printing came to the fore, Europeans finally escaped their geographical cul de sac and sent ships for commerce, subjugation, and spiritual blessings to the very ends of the earth. And as a part of the reform, the Protestant Reformation now loomed on the horizon: that great, permanent, cultural decentralization of Europe.

Protestants often think of the Reformation as a legitimate reaction against the evils of a monstrous Christian bureaucracy sunken in corruption. But it must be admitted that the Reform was not just a reaction against decadence in the Christian movement. This great decentralization of Christendom was in many respects the result of an increasing vitality which, unknown to most Protestants, was as evident in the return to a study of the Bible and to the appearance of new life and evangelical preaching in Italy, Spain, and France as in Moravia, Germany, and England.

In the Reformation, the gospel finally succeeded in allowing Christians to be German, not merely permitting Germans to be Roman Christians. Unfortunately, the emphasis on justification by faith (which was preached as much in Italy and Spain as in Germany at the time Luther loomed into view) became identified with German nationalistic hopes and thus was suppressed as a dangerous doctrine by political powers in the South. But it is merely a typical Protestant misunderstanding that there was not as much a revival of deeper life, Bible study, and prayer in Southern Europe as in Northern Europe at the time of the Reformation. The issue may have appeared to the Protestants as faith vs. law, or to the Romans as unity vs. division, but popular scales are askew because it was much more Latin uniformity vs. national diversity. The vernacular had to eventually conquer. Paul had not demanded that the Greeks become Jews, but the Germans had been obliged to become Roman. The Anglo-Saxons and the Scandinavians had at least been allowed their vernacular to an extent unknown in Christian Germany. Germany was where the revolt would have to take place. Italy, France, and Spain, formerly part of the Roman Empire and extensively assimilated culturally in that direction, had no nationalistic steam behind their reforming movements, which became almost lost in the shuffle that ensued.

However, despite the fact that the Protestants won on the political front and to a great extent gained the power to formulate anew their own Christian tradition, they did not even talk of mission outreach, and the period ended with Roman Europe expanding both politically and religiously on the seven seas. Thus, entirely unshared by Protestants, for at least two centuries, there ensued a worldwide movement of unprecedented scope in the annals of mankind in which there was greater Christian missionary presence than ever before.

16. How did cultural issues play a significant part in the Protestant Reformation?

_____

_____

_____

_____

Period 5

The emergence of nationalized forms of Christianity and the discovery and exploration of vast new portions of the globe set the stage for a tremendous surge in the Christian expansion. The next two centuries were to see vigorous missionary activity by the Roman Church. It took Protestants over 200 years to wake up to their own responsibility to be a blessing to the ends of the earth.

III. The Final Thrust

To the ends of the earth (1600-2000 A.D.)

The period from 1600 to 2000 began with European footholds in the rest of the world. Apart from taking over what was almost an empty continent by toppling the Aztec and Inca Empires in the Western hemisphere, Europeans had only tiny enclaves of power in the heavily populated portions of the non-Western world. By 1945, Europeans had virtual control over 99.5 percent of the non-Western world. Twenty-five years later, the Western nations had lost control over all but five percent of the non-Western population of the world. This 1945-1969 period of the sudden collapse of Western control, coupled with the unexpected upsurge of significance of the Christian movement in the non-Western world, I have elsewhere called "the 25 unbelievable years." If we compare this period to the collapse of

Figure 4-7. To the Ends of the Earth

the Western Roman Empire's domination over its conquered provinces of Spain, Gaul, and Britain, and to the breakdown of control over non-Frankish Europe under Charlemagne's successors, we can anticipate—at least by the logic of sheer parallelism—that by the year 2000 the Western world itself will be dominated by non-Westerners.

Indeed, ever since the collapse of Western power became obvious (during "the 25 unbelievable years"), there have been many who have decried the thought of any further missionary effort moving from the West to the non-Western world, perhaps confusing the absence of political control for the absence of the need for foreign missions. The true situation is actually very different. Rather, the absence of political control for the first time in many areas has now begun to allow non-Western populations to yield to the Kingdom of Christ without simultaneously yielding to the political kingdoms of the Western world. Here we see a parallel to the Frankish tribespeople accepting the faith of Rome only after Rome had become politically powerless, and the continued relative acceptability of the Roman faith among the Anglo-Saxons, Germans, and Scandinavians up until the point where the emergence of strong papal authority mixed with power politics became a threat to legitimate national ambitions and led to a reformation which allowed nationalized forms of Christianity.

The present spectacle of a Western world flaunting the standards of Christian morality in more obvious ways than ever is not as likely, therefore, to dissuade others from embracing the Christian faith in non-Christian lands as it is to disassociate the treasure of Christian ideals from a Western world which has, until this age, been their most prominent sponsor. When Asians accuse Western nations of immorality in warfare, they are appealing to Christian values, certainly not the values of their own pagan past. In this sense, Christianity has already conquered the world. No longer, for example, is the long-standing Chinese tradition of skillful torture likely to be boasted about in China nor highly respected anywhere else, at least in public circles.

But this worldwide change has not come about suddenly. Even the present, minimal attainment of world Christian morality on a tenuous public level has been accomplished only at the cost of a great

amount of sacrificial missionary endeavor (during the four centuries of Period Five), labors which have been mightier and more deliberate than at any time in 2,000 years. The first half (1600-1800) of this Fifth Period was almost exclusively a Roman show. By the year 1800, it was painfully embarrassing to Protestants to hear Roman missionaries writing off the Protestant movement as apostate simply because it was not sending missionaries. But by the year 1800, Roman missionary effort had been forced into sudden decline due to the curtailment of the Jesuits and the combined effect of the French Revolution and ensuing chaos in the cutting of the European economic roots of Catholic missions.

The year 1800 marks the awakening of the Protestants from two and a half centuries of inactivity, if not actual slumber, in regard to missionary outreach across the world.

However, the year 1800 marks the awakening of the Protestants from two and a half centuries of inactivity, if not actual slumber, in regard to missionary outreach across the world. Now, for the first time, Protestants equipped themselves with structures of mission comparable to the Catholic orders and began to make up for lost time. Unheralded, unnoticed, all but forgotten in our day except for ill-informed criticism, Protestant missionary efforts in this period, more than Catholic missions, led the way in establishing all around the world the democratic apparatus of government, the schools, the hospitals, the universities, and the political foundations of the new nations. Rightly understood, Protestant missionaries along with their Roman brethren are surely not less than the prime movers of the tremendous energy that is mushrooming in the Third World today. Take China, for example. Two of its greatest modern leaders, Sun Yat Sen and Chiang Kai-shek, were both Christians.

If the Western home base is now to falter and to fail as the tide is reversed by the new power of its partially evangelized periphery (as is the pattern in the earlier periods), we can only refer to Dawson's comment on the devastation wrought by the

Vikings—that this will not be a "victory for paganism." The fall of the West will be due in part to a decay of spirit. It will be due in part to the pagan power in the non-Western world emboldened and strengthened by its first contact with Christian faith. It may come as a most drastic punishment to a Western world that has always spent more on cosmetics than it has on foreign missions—and lately 10 times as much. From a secular or even nationalistic point of view, the next years may be a very dark period for the Western world, in which the normal hope and aspirations of Christian people for their own country may find only a very slight basis for optimism. But if the past is any guide at all, even this will have to be darkness before the dawn. While we may not be able to be sure about our own country, we have no reason to suppose—there is no historic determinism that assures us—that the Christian faith will not survive. The entire Western world in its present political form may be radically altered.

For one thing, we can readily calculate, in regard to population trends, that by the year 2000 Westerners will constitute less than half as large a percentage of the world (8%) as they did in the year 1900 (18%). This does seem inevitable. But certainly, judging by the past, we cannot ultimately be pessimistic. Beyond the agony of Rome was the winning of the Barbarians. Beyond the agony of the Barbarians was the winning of the Vikings. Beyond the agony of the Western world we can only pray that there will be the winning of the "two billion" who have not yet heard. And we can only know that there is no basis in the past or in the present for assuming that things are out of the control of the living God.

> *If we in the West insist on keeping our blessings instead of sharing them, then we will have to lose our blessings for the remaining nations to receive them.*

If we in the West insist on keeping our blessings instead of sharing them, then we will, like other nations before us, have to lose our blessings for the remaining nations to receive them. God has not changed His plan in the last 4,000 years. But how much better not to lose but to use our blessings, without reserve, in order "to be a blessing to all the families of the earth"? That is the only way we can continue in God's blessing. The expanding Kingdom is not going to stop with us. "This gospel must be preached in the whole world as a testimony to all people groups, and then shall the end come" (Matt. 24:14).

17. Compare the current state of the West with dominant Christian societies in past epochs. What parallels do you see with the situation that now exists in your own country?

_____

_____

_____

18. During the past 200 years, the gospel has spread widely throughout the non-Western world. Considering past patterns, how might vigorous new churches in these parts of the globe respond to the blessings they now enjoy?

_____

_____

_____

Before we leave our reflection on the past, it is healthy to see the tremendous positive influence the world Christian movement has already had. Renowned historian Kenneth Scott Latourette summarizes these effects from his lifelong study of the history of the expansion of Christianity.

❑ *The Effect of Christianity* *

Kenneth Scott Latourette **

In the relatively brief nineteen and a half centuries of its existence, in spite of its seemingly unpromising beginning, Christianity had spread over most of the earth's surface and was represented by adherents in almost every tribe and nation and in nearly every inhabited land. It had gone forward by pulsations of advance, retreat, and advance. Measured by the criteria of geographic extent, inner vigour as shown by new movements from within it, and the effect on mankind as a whole, each major advance had carried it further into the life of the world than the one before it, and each major recession had been less severe than its predecessor. In spite of this spread, in the middle of the 20th century Christianity was still the professed faith of only a minority of men, in some of the largest countries only a small minority. Of those who bore the Christian name, especially in lands where they were in the majority, only a minority made the thoroughgoing commitment required by the genius of the faith.

What effect had Christianity had across the centuries, operating as it did through this minority? Often we cannot know whether Christianity was at all an element in a particular movement or action. In many other instances we can be reasonably sure that it entered as a factor but so compounded with other causes that we cannot accurately appraise the extent of its responsibility. Among these were the emergence of universities in the Middle Ages, the Renaissance, the rise of the scientific method, the geographic discoveries by Europeans in the 15th,

16th, and 17th centuries, democracy of the Anglo-Saxon kind, and communism. Whether in any of these it was determinative, so that but for it they would not have come into being, we are not and probably cannot be sure. We can be clear that in some movements Christianity was dominant. Such were the appearance and development of the various churches, monasticism in its several manifestations, the Protestant and Catholic Reformations, the formulation of the great creeds of the first few centuries, and the construction of most of the systems of theology. Yet in none of these was Christianity the only cause. Indeed, what we call Christianity changed from time to time. In most of its forms what came from Jesus and His apostles was regarded as primary and determinative, but other contributions entered, among them the cultural background of individuals and groups, the personal experiences of outstanding leaders, and inherited religions and philosophical conceptions.

The fruits of the faith

In spite of these uncertainties and complicating factors, we can be fully assured of some of the fruits of what constitutes the core of the Christian faith and of Christianity, namely, the life, teachings, death, and resurrection of Jesus. We can, of course, be clear that without this core Christianity and the churches would not have been. It is by no means responsible for all that was done in the guise of Christianity or under the aegis of the churches, and much was performed in its name which was quite contrary to

* Latourette, K. S. (1953). *A history of Christianity* (pp. 1471-1474). New York: Harper & Bros.

** Kenneth Scott Latourette was probably the premier historian of the Christian movement. A member of the Student Volunteer Movement at Yale early in the 20th century and very active in a vast network of student Bible study groups, Latourette sailed for China but returned after a year because of illness. He taught from 1921 to 1953 at Yale as Professor of Missions and Oriental History. He was also a prolific author and is best known for his seven-volume *History of the Expansion of Christianity*, five-volume *Christianity in a Revolutionary Age*, and two-volume *History of Christianity*.

it. However, the perversion of the gospel is one of the facts of which an appraisal of the results of Christianity must take account. It is incontestable that from Christ issued unmeasured and immeasurable power in the life of mankind. We know that because of Him across the centuries untold thousands of individuals have borne something of His likeness. Thousands have been so reared in the knowledge of Him that from childhood and without striking struggle they have followed Him and have increasingly shown the radiance of the faith, hope, and self-giving love which were in Him. Other thousands have come to the same path and goal through deep sorrow, initial moral defeat, and soul-wrenching struggles. Some have been famous and have passed on to other thousands the light which has come from Him. More have been obscure and have been known only to a limited circle, but within that circle they have been towers of strength.

From individuals who have been inspired by Christ and from the church has issued movement after movement for attaining the Christian ideal.

Through Christ there has come into being the Church. The Church is never fully identical with ecclesiastical organizations. It is to be found in them, but not all of their members belong to it and it is greater than the sum of them all. Yet, though never fully visible as an institution, the Church has been and is a reality, more potent than any one or all of the churches. "The blessed company of all faithful people," it constitutes a fellowship which has been both aided and hampered by the churches, and is both in them and transcends them.

From individuals who have been inspired by Christ and from the Church has issued movement after movement for attaining the Christian ideal. That ideal has centered around the kingdom of God, an order in which God's will is done. It sets infinite value upon the individual. Its goal for the individual is to become a child of God, to "know the love of Christ which passeth knowledge" and to "be filled unto all the fullness of God"—God who is Creator and Father, who revealed His true nature, self-giving love, by becoming incarnate in Jesus Christ, and

permitting the seeming defeat and frustration of the cross, and who is ever active in history in individuals and the collective life of mankind. Its goal for the individual cannot be completely attained this side of the grave, but is so breath-taking that within history only a beginning is possible. Nor can it be reached in isolation, but only in community. In Christ's teaching, love for God, as the duty and privilege of man, is inseparably joined with love for one's neighbor.

The ideal and the goal have determined the character of the movements which have been the fruits of Christianity. Although men can use and often have used knowledge and education to the seeming defeat of the ideal, across the centuries Christianity has been the means of reducing more languages to writing than have all other factors combined. It has created more schools, more theories of education, and more systems than has any other one force. More than any other power in history it has impelled men to fight suffering, whether that suffering has come from disease, war, or natural disasters. It has built thousands of hospitals, inspired the emergence of nursing and medical professions, and furthered movements for public health and the relief and prevention of famine. Although explorations and conquests which were in part its outgrowth led to the enslavement of Africans for the plantations of the Americas, men and women whose consciences were awakened by Christianity and whose wills it nerved brought about the abolition of Negro slavery. Men and women similarly moved and sustained wrote into the laws of Spain and Portugal provisions to alleviate the ruthless exploitation of the Indians of the New World. Wars have often been waged in the name of Christianity. They have attained their most colossal dimensions through weapons and large scale organization initiated in Christendom. Yet from no other source have there come as many and as strong movements to eliminate or regulate war and to ease the suffering brought by war. From its first centuries the Christian faith has caused many of its adherents to be uneasy about war. It has led minorities to refuse to have any part in it. It has impelled others to seek to limit war by defining what, in their judgment, from the Christian standpoint is a "just war." In the turbulent middle ages of Europe it gave rise to the Truce of God and the Peace of God. In a later era it was the main impulse in the formulation of international law. But for it the League of Nations and the United Nations would not have been. By its name and symbol the most extensive organization ever created for the relief of the suffering caused by war, the Red Cross, bears witness to its Christian origin. The list might go on indefinitely. It includes many other humanitarian projects and movements, ideals in government, the reform of prisons and the emergence of criminology, great art and architecture, and outstanding literature. In geographic extent and potency the results were never as marked as in the 19th and 20th centuries.

19. Why does Latourette suggest that the Christian ideal can be reached only in community, never in isolation?

_____

_____

_____

_____

Where is the world Christian movement headed? The church has been planted around the globe, and the blessing has touched every country. Yet half the world's population still has not had a reasonable opportunity to know the power of the gospel in a personal way. Missiologists are calling the church to a strategy of *closure*, a concerted effort by the whole church to finish the Great Commission task.

Where will the resources come from which will bring the Great Commission task to completion? Can the seeming apathy of a self-indulgent Western church be overcome? Will the spirited young churches of the Two Thirds World* respond to this challenge? If history repeats itself, the West may be entering a period of decline. The reversal of this decline will be difficult if the West does not dedicate itself fully to being a blessing to the nations. Yet, even if this demise is imminent, beyond this "agony of the West" lies the bright promise of the new churches of the more recently evangelized continents. These churches are already rising up to take on the Great Commission challenge. In the following article, Theodore Williams and William Taylor describe the historical emergence of "sending" from former missionary "receiving" countries and the issues surrounding this great movement.

---

* The term "Two Thirds World" is being used increasingly by missiologists to speak of countries which are non-Western but contain now over two-thirds of the world's population and a great majority of the world's Christians. "Two Thirds World" replaces the term "Third World," which was coined as a political denotation and which has developed negative connotations over the years. Some people also use the term "Non-Western World" interchangeably with "Two Thirds World."

❏ *Two Thirds World Missions*

Theodore Williams and William Taylor *

The amazing story Thomas shared profoundly moved us as we marveled at God's creativity and power. Over 25 years ago, Thomas and another young Indian colleague went with the gospel to an isolated, unreached people of northern India. Called the "Valley of the Gods" for its bondage to the evil one, the area knew spiritual warfare as a dominant reality. In spite of opposition, God blessed His Word and the proclamation of the unique Christ in this religiously pluralistic society. Today the church flourishes in this valley and is sending out its own missionaries!

Missionaries with names like Suraja, Francisco, Kim, and Bayo come from different continents and represent an amazing and relatively new missionary force, perhaps 40,000 strong. We speak of one of the most significant phenomena in current church history—the rapid growth of indigenous missions in the Two Thirds World.

Indigenous missions began in the early 1900s. Non-Western missionaries sailed in canoes from island to island in the South Pacific. (Interestingly, this "deep sea canoe" vision is being revived again.) The real growth of Two Thirds World missions, however, began in the 1960s and mushroomed in the 1970s and 1980s. Research done on the size of this new force illustrates this growth, which we give in rounded figures:**

Year	Approximate Number of Two Thirds World Missionaries
1972	5,000
1982	15,000
1992	40,000

Significantly, the number of Two Thirds World missionaries is increasing faster than that of Western missionaries. By the year 2000 it is predicted that there will be more non-Western missionaries than their Western counterparts.

Where do these missionaries serve? They are going everywhere! In some cases, such as India and Nigeria, we see them concentrated within their own countries, where there are many totally unreached people groups. Thousands of others have moved internationally, such as the Koreans, Singaporeans, and Brazilians. In Africa, Nigeria has the highest number of missionaries. India sends the most cross-cultural missionaries from Asia, with the majority serving within the country. Brazil leads the Latin American continent in numbers of missionaries.

Factors producing the movement

What has caused the mushrooming of these Two Thirds World missions? Sadly, in most countries, Western missionaries did not impart the cross-cultural missionary vision to the churches that they

---

* Theodore Williams is the founder and director of India Evangelical Mission, an indigenous mission organization ministering primarily in northern India. He also travels extensively as President of the Missions Commission of the World Evangelical Fellowship.

William D. Taylor was born of missionary parents in Costa Rica and served 17 years as a missionary in Guatemala. He is currently the Executive Secretary for the Missions Commission of the World Evangelical Fellowship.

** We use general numbers as interpreted from different sources. There is no clear consensus of opinion on these statistics.

planted, so the movement cannot be attributed directly to missionary influence. Although we will attempt to trace this phenomenon to some other causes, we recognize that the primary initiator of this phenomenon is the Supreme Lord, who acts in a sovereign and timely manner in the history of missions.

Many nations in the Two Thirds World became independent from colonial rule in the period 1940-1960. The spirit of nationalism identified the native non-Christian religions with national culture and patriotism and regarded Christianity as a product of colonialism. This produced a compelling zeal on the part of national Christians and churches to accept responsibility for evangelizing their own people. The Sovereign Lord used this spirit of national pride to cause the churches to see their international responsibility.

Also, restrictions were placed on the entry of expatriate missionaries into many countries. Even if missionaries were given visas, they often were not permitted to go to certain unreached peoples, as in India. This reality stirred the national Christians and churches to accept responsibility to reach the unreached peoples in their own countries.

In some countries of the world the church has grown phenomenally. In Latin America, this is true in Brazil, Costa Rica, El Salvador, and Guatemala. In Asia, growth is evident in Singapore, Indonesia, and Korea. It is happening in Nigeria, Kenya, and other African nations also. Look at the figures:

Year	Percent of the World's Christians Living in the Two Thirds World*
1800	1%
1900	9%
1950	32%
1980	50%
1992	75%

* Includes Asia, Africa, Latin America, the South Pacific, and the Middle East

Not only is there church growth, but there is also spiritual revival in several countries of the Two Thirds World. The Christians have become more aware of their Christian discipleship and responsibilities. There is deep zeal for prayer and fasting, an understanding of spiritual warfare, and a concern to bring others to Christ. In the history of the church, whenever and wherever there is true revival, missions has resulted. It is not surprising that strong missionary movements have arisen in Two Thirds World countries.

20. *What factors have worked together to produce missions movements in the Two Thirds World?*

_____

_____

_____

Challenges and concerns

1. Most of the Two Thirds World missions are involved in pioneer evangelism and church planting. This is encouraging. It is reported that there are still 11,000 unreached people groups in the world. Most of them are in the non-Western world. Missions from the Two Thirds World must accept their responsibility for these and join the worldwide missionary movement to accomplish this task. This will require sacrifice, creativity and long-term commitments.

2. The Western missionary movement is still associated with colonialism and imperialism in many parts of Asia and Africa. It is regarded as a threat to national identity and native cultures because

it comes with money power from the West. Two Thirds World missions can be free from this accusation because they generally come from a background of poverty and powerlessness. Because of cultural similarities and less disparity in economic levels, missionaries from the Two Thirds World may have certain advantages when they go to people groups in the Two Thirds World. Because they and some of their parents suffered when the gospel came to their area, they are now willing to suffer for our Lord.

3. Most of the Two Thirds World consists of economically poor, developing countries. The gross national product is low in these countries, and some of them are hit with staggering inflation rates. The national and international debts, coupled with internal corruption and mismanagement, are crushing burdens. But these factors must not create a "poverty complex" leading to a dependent, helpless mentality. The Two Thirds World church must seriously face the challenge of sacrifice for the sake of our Lord.

Two Thirds World missions should not make the mistake of doing missions by depending on the flow of funds from the West, without any cost to their own churches and Christians.

Two Thirds World missions should not make the mistake of doing missions by depending on the flow of funds from the West, without any cost to their own churches and Christians. These Christians may not be developed economically and technologically, but they are rich in cultural heritage and in human and spiritual resources potential. They can break the mentality which downgrades them and seek with God's help to rise to the challenge of His missionary mandate. This can be done by creating missions awareness in the churches through consistent, systematic education and mobilization of congregations in missions. Appropriate missionary infrastructures must be developed for the new movements to prosper.

4. The world increasingly seems to limit traditional missionary work. Two-thirds of the countries in the world today are in the Restricted Access category for missions. These countries can be reached only by bivocational, tentmaking, cross-cultural servants. There are already thousands of Two Thirds World believers who travel to other countries to make a living, whether simply in search of better jobs or in conscious cross-cultural service to Christ. They may be Filipino maids in Saudi Arabia; Nigerian agriculturalists in Libya; Middle East doctors in Muslim Africa; Indonesian engineers in Cambodia; Singaporean English teachers in China; Latin businessmen in North Africa; Korean fish farmers in India. The fact is that they are there. They need to be equipped as missionaries and then sent out by their churches with training and full prayer support.

5. In many countries of the Two Thirds World, there are strict foreign exchange regulations, and so money cannot be sent out of the country for missionary support. To overcome this hurdle, these missions should move beyond traditional patterns of missionary support, seeking innovative ways from the Holy Spirit. They need not organize themselves on Western patterns of administration, structure, and finance. They can learn from them and yet work out their own patterns that are culturally suitable. This is happening!

6. There are relatively few Two Thirds World mission agencies to care for the number of missionary volunteers. Many of the existing agencies are weak in their administrative structures and in providing adequate pastoral care for their missionaries. Several do not have full-time executive officers. This handicap results in inadequate communication with missionaries. The emphasis is often on recruiting and sending, but missionaries should not be sent unless there is proper home selection and financial support, followed by field placement and supervision, strategizing and shepherding. This area must be remedied as missions develop creative and contextualized infrastructure. Again, these missions can examine

the strengths and weaknesses of the methods and practices of the West and learn from them.*

7. Two Thirds World missions must develop networking systems and partnerships among themselves and with Western missions. There is no place for a nationalistic, do-it-alone attitude, as missions flow from all nations to all nations in the world today.

There is no place for a nationalistic, do-it-alone attitude, as missions flow from all nations to all nations in the world today.

---

8. This newer missionary movement needs effective and carefully designed training programs and centers. The sad fact is that most of this cross-cultural force has been sent out with very limited prefield training. And the results are coming in: too many young missionaries are returning home after only a shortened first term, never to return; they encountered obstacles (spiritual, human, political, economic) that no one told them about before leaving for the field; some simply are so proud and ethnocentric that they frustrate themselves and the people they

minister to; others left with financial and prayer support promises which soon dried up. Many of these problems can be corrected with proper selection and adequate training.

The Western movement has tended to create a costly training system that is primarily dependent upon formal and academic schooling models. But the non-Western missions are in the enviable position of learning from the West and then designing new training models which have contextualized instruction and practice, combining formal, nonformal, and informal dimensions.

Conclusion

We are profoundly thankful to God for His marvelous new creation of this additional missionary force. The Western force joins hearts and hands with this massive international team. Missionaries from the West will increasingly serve alongside and under non-Western counterparts, and this is a unique challenge to cross-cultural servanthood. There is no room to call a moratorium on Western missions. This is anti-biblical. We need a global call for all churches to be sending missionaries and establishing training bases to further the kingdom of Christ.

---

21. *Which of the preceding challenges and concerns do you think can be met most effectively through cooperative efforts between Western and non-Western missions?*

_____

_____

_____

---

* See Lane, D. (1990). *Tuning God's new instruments: A handbook for missions from the Two Thirds World*. OMF Books.

Summary

In broad brush strokes, this chapter has painted the world Christian movement from its tentative first century beginnings to today's stirring developments in the Two Thirds World. As Winter has so aptly illustrated through his whirlwind tour of the ten 400-year epochs of mission history, much of the frontier mission work has been done by a reluctant church being sent through involuntary means. Yet God's determination that some from every nation know His sovereignty and blessing has permitted Christianity to spread relentlessly from one cultural basin to another, even though the experience hasn't always been joyful for the messengers.

After the conquest of Rome by Christianity in 375 A.D., the unshared blessings of Christianity were appropriated by force through the invasion of the Barbarians. These northern European peoples adopted fully the religion of those they conquered, and Christianity thus spread. The mistake of not purposefully evangelizing the next frontier, the Vikings, allowed the gospel to be spread to these people through involuntary means: slaves and concubines taken from raided Christian communities. When these Christianized but warlike Scandinavian peoples turned their attention to spreading Christianity, it resulted in a sad, misdirected attempt to regain the Holy Land through expulsion of the Saracens. This bloody page of mission history, while a form of voluntary going, still represents a major obstacle in evangelization of Muslims.

The final epoch of Christian growth began about the 17th century and coincided with European colonial expansion. It has been an epoch characterized by the voluntary sending of missionaries. The Roman Catholic church led the way in mission advance in the first two centuries in this epoch. Protestants did not awaken to their mission responsibility till the early 19th century. When they did, they launched a tremendous mission effort which continues to this day. In spite of its many shortcomings, the world Christian movement has affected mankind much more profoundly than any other organized religion or philosophical expression and remains the most significant movement in the history of the world. Yet, as if guided by historical determinism, the West, which so long has enjoyed the blessing of Christianity, now seems to be in decline, while the churches of the most recently evangelized regions of the world take up the torch for world evangelization. Abdication of this role to this vigorous newer element of Christian expansion, however, would be a serious and unpardonable mistake by the Western church. The Great Commission task belongs to all churches everywhere.

Integrative Assignment

1. *Explain Winter's statement that history is a "single, coherent drama." What is the plot of the drama? Who are the main characters? How many "acts" does the play have?*

2. *How can you see the come/go, voluntary/involuntary mechanisms at work in your own country today? What strategies or responsibilities might these mechanisms suggest to you and your church?*

3. *Prepare a short talk entitled, "Share Your Blessings or Have Them Taken Away." Illustrate your talk from Scripture and history. Scriptures you might want to use are Luke 19:11-27, Mark 4:21-25, Matthew 21:42-44, and Romans 11.*

Questions for Reflection

Someone has said, "Share your faith or lose it." Although losing one's faith is tragic, history has demonstrated that we stand to lose more than just our faith if we are unwilling to share God's blessing with others. In what ways can you be involved in sharing God's blessings with those who are culturally different from you and still beyond the reach of the gospel? Think of specific ways you can become involved. Then prayerfully commit yourself to a plan of action. Record your thoughts and plans below.

_____

_____

_____

_____

_____

_____

_____

_____

_____

_____

_____

_____

CHAPTER 5

Eras, Pioneers, and Transitions

The God of history has moved governments, kingdoms, armies, and entire peoples in His desire to bring men and nations to know His loving rule. A study of His work through the centuries opens our eyes to an understanding of the depth of His determination to accomplish His mission purpose. As we adjust our own course to cooperate with His purpose, we can learn from history and from those who have served in His cause.

In the previous chapter, Ralph Winter led us on a whirlwind tour of the epochs of the expansion of Christianity. In this section, we will look more closely at the Fifth Period, the last 200 years of mission history. This period of active Protestant involvement in mission is marked by astounding advances in the world Christian movement. Many valuable lessons can be learned from this period—lessons that can help our generation as we work towards closure of the Great Commission mandate.

I. Three Eras of Expansion

The last two centuries of Christian expansion can be understood in terms of three distinct "eras." In the First Era, lasting from 1792 to 1910, missionary efforts focused on reaching the coastlands of the major unreached continents. The Second Era, spanning 1865 to 1980, concentrated on inland regions. The Third Era, 1934 to the present, has targeted hidden and unreached peoples who were hitherto bypassed. In the following excerpts, Ralph Winter describes each of these eras, the advances for the kingdom made during each period, and persons who played key roles in pioneering these advances.

COASTLANDS | INLAND REGIONS | UNREACHED PEOPLES

1800   2000 A.D.

THE FINISHED TASK

❑ *Four Men, Three Eras, Two Transitions* *

Ralph D. Winter

The First Era:
Reaching the coastlands

An "under 30" young man, William Carey, got into trouble when he began to take the Great Commission seriously. When he had the opportunity to address a group of ministers, he challenged them to give a reason why the Great Commission did not apply to them. They rebuked him, saying, "When God chooses to win the heathen, He will do it without your help or ours." He was unable to speak again on the subject, so he patiently wrote out his analysis, "An Enquiry Into the Obligations of Christians to Use Means for the Conversion of the Heathens."

William Carey's little book, in combination with the Evangelical Awakening, quickened vision and changed lives on both sides of the Atlantic.

The resulting small book convinced a few of his friends to create a tiny missions agency, the "means" of which he had spoken.** The structure was flimsy and weak, providing only the minimal backing he needed to go to India. However, the impact of his example reverberated throughout the English-speaking world, and his little book became the Magna Carta of the Protestant mission movement.

William Carey was not the first Protestant missionary. For years the Moravians had sent people to Greenland, America, and Africa. But his little book, in combination with the Evangelical Awakening, quickened vision and changed lives on both sides of the Atlantic. Response was almost instantaneous: a second missionary society was founded in London;

two in Scotland; one in Holland; and then still another in England. By then it was apparent to all that Carey was right when he had insisted that organized efforts in the form of missions societies were essential to the success of the missionary endeavor.

In America, five college students, aroused by Carey's book, met to pray for God's direction for their lives. This unobtrusive prayer meeting, later known as the "Haystack Prayer Meeting," resulted in an American "means"—the American Board of Commissioners for Foreign Missions. Even more important, they started a student mission movement which became the example and forerunner of other student movements in missions to this day.

In fact, during the first 25 years after Carey sailed to India, a dozen mission agencies were formed on both sides of the Atlantic, and the First Era in Protestant missions was off to a good start. Realistically speaking, however, missions in this First Era was a pitifully small shoestring operation, in relation to the major preoccupations of most Europeans and Americans in that day. The idea that we should organize in order to send missionaries did not come easily, but it eventually became an accepted pattern.

Carey's influence led some women in Boston to form women's missionary prayer groups, a trend which led to women becoming the main custodians of mission knowledge and motivation. After some years women began to go to the field as single missionaries. Finally, by 1865, unmarried American women established women's mission boards which, like Roman Catholic women's orders, only sent out single women as missionaries and were run entirely by single women at home.

---

* Winter, R. D. (1992). Four men, three eras, two transitions. In R. D. Winter & S. C. Hawthorne (Eds.), *Perspectives on the world Christian movement: A reader* (rev. ed.) (pp. B35-B43). Pasadena: William Carey Library.

** Carey's thesis was that committed societies needed to be founded to advance the gospel in other cultures. These societies were the "means" to which he referred in his book.

There are two very bright notes about the First Era. One is the astonishing demonstration of love and sacrifice on the part of those who went out. Africa, especially, was a forbidding continent. All mission outreach to Africa, prior to 1775, had totally failed. Of all Catholic efforts, all Moravian efforts, nothing remained. Not one missionary of any kind existed on the continent on the eve of the First Era. The gruesome statistics of almost inevitable sickness and death that haunted, yet did not daunt, the decades of truly valiant missionaries who went out after 1790 in virtually a suicidal stream cannot be matched by any other era or by any other cause. Very few missionaries to Africa in the first 60 years of the First Era survived more than two years. As I have reflected on this measure of devotion, I have been humbled to tears, for I wonder—if I or my people today could or would match that record. Can you imagine our Urbana students today going out into missionary work if they knew that for decade after decade 19 out of 20 of those before them had died almost on arrival on the field?

Can you imagine our Urbana students today going out into missionary work if they knew that for decade after decade 19 out of 20 of those before them had died almost on arrival on the field?

A second bright spot in this First Era is the development of high-quality insight into mission strategy. The movement had several great missiologists. In regard to home structure, they clearly understood the value of the mission structure being allowed a life of its own. For example, we read that the London Missionary Society experienced unprecedented and unequalled success, "due partly to its freedom from ecclesiastical supervision and partly to its formation from an almost equal number of ministers and lay-men." In regard to field structure, we can take a note from Henry Venn, who was related to the famous Clapham evangelicals* and the son of a founder of the Church Missionary Society. Except for a few outdated terms, one of his most famous paragraphs sounds strangely modern:

> Regarding the ultimate object of a Mission, viewed under its ecclesiastical result, to be the settlement of a Native Church under Native Pastors upon a self-supporting system, it should be borne in mind that the progress of a Mission mainly depends upon the training up and the location of Native Pastors; and that, as it has been happily expressed, the "euthanasia of a Mission" takes place when a missionary, surrounded by well-trained Native congregations under Native Pastors, is able to resign all pastoral work into their hands, and gradually relax his superintendence over the pastors themselves, 'til it insensibly ceases; and so the Mission passes into a settled Christian community. Then the missionary and all missionary agencies should be transferred to the "regions beyond."

These missiologists were recognizing the stages of mission activity recently described in the alliterative sequence:

- Stage 1: A Pioneer stage – First contact with a people group.

- Stage 2: A Paternal stage – Expatriates train national leadership.

- Stage 3: A Partnership stage – National leaders work as equals with expatriates.

- Stage 4: A Participation stage – Expatriates are no longer equal partners, but only participate by invitation.

---

* The Clapham evangelicals were a group of influential evangelicals in England during the early 1800s.

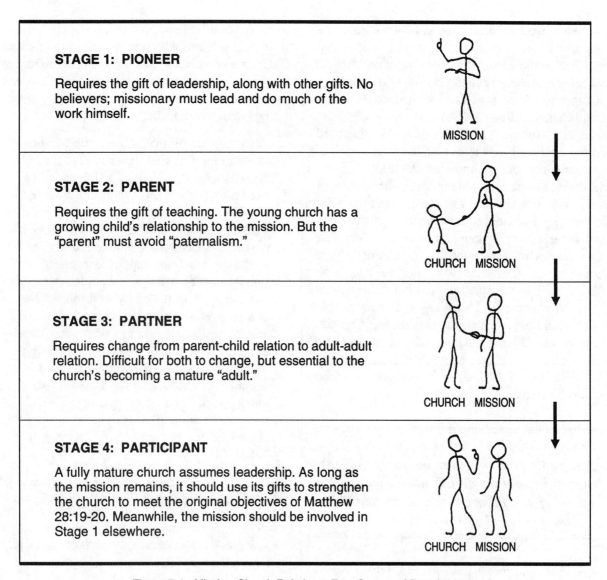

STAGE 1: PIONEER

Requires the gift of leadership, along with other gifts. No believers; missionary must lead and do much of the work himself.

MISSION

STAGE 2: PARENT

Requires the gift of teaching. The young church has a growing child's relationship to the mission. But the "parent" must avoid "paternalism."

CHURCH   MISSION

STAGE 3: PARTNER

Requires change from parent-child relation to adult-adult relation. Difficult for both to change, but essential to the church's becoming a mature "adult."

CHURCH   MISSION

STAGE 4: PARTICIPANT

A fully mature church assumes leadership. As long as the mission remains, it should use its gifts to strengthen the church to meet the original objectives of Matthew 28:19-20. Meanwhile, the mission should be involved in Stage 1 elsewhere.

CHURCH   MISSION

Figure 5-1. Mission-Church Relations: Four Stages of Development

1. *What outstanding "bright spots" characterized the First Era of modern Protestant missions? Discuss these in light of what you observe to be the current state of missions activity, particularly in your own church or denomination.*

_____

_____

_____

_____

_____

Four stages of development

Slow and painstaking though the labors of the First Era were, they did bear fruit, and the familiar series of stages can be observed which goes from no church in the pioneer stage to infant church in the paternal stage and to the more complicated mature church in the partnership and participation stage. Samuel Hoffman of the Reformed Church in America Board puts it well: "The Christian missionary who was loved as an evangelist and liked as a teacher, may find himself resented as an administrator."

Lucky is the missionary in whose own career this whole sequence of stages takes place. More likely the series represents the work in a specific field with a succession of missionaries, or it may be the experience of an agency which in its early period bursts out in work in a number of places and then after some years finds that most of its fields are mature at about the same time. But rightly or wrongly, this kind of succession is visible in the mission move-ment globally, as the fever for change and nationalization sweeps the thinking of almost all executives at once and leaps from continent to continent, affecting new fields still in earlier stages as well as old ones in the latter stages.

At any rate, by 1865 there was a strong consensus on both sides of the Atlantic that the missionary should go home when he had worked himself out of a job. Since the First Era focused primarily upon the coastlands of Asia and Africa, we are not surprised that literal withdrawal would come about first in a case where there were no inland territories. Thus, symbolizing the latter stages of the First Era was the withdrawal of all missionaries from the Hawaiian Islands, then a separate country. This was done with legitimate pride and fanfare and fulfilled the highest expectations, then and now, of successful progress through the stage of missionary planting, watering, and harvest.

2. *Why is an understanding of the four stages of mission-church relations important for the evaluation of work in any field?*

_____

_____

   The First Era of Protestant missions was fueled by an intense, almost reckless compassion for the lost, as well as a measured attempt to understand the task and the implications for the long haul. From this era, Protestant missions learned that service for God does require heart and soul, but also mind and strength.

   An awakened Protestant church in Europe and America applied herself to using "means" in carrying out her responsibility for world evangelization. Mission agencies (mostly related to denominations) which were organized as the "means" of promoting and directing that effort proved to be one of the most significant aspects of this awakening. The First Era also aroused missions leaders to the fact that the missionary task required not only compassion and prayer, but also an understanding of the process which would lead to effectiveness in completing the worldwide task. An emerging *missiology* * helped define their task and gave them tools to evaluate and organize their work, especially in planning to build the national church. It became clear: *Effective mission requires compassion and prayer. It also requires research and planning.*

_____

   * Missiology is the "science" of mission. It employs theology, linguistics, the social sciences, and other academic disciplines important to the training of missionaries and the effective formulation and implementation of mission strategy.

As First Era missiologists understood it, the completion of the four stages of mission-church relations signaled the end of the missionary task. In Hawaii, the South Sea islands, and some coastal regions, completion occurred relatively quickly, and the feeling prevailed that a missionary presence was no longer necessary. In other parts of the world, however, the stages were not completed, or if they were completed, much pioneer work was often still needed. Confusion ensued with supporting constituencies divided on whether missionaries in general were still needed or not. In the midst of this disorientation, God began to provide a clearer focus during a Second Era, as Winter explains below.

The Second Era:
Penetrating the inland regions

A second symbolic event of 1865 is even more significant, at least for the inauguration of the Second Era. A young man, after a short term and like Carey still under 30, in the teeth of surrounding counter-advice, established the first of a whole new breed of missions emphasizing the inland territories. This second young upstart was given little but negative notice, but like William Carey, brooded over statistics, charts, and maps. When he suggested that the inland peoples of China needed to be reached, he was told you could not get there, and he was asked if he wished to carry on his shoulders the blood of the young people he would thus send to their deaths.

The Student Volunteer Movement was history's single most potent mission organization. It netted 100,000 volunteers who gave their lives to missions.

With only trade school medicine, without any university experience, much less missiological training, and a checkered past in regard to his own individualistic behavior while he was on the field, he was merely one more of the weak things that God used to confound the wise. Even his early anti-church-planting missionary strategy was breathtakingly erroneous by today's church-planting standards. Yet God strangely honored him because his gaze was fixed upon the world's least-reached peoples. Hudson Taylor had a divine wind behind him. The Holy Spirit spared him from many pitfalls, and it was his organization, the China Inland Mission [now called Overseas Missionary Fellowship]—the most cooperative, servant organization yet to appear—that eventually served in one way or another over 6,000 missionaries, predominantly in the interior of China. It took 20 years for other missions to begin to join Taylor in his special emphasis—the unreached, inland frontiers.

One reason the Second Era began slowly is that many people were confused. There were already many missions in existence. Why more? Yet as Taylor pointed out, all existing agencies were confined to the coastlands of Africa and Asia, or islands in the Pacific. People questioned, "Why go to the interior if you haven't finished the job on the coast?"

I am not sure the parallel is true today, but the Second Era apparently needed not only a new vision but a lot of new organizations. Taylor not only started an English frontier mission, he went to Scandinavia and the Continent to challenge people to start new agencies. As a result, directly or indirectly, over 40 new agencies took shape to compose the faith missions that rightly should be called frontier missions, as the names of many of them still indicate: China Inland Mission, Sudan Interior Mission, Africa Inland Mission, Heart of Africa Mission, Unevangelized Fields Mission, Regions Beyond Missionary Union.

As in the early stage of the First Era, when things began to move, God brought forth a student movement. This one was more massive than before—the Student Volunteer Movement for Foreign Missions—history's single most potent mission organization. In the 1880s and '90s there were only 1/37th as many college students as there are today, but the Student Volunteer Movement netted 100,000 volunteers who gave their lives to missions. Twenty thousand actually went overseas. As we see it now, the other 80,000 had to stay home to rebuild the foundations of the missions endeavor. They began the

Laymen's Missionary Movement and strengthened existing women's missionary societies.

However, as the fresh new college students of the Second Era burst on the scene overseas, they did not always fathom how the older missionaries of the First Era could have turned responsibility over to

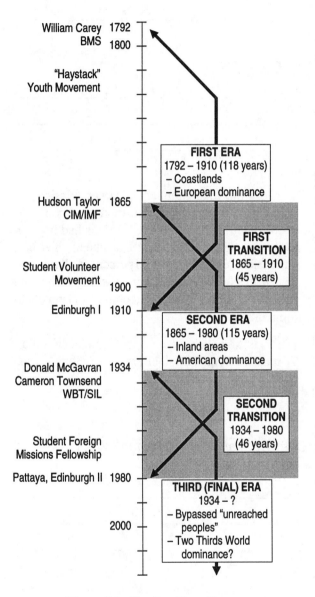

Figure 5-2. The Two Transitions

national leadership at the least educated levels of society. First Era missionaries were in the minority now, and the wisdom they had gained from their experience was bypassed by the large number of new college-educated recruits. Thus, in the early stages of the Second Era, the new missionaries, instead of going to new frontiers, sometimes assumed leadership over existing churches, forcing First Era missionaries and national leadership (which had been painstakingly developed) into the background. In some cases this caused a huge step backward in mission strategy.

By 1925, however, the largest mission movement in history was in full swing. By then, Second Era missionaries had finally learned the basic lessons they had first ignored and produced an incredible record. They had planted churches in a thousand new places, mainly "inland," and by 1940 the reality of the "younger churches" around the world was widely acclaimed as the "great new fact of our time." The strength of these churches led both national leaders and missionaries to assume that all additional frontiers could simply be mopped up by the ordinary evangelism of the churches scattered throughout the world. More and more people wondered if, in fact, missionaries weren't needed so badly! Once more, as in 1865, it seemed logical to send missionaries home from many areas of the world.

For us today it is highly important to note the overlap of these first two eras. The 45-year period between 1865 and 1910 (compare 1934 to 1980 today) was a transition between the strategy appropriate to the mature stages of Era 1, the Coastlands Era, and the strategy appropriate to the pioneering stages of Era 2, the Inland Era.

3. What advances were made in the Second Era? What mistakes did missionaries have to overcome? How could the mistakes have been avoided?

_____

_____

_____

_____

_____

4. Why does Winter draw our attention to the periods of transition?

_____

_____

_____

Shortly after the World Missionary Conference in Edinburgh in 1910, there ensued the shattering World Wars and the worldwide collapse of the colonial apparatus. By 1945 many overseas churches were prepared not only for the withdrawal of the colonial powers, but for the absence of the missionary as well. While there was no very widespread outcry, "Missionary Go Home," as some supposed, nevertheless things were different now, as even the people in the pews at home ultimately sensed. Pioneer and paternal were no longer the relevant stages, but partnership and participation.

In 1967, the total number of career missionaries from America began to decline (and it has continued to do so to this day). Why? Christians had been led to believe that all necessary beachheads had been established. By 1967, over 90 percent of all missionaries from North America were working with strong national churches that had been in existence for some time.

The facts, however, were not that simple. Unnoticed by most everyone, another era in missions had begun.

5. Contrast and compare the First and Second Eras. What similarities existed? What significant changes in focus characterized the Second Era?

_____

_____

_____

_____

_____

_____

The Second Era met the challenge of the geographically isolated interiors of the continents. Hudson Taylor's vision spawned the formation of nearly 40 new mission societies, often called "faith missions," * which undertook this new focus of concern. These mission societies deployed thousands of recruits from the Student Volunteer Movement. The result was tens of thousands of churches established throughout previously unevangelized parts of the globe.

At the same time, special problems arose. How was the new wave of missionaries to be appropriately integrated into the work? When should these workers learn from the past, and when should they forge new paths? These challenges still arise today.

The Third Era:
Reaching the unreached peoples

This era was begun by a pair of young men of the Student Volunteer Movement: Cameron Townsend and Donald McGavran. Cameron Townsend was in so much of a hurry to get to the mission field that he didn't bother to finish college. He went to Guatemala as a Second Era missionary, building on work which had been done in the past. In that country, as in all other mission fields, there was plenty to do by missionaries working with established national churches.

But Townsend was alert enough to notice that the majority of Guatemala's population did not speak Spanish. As he moved from village to village, trying to distribute scriptures written in the Spanish language, he began to realize that Spanish evangelism would never reach all Guatemala's people. He was further convinced of this when an Indian asked him, "If your God is so smart, why can't He speak our language?" He was just 23 when he began to move on the basis of this new perspective.

Surely in our time one person comparable to William Carey and Hudson Taylor is Cameron Townsend. Like Carey and Taylor, Townsend saw that there were still unreached frontiers, and for almost a half century he has waved the flag for the overlooked tribal peoples of the world. He started out hoping to help older boards reach out to tribal people. Like Carey and Taylor, he ended up starting his own mission, Wycliffe Bible Translators, which is dedicated to reaching these new frontiers. At first he

> *Cameron Townsend saw that there were still unreached frontiers, and for almost a half century he has waved the flag for the overlooked tribal peoples of the world.*

thought there must be about 500 unreached tribal groups in the world. (He was judging by the large number of tribal languages in Mexico alone.) Later, he revised his figure to 1,000, then 2,000, and now it is closer to 5,000. As his conception of the enormity of the task has increased, the size of his organization has increased. Today it numbers over 4,000 adult workers.

6. In what ways was Townsend similar to Carey and Taylor?

_____

_____

_____

* Faith missions are independent, non-denominationally aligned missions funded primarily through the freewill offerings of churches and individuals.

At the very same time Townsend was ruminating in Guatemala, Donald McGavran was beginning to yield to the seriousness, not of linguistic barriers, but of India's amazing social barriers. Townsend "discovered" the tribes; McGavran discovered a more nearly universal category he labeled "homogeneous units," which today are more often called "people groups."

Once such a group is penetrated, diligently taking advantage of that missiological breakthrough along group lines, the strategic "bridge of God" to that people group is established. The corollary of this truth is the fact that *until* such a breakthrough is made, normal evangelism and church planting cannot take place.

Donald McGavran's active efforts and writings spawned both the Church Growth Movement and the Frontier Mission Movement.

McGavran did not found a new mission. (Townsend did so only when the existing missions did not properly respond to the tribal challenge.) McGavran's active efforts and writings spawned both the Church Growth Movement and the Frontier Mission Movement, the one devoted to expanding within already penetrated groups and the other devoted to deliberate approaches to the remaining unpenetrated groups.

As with Carey and Taylor before them, for 20 years Townsend and McGavran attracted little attention. But by the 1950s both had wide audiences. By 1980, 46 years from 1934, a 1910-like conference was held, focusing precisely on the forgotten groups these two men emphasized. The Edinburgh-1980 World Consultation on Frontier Missions was the largest mission meeting in history, measured by the number of mission agencies sending delegates. And wonder of wonders, 57 Third World agencies sent delegates. This is the sleeper of the Third Era! Also, a simultaneous youth meeting, the International Student Consultation on Frontier Missions, pointed the way for all future mission meetings to include significant youth participation.

As happened in the early stages of the first two eras, the Third Era has spawned a number of new mission agencies. Some, like the New Tribes Mission, carry in their names reference to this new emphasis. The names of others, such as Gospel Recordings and Mission Aviation Fellowship, refer to the new technologies necessary for the reaching of tribal and other isolated peoples of the world. Some Second Era agencies, like Regions Beyond Missionary Union, have never ceased to stress frontiers and have merely increased their staff so they can penetrate further—to people groups previously overlooked.

More recently many have begun to realize that tribal peoples are not the only forgotten peoples. Many other groups, some in the middle of partially Christianized areas, have been completely overlooked. These peoples are being called the "Unreached Peoples" and are defined by ethnic or sociological traits to be people so different from the cultural traditions of any existing church that missions (rather than evangelism) strategies are necessary for the planting of indigenous churches within their traditions.

If the First Era was characterized by reaching coastland peoples and the Second Era by inland territories, the Third Era must be characterized by the more difficult-to-define, non-geographical category which we have called "Unreached Peoples"—people groups which are socially isolated. Because this concept has been so hard to define, the Third Era has been even slower getting started than the Second Era. Cameron Townsend and Donald McGavran began calling attention to forgotten peoples over 40 years ago, but only recently has any major attention been given to them. More tragic still, we have essentially forgotten the pioneering techniques of the First and Second Eras, so we almost need to reinvent the wheel as we learn again how to approach groups of people completely untouched by the gospel!

We know that there are about 11,000 people groups in the "Unreached Peoples" category, gathered in clusters of similar peoples, these clusters numbering not more than 3,000. Each individual people will require a separate, new missionary beachhead. Is this too much? Can this be done? Is there any realism in the slogan gaining currency, "A church for every people by the year 2000"?

7. *What characteristics distinguish the Third Era from its predecessors?*

_____

_____

_____

The Third Era is gaining momentum. Through the efforts of the U.S. Center for World Mission in Pasadena, California, and organizations with a similar focus around the world, the church has been alerted to the ultimate objective of this third and final era of mission history. Hundreds of new efforts are being initiated to reach the "unreached peoples"—groups socially, ethnically, or linguistically isolated from the gospel. In this burgeoning enthusiasm for reaching the final goal, let us be like the "head of a household, who brings out of his treasure things new and old" (Matt. 13:52). While responding to this tremendous new challenge and considering new realities, let us not forget to look at the old lessons learned by those who went before us. The study of mission history and the pioneers who led the way can save us from many mistakes.

II. Four Pioneers

From the study of the eras of mission history, we learn that every major trend in missions has been led by men to whom God gave a specific vision. Selections from the writings of pioneers such as Carey, Taylor, Townsend, and McGavran provide a rich source of insight that is stirring and instructive. Many of the issues these men grappled with are still current today. In this section, Meg Crossman guides us as we look in more detail at the lives of these four pioneers and the principal concepts they imparted through their writings.

❏ *Mission Pioneers*

Meg Crossman

William Carey: Pioneer to the coastlands

There is a curiously contemporary quality to the writings of William Carey, the 18th century shoe-maker who has come to be called "The Father of Modern Missions." Carey, with little formal education, was stirred to concern by reading the reports of Captain Cook's Pacific explorations. He learned all he could about the people and cultures of other countries. The plight of unevangelized continents so burdened him that he covered his walls with maps, praying as he repaired shoes.

In 1792, the British had been in India (through the East India Company) for more than 150 years. In all

that time not one verse of Scripture had been translated into any native language. Carey had early demonstrated linguistic gifting, teaching himself Greek with the help of a New Testament commentary. He also learned French and Dutch in a matter of weeks. He began to ponder the responsibility of Christians to reach the unsaved with the Word of God.

This impoverished part-time pastor, hoping to convince his tiny denomination to act in reaching other nations, wrote a small pamphlet: "An Enquiry Into the Obligations of Christians to Use Means for the

Conversion of the Heathens." This "little book with the long name" produced an upheaval that affected all of Christianity. The following sections summarize some of Carey's most significant concepts.*

Pray and act

As our blessed Lord has required us to pray that His kingdom may come and His will be done on earth as it is in heaven, it becomes us not only to express our desires of that event by word, but to use every lawful method to spread the knowledge of His name.

Carey saw that prayer required a response of obedience. He was also convinced that in order for the church to carry out her kingdom obligation, the members must first be informed of the actual situation. With these things in mind, Carey prepared detailed demographic charts of the unreached continents to inform and motivate the church to action.

8. What missions relevance does Carey attach to the Lord's command that we pray, "Thy kingdom come, Thy will be done on earth as it is in heaven"?

_____

_____

_____

Overcoming resistance at home

One of the greatest obstacles Carey faced in motivating the church towards her obligation was the then-popular theological opinion that the Great Commission was binding *only* on the apostles. Among other arguments to dispel this notion, Carey pointed out:

If the command of Christ to teach all nations be restricted to the apostles, or those under the immediate inspiration of the Holy Ghost, then that of baptizing should be so, too; and every denomination of Christian, except the Quakers, do wrong in baptizing with water at all.

Next Carey dealt with an objection that is still current: "There is so much to be done here at home!" Although the language may seem stilted, the argument is fresh:

It has been objected that there are multitudes in our own nation and within our immediate spheres of action, who are as ignorant as the South-Sea savages, and that therefore we have work enough at home, without going into other countries. That there are thousands in our own land as far from God as possible, I readily grant, and that this ought to excite us to ten-fold diligence to our work, and in attempts to spread divine knowledge amongst them is a certain fact; but that it ought to supersede all attempts to spread the gospel in foreign parts seems to want proof. Our own countrymen have the means of grace, and may attend on the word preached if they choose it. They have the means of knowing the truth, and faithful ministers are placed in almost every part of the land, whose spheres of action might be much extended if their congregations were but more hearty and active in the cause; but with them the case is widely different, who have no Bible, no written language (which many of them have not), no ministers, no good civil government, nor any of those advantages which we have. Pity therefore, humanity, and much more Christianity, call loudly for every possible exertion to introduce the gospel amongst them.

* Carey, W. (1962). *An enquiry into the obligations of Christians to use means for the conversion of the heathens* (New Facsimile ed.). London: Carey Kingsgate Press. (Original work published 1792)

9. Summarize Carey's response to the objection, "We have so many problems here at home."

_____

_____

_____

_____

A call to action

Carey researched extensively the state of the unsaved world in his day. In more than 20 charts covering information about every continent, he demonstrated the tremendous need. After evaluating the compelling nature of the gathered information, he called the church to act:

> The impediments in the way of carrying the gospel among the heathen must arise, I think, from one or other of the following things;—either their distance from us, their barbarous and savage manner of living, the danger of being killed by them, the difficulty of procuring the necessities of life, or the unintelligibleness of their language.

Carey dealt with each of these objections, pointing out that none of these considerations restrained commercial interests. If people could go for gain, could they not go for God? Certainly, these excuses did not stop "the apostles and their successors, who went among the barbarous *Germans* and *Gauls*, and still more barbarous *Britons!*" As for being killed, Carey pointed out that acts of savagery were usually provoked by hostility on the part of newcomers and that missionaries such as the Moravians were seldom molested.

The use of means

One of Carey's most important contributions was his concept of the use of "means":

> Suppose a company of serious Christians, ministers and private persons, were to form themselves into a society, and make a number of rules respecting the regulation of the plan, and the persons who are to be employed as missionaries, the means of defraying the expense, etc., etc. This society must consist of persons whose hearts are in the work, men of serious religion, and possessing a spirit of perseverance; there must be a determination not to admit any person who is not of this description, or to retain him longer than he answers to it.

> From such a society a *committee* might be appointed, whose business it should be to procure all the information they could upon the subject, to receive contributions, to enquire into the characters, tempers, abilities, and religious views of the missionaries, and also to provide them with necessaries for their undertakings.

10. What practical steps does Carey suggest for the carrying out of God's intended purposes? Why was this idea revolutionary?

_____

_____

_____

_____

Carey acts on his own proposal

From this inauspicious beginning, the modern Protestant missions movement arose. The Baptist Missionary Society was formed, the first of many denominational mission agencies. Carey did not suggest to others what he was not willing to do himself. In 1793, he went out with his family to India as a missionary for BMS.

The hurdles Carey had to overcome in getting to the field are similar to the kind missionaries contend with today. First, Carey had to combat universalism and other theological objections. Next, he met severe resistance to his new idea of "means," essentially a "parachurch organization." He struggled to raise his outgoing expenses, an overwhelming amount at the time.

> **William Carey lived out his great watchword, "Expect great things from God; attempt great things for God."**

Once Carey was on the field, his promised support dried up, and he was forced to undertake secular employment, much like today's "tentmakers." * His target, India, was firmly "closed" to missionary work, and the population was highly resistant to the gospel. Although Carey's supporting base back home was always marginal, the group still attempted to control the work from England.

Carey worked in India for eight years, all the while battling the continuing hostility of the East India Company. At last he found refuge in the Danish-held city of Serampore, near Calcutta. With coworkers Joshua Marshman and William Ward, Carey formed a team known as the Serampore Trio that would work together for many years. Even during this time, Carey supported his work almost entirely through his well-paid and prestigious position as professor of oriental languages at Fort William College in Calcutta. The team's publication work was financed largely through the sale of published materials.

In spite of personal tragedy (Carey's wife died insane, and several children perished as well) and ministry setbacks (a fire in 1812 destroyed priceless manuscripts and whole translations), Carey continued doggedly. He once said, "I can plod. I can persevere in any definite pursuit. To this I owe everything."

Carey lived out his great watchword, "Expect great things *from* God; attempt great things *for* God." He translated the entire Bible into Bengali, Sanskrit, and Marathi. Together the team completed 46 translations, New Testaments, and portions in various languages and dialects. Carey founded Serampore College to train national leaders and church planters.

Carey died in 1834, but as Dr. Ruth Tucker notes, "not before leaving his mark on India and on missions for all time. His influence in India went beyond his massive linguistic accomplishments.... He also made a notable impact on harmful Indian practices through his long struggle against widow burning and infanticide. But otherwise he sought to leave the culture intact." **

---

* Tentmakers are committed Christians with marketable occupational skills who are working overseas while effectively sharing their faith in Jesus Christ. The term is taken from the Apostle Paul's practice of making tents to help support himself during his missionary journeys (Acts 18:3).

** Tucker, R. H. (1983). *From Jerusalem to Irian Jaya* (p. 121). Grand Rapids: Zondervan.

11. What impressions impact you most from the life and writings of William Carey?

_____

_____

_____

_____

Hudson Taylor: Champion of the inland regions

Like Carey, the young Englishman who would launch the movement to the inland regions had an unprepossessing start. At the age of 17, Hudson Taylor experienced a compelling call to China. He began to learn about China and prepare himself to work there.

The call to service *

Well do I remember, as in unreserved consecration I put myself, my life, my friends, my all, upon the altar, the deep solemnity that came over my soul with the assurance that my offering was accepted. The presence of God became unutterably real and blessed; and though but a child under sixteen, I remember stretching myself on the ground and lying there silent before Him with unspeakable awe and unspeakable joy.

"Move men through God by prayer alone," became Hudson Taylor's motto and deeply affected his view of ministry.

While pursuing medical studies, Taylor began, in a disciplined way, to prepare himself for missionary service. He trained himself to live simply and frugally. He practiced trusting God for practical provision, letting the Lord provide his needs, even when it was within his power and rights to ask things of others. "Move men through God by prayer alone," became his motto and deeply affected his view of ministry.

I began to take more exercise in the open air to strengthen my physique. My feather bed I had taken away and sought to dispense with as many other home comforts as I could in order to prepare myself for rougher lines of life. I began also to do what Christian work was in my power, in the way of tract distribution, Sunday-school teaching, and visiting the poor and sick, as opportunity afforded.

… More time was given in my solitude to the study of the Word of God, to visiting the poor, and to evangelistic work on summer evenings than would otherwise have been the case. Brought into contact in this way with many who were in distress, I soon saw the privilege of still further economizing, and found it not difficult to give away much more than the proportion of my income I had at first intended.

Besides living in very simple accommodations, Taylor periodically went through his books and his wardrobe to see what he could give to others. As his guideline, he asked what he would be ashamed of still having if the Lord were to return that day.

---

* Taylor, J. H. (n.d.). *A retrospect* (pp. 10-14). Philadelphia: China Inland Mission.

12. *In what practical ways did Taylor develop himself for missionary labor?*

_____

_____

_____

A new agency needed *

In 1854 Taylor arrived in Shanghai, China. He worked with some missionaries there but began to take trips into the interior where no missionaries had yet gone. To make himself more understandable to the Chinese, he adopted the dress of a Mandarin scholar, including blacking his hair and wearing a pigtail. British colleagues were horrified, but the increase in effectiveness with the nationals convinced Taylor of the wisdom of his actions. Even when he had to go home for health reasons, God used the apparent setback for ultimate good:

> To me it seemed a great calamity that failure of health compelled my relinquishing work for God in China, just when it was more fruitful than ever before.... Little did I then realize that the long separation from China was a necessary step towards the formation of a work which God would bless as He has blessed the China Inland Mission.
>
> Months of earnest prayer and not a few abortive efforts had resulted in a deep conviction that a special agency was essential for the evangelization of Inland China.... The grave difficulty of possibly interfering with existing missionary operations at home was foreseen; but it was concluded that, by simple trust in God, a suitable agency might be raised up and sustained without interfering injuriously with any existing work. I had also a growing conviction that God would have *me* to seek from Him the needed workers, and to go forth with them. But for a long time unbelief hindered my taking the first step.

Taylor's great struggle in prayer centered not on God's ability to give workers, but on the dangers, difficulties, and trials those workers might face on the field. The struggle climaxed on a beach in Brighton, England.

> On Sunday, June 25th, 1865, unable to bear the sight of a congregation of a thousand or more Christian people rejoicing in their own security, while millions were perishing for lack of knowledge, I wandered out on the sands alone, in great spiritual agony; and there the Lord conquered my unbelief, and I surrendered myself to God for this service. I told Him that all the responsibility as to issues and consequences must rest with Him; that as His servant, it was mine to obey and follow Him—His, to direct, to care for, and to guide me and those who might labour with me. Need I say that peace at once flowed into my heart?

13. *Why was a new society needed at this time?*

_____

_____

_____

_____

* Taylor, J. H. (n.d.). *A retrospect* (pp. 105-109). Philadelphia: China Inland Mission.

Taylor's society was unique, developed around the experiences and person of its founder. It was not linked to a denomination. It appealed to the working classes instead of demanding years of study and training. Its headquarters was in China, rather than far away in England, so it could be more responsive to field situations. Like Taylor, the missionaries were to adopt Chinese dress.

Hudson Taylor's missionaries were not to ask for funds but to trust God entirely for their needs, believing that "God's work, done God's way, will never lack for God's supply."

Taylor gladly accepted single women and expected missionary wives to be full partners in the enterprise. Most distinctive of all, the missionaries were not to ask for funds but to trust God entirely for their needs, believing that "God's work, done God's way, will never lack for God's supply." From this principle came the appellation, "faith missions."

Extending the kingdom to China *

Besides maintaining an extensive speaking schedule, Taylor mobilized many through the book he wrote with his wife, Maria, called *China's Spiritual Needs and Claims*. Like Carey, Taylor used charts and research as well as scriptural evidence in presenting his case.

> Think of the over eighty millions beyond the reach of the Gospel in the seven provinces, where missionaries have longest laboured; think of the over 100 millions in the other eleven provinces of China Proper, beyond the reach of the few missionaries labouring there; think of the over twenty millions who inhabit the vast regions of Manchuria, Mongolia, Thibet, and the Northwestern Dependencies, which exceed in extent the whole of Europe—an aggregate of over 200 millions beyond the reach of all existing agencies—and say, how shall
>
> > God's name be hallowed by them,
> > His kingdom come among them, and
> > His will be done by them?
>
> His name and His attributes they have never heard. His kingdom is not proclaimed among them. His will is not made known to them!
>
> We have now presented a brief and cursory view of the state and claims of China.... We have sought to press the great command of our risen *Savior*, "*Go ye, into all the world*, and preach the gospel to *every creature*," and would point out that in the parable of our *Lord*, contained in Matt. 25, it was not a *stranger*, but a *servant*; not an *immoral* but an *unprofitable* one who was to be cast into outer darkness, where there is weeping and gnashing of teeth.... We cannot but believe that the contemplation of these solemn facts has awakened in many the heartfelt prayer, "Lord, what wilt Thou have me to do, that Thy name may be hallowed, Thy kingdom come, and Thy will be done in China?"

14. *How does Taylor's understanding of the prayer "Thy kingdom come" influence his call for workers?*

---

* Taylor, J. H. (1887). *China's spiritual needs and claims* (7th ed.) (pp. 38, 47-48). London: Morgan & Scott.

In 1865, the China Inland Mission was officially organized, and the following year Taylor left with Maria, his four children, and 15 recruits for China. While extensive work was done and the force of laborers grew, there were also problems to be overcome and dangers to be faced. One such incident occurred in 1900, when 153 missionaries and 53 missionary children were killed in the hostility unleashed by the Boxer rebellion.

Hudson Taylor's agency, the China Inland Mission, became a model for more than 40 new "faith missions."

Taylor lived to see a company of over 1,500 workers committed to the vast inland regions of China. His agency became a model for more than 40 new "faith missions." His vision for the inlands stirred new zeal for the interior populations of Africa, Asia, and Latin America as well.

Townsend and McGavran: To see with new eyes

Two very different men ushered in the Third Era. Cameron Townsend dropped out of college to go to work on the field. Donald McGavran, son and grandson of missionaries, left the field to seek a secular career. Townsend gloried in the fact that he never had a degree. McGavran finished his Ph.D. in his 30s. Townsend served in Guatemala. McGavran returned to work in India. Once again, it was not from the institutional church but from its periphery that new movements began.

The impact of each of these men was extensive. Townsend's agency became the largest in the Protestant world. McGavran did not found an agency, but his writings affected every agency. These two unique individuals, captured by provocative insights, tempered by field experience, changed forever the face of world missions.

Cameron Townsend: Visionary for tribes and translations

Cam Townsend, or "Uncle Cam" as he would affectionately be known, was led to the Lord by his deaf father, Will. He began his work on the field selling Bibles. Confronted by an Indian who could not read the Spanish testaments, he determined to help those who did not have Scripture in their own language. His own words tell of his growing conviction:*

> "Don't be a fool," friends told me fifty years ago when I decided to translate the Word for the Cakchiquel Indians, a large tribe in Central America. "Those Indians aren't worth what it would take to learn their outlandish language and translate the Bible for them. They can't read anyhow. Let the Indians learn Spanish," they said.
>
> My friends used these same arguments fourteen years later, when, after having seen the transformation the Word brought to the Cakchiquels, I dreamed of reaching all other tribes. When I included even the small primitive groups in Amazonia in my plan, my friends added other arguments. "They'll kill you," said one old, experienced missionary. "Those jungle tribes are dying out anyway. They kill each other as well as outsiders with their spears, or bows and arrows. If they don't kill you, malaria will get you, or your canoe will upset in the rapids and you'll be without supplies and a month away from the last jumping-off place. Forget the other tribes, and stay with the Cakchiquels."
>
> But I couldn't forget them. And one day God gave me a verse that settled the matter for me. He said: "The Son of Man is come to save that which was lost. How think ye? If a man have a hundred sheep and one of them be gone astray, doth he not leave the ninety and nine, and goeth into the mountains and seeketh that which is gone astray?" (Matt. 18:11-12).

---

* Townsend, W. C. (1963). Tribes, tongues, and translators. In Wycliffe Bible Translators, Inc., in cooperation with the Summer Institute of Linguistics, *Who brought the Word* (pp. 7-8). Santa Ana, CA: Wycliffe.

That verse guided me; I went after the "one lost sheep," and four thousand young men and women have followed suit.

As Townsend began to see the need to develop a unique work with each tribal and language group, he was also forced to realize that a new agency was needed as well. The complex work of translation required a great degree of both specialization and support.

We call ourselves the "Wycliffe Bible Translators," in memory of John Wycliffe who first gave the whole Bible to the speakers of English. Half our members are dedicated to linguistic and translation work among the tribespeople, bringing them the Word. The other half are support personnel; teachers, secretaries, pilots, mechanics, printers, doctors, nurses, accountants, and others who man the supply lines.... Our tools are linguistics and the Word, administered in love and in the spirit of service to all without discrimination.

... Tribesmen formerly lost to the lifestream of their respective nations are being transformed by the Word. And whether the transformation occurs in the mountains of Southern Mexico, the jungles of Amazonia, or the desert plains of Australia, it is a spectacular leap out of the old into the new.

Townsend maintained that "The greatest missionary is the Bible in the Mother tongue. It never needs a furlough, is never considered a foreigner."[*] His leadership and drive brought into being Wycliffe, the Summer Institute of Linguistics, and JAARS (Jungle Aviation and Radio Service). Through these organizations' service together, more than 300 translations have been dedicated, each for a different tribe or language group.

> *"The greatest missionary is the Bible in the Mother tongue. It never needs a furlough, is never considered a foreigner."*
> — *Cameron Townsend*

With personnel from more than 30 countries, Wycliffe currently fields more than 6,000 people into over 80 nations. Although Townsend continued to defend the value of non-degreed workers for translation work, Wycliffe probably has more Ph.D.'s than any other mission agency. Ruth Tucker credits Townsend with being "the one individual most responsible for the 20th century surge in Bible translation."[**] That surge produced not only Townsend's organization, but nearly 20 others worldwide.

15. Why was Townsend's concern for the tribes a new level of missiological insight?

_____

_____

_____

_____

---

[*] Hefley, J., & Hefley, M. (1974). *Uncle Cam* (p. 182). Waco, TX: Word.

[**] Tucker, R. A. (1983). *From Jerusalem to Irian Jaya* (p. 351). Grand Rapids: Zondervan.

Donald McGavran:
Voice for hidden peoples

At virtually the same time as Townsend, on the other side of the globe, Donald McGavran was beginning to ask some related questions. Born of missionary parents and raised in India, McGavran thought to pursue a career in law. The Lord changed his mind during meetings of the Student Volunteer Movement, and McGavran returned to work in India, where he was occupied as an administrator. When the mission with which he was working decided to open a work among the Satnamis people, McGavran's colleagues selected him for the task. Through this experience and his long-term observation of missions in India, McGavran became fascinated with the question of how people become Christians.*

> This book asks how clans, tribes, castes, in short how *Peoples* become Christian. Every nation is made up of various layers of strata of society. In many nations each stratum is clearly separated from every other. The individuals in each stratum intermarry chiefly, if not solely, with each other. Their intimate life is therefore limited to their own society, that is, to their own people. They may work with others, they may buy from and sell to individuals of other societies, but their intimate life is wrapped up with the individuals of their own people. Individuals of another stratum, possibly close neighbours, may become Christians or Communists without the first stratum being much concerned. But when individuals of their own kind start becoming Christians, that touches their very lives. How do chain reactions in these strata of society begin? *How do Peoples become Christian?*

Western individualism vs. group decisions

It was the understanding of the uniqueness of various strata of society that started McGavran's quest for answers. Where but in India with its multi-layered caste system could this idea of strata come

into such sharp focus? McGavran also recognized that the way *decisions* are made in most cultures is a key factor in the way the society becomes Christian.

The way decisions are made in most cultures is a key factor in the way the society becomes Christian.

> In the West, Christianization is an extremely individualistic process. This is due to various causes. For one thing, in Western nations there are few exclusive subsocieties. Then too, because freedom of conscience exists, one member of a family can become Christian and live as a Christian without being ostracized by the rest of the family. Furthermore, Christianity is regarded as true, even by many who do not profess it. It is considered a good thing to join the Church.... Thus individuals are able to make decisions as individuals without severing social bonds.

This way of thinking was exported with Western missionaries. However, it caused serious problems in other cultures.

> Peoples were thought of as aggregates of individuals whose conversion was achieved one by one. The social factor in the conversion of peoples passed unnoticed because people were not identified as separate entities.

> However, a people is not an aggregation of individuals. In a true people, intermarriage and the intimate details of social intercourse take place within the society. In a true people, individuals are bound together not merely by common social practices and religious beliefs but by common blood. A true people is a

---

* McGavran, D. A. (1955). *The bridges of God: A study in the strategy of missions* (pp. 1, 8-13). New York: Friendship Press.

social organism which, by virtue of the fact that its members intermarry very largely within its own confines, becomes a separate race in their minds. Since the human family, except in the individualistic West, is largely made up of such castes, clans, and peoples, the Christianization of each nation involves the prior Christianization of its various peoples as peoples.

McGavran goes on to explain how most cultures make decisions and the implications for Christianizing the culture. There he finds significant answers for his driving question.

> To understand the psychology of the innumerable subsocieties which make up non-Christian nations, it is essential that the leaders of the Churches and missions strive to see life from the point of view of a people, to whom individual action is treachery. Among those who think corporately, only a rebel would strike out alone, without consultation and without companions. The individual does not think of himself as a self-sufficient unit, but a part of the group. His business affairs, his children's marriages, his personal problems, or the difficulties he has with his wife are properly settled by group thinking. Peoples become Christian as their group-mind is brought into a lifegiving relationship to Jesus as Lord.
>
> It is important to note that the group decision is not the sum of separate individual decisions. The leader makes sure that his followers will follow. The followers make sure that they are not ahead of each other. Husbands sound out wives. Sons pledge their fathers. "Will we as a group move if so-and-so does not come?" is a frequent question. As the group considers becoming Christian, tension mounts and excitement rises. Indeed, a prolonged informal vote-taking is under way. A change of religion involves community change. Only as its members move together, does change become healthy and constructive.

Peoples become Christian as a wave of decision for Christ sweeps through the group mind, involving many individual decisions but being far more than merely their sum.

> Peoples become Christian as a wave of decision for Christ sweeps through the group mind, involving many individual decisions but being far more than merely their sum. This may be called a chain reaction. Each decision sets off others and the sum total powerfully affects every individual. When conditions are right, not merely each sub-group, but the entire group concerned decides together.

16. *Are group decisions valid? What questions would you have about the pros and cons of this approach?*

_____

_____

_____

_____

_____

This group decision when "the entire group decides together" was called by McGavran a "People Movement." In contrast to the laborious strategy of one-by-one decisions, a people movement is a much more culturally acceptable method of decision making. McGavran's research proved it is also historically a far more stable type of conversion and has happened many times, often without the knowledge or approval of the missionary!

McGavran returned from India to become the first Dean of the Fuller School of World Mission. His prolific writing exposed the entire missions world to his research. From his efforts grew the Church Growth Movement, devoted to expanding within already penetrated groups, and the Frontier Mission Movement, focused on reaching unpenetrated groups.

These two very different men, Townsend and McGavran, with their unique perspectives, began to see the necessity of looking at missions not in terms of geography, but in terms of particular ethnic groups, now referred to as "peoples." The effect of their vision completely changes our understanding of the task ahead.

III. Transitions and Movements

The pioneers of the different eras inspired their generations with key concepts and clear objectives. Others followed who tested and carried out the challenges. In this section, we will continue to explore missions history to glean principles and truth that may be applied today. The "transition" periods, during which missions from one era overlap with those of the following era (see Figure 5-3), have been and continue to be challenging times. We also want to look at the movements produced during each era to try to recognize how God is working today. We will end our review of mission history with a forward look, hoping to catch a glimpse of things to come.

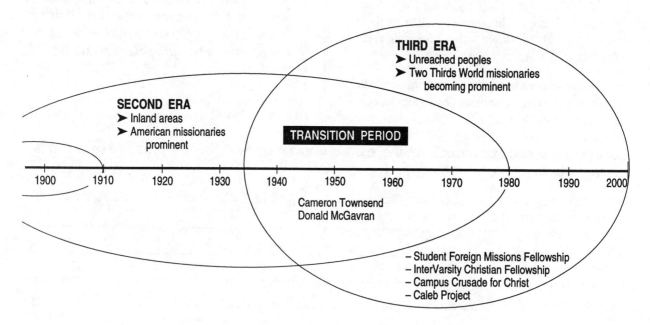

Figure 5-3. The Transition Period Between the Second and Third Eras

In the following article, Harry Larson takes us through a discussion of transition periods in seeking an understanding of critical issues facing us today.

❏ *Responding to the Challenge of the Transitions*

Harry Larson *

In every generation, God has given individuals a passion for the unpenetrated frontiers. Paul strove to "preach the gospel, not where Christ was named" (Rom. 15:20) and "to preach the gospel in the regions beyond" (2 Cor. 10:16). Every new move of God in mission history has incorporated this driving desire to go beyond the current frontiers of the gospel. Each new effort has also built on the accomplishments of the previous one. The transitions from one period to another, however, have not always been smooth. Eager young missionaries, impatient to get on with their pioneer work, have often trampled on the insights, achievements, and feelings of their predecessors. This approach has produced pain, and in many cases the work of God has been greatly hindered.

God is moving all history towards the completion of world evangelization. We know we are currently in an exciting transition period between Second Era missions and the final thrust of Third Era missions. Those who grasp what God is doing may become impatient with those of God's people who are slower to understand this new direction of the Spirit. Historical study of the transition periods can make us aware of these tensions and help us avoid the painful mistakes of the past. The many lessons to be learned can not only help Second and Third Era missionaries avoid unnecessary conflict and hurt, they may also provide a key for raising up the tremendous movements needed to complete the remaining task.

Transitions are seldom easy. In the current transition in mission history, the workers in the era being completed are turning the work over to the national church and stepping away from the level of involvement required of them in initial stages. However, the workers in the newly started era must enter unengaged fields in pioneering roles. This difference in roles can cause various kinds of conflict and misunderstanding.

Those who are ready to exit may be critical of those who are beginning to enter. The new strategies necessary for the new work may cause some to think that the earlier work was "wrong" or "inappropriate." The valid reasons for moving on from a completed work may be incorrectly applied to say that all cross-cultural workers in every field should "go home." This thinking can produce confusion, both in the national church and in the sending church at home.

> *When workers accept the fact that a transition is in progress, confusion can be replaced by understanding.*

Such difficulties are particularly true in the transition from the Second to Third Era, since there may be both reached and unreached fields in the same geographical location. The Philippines, for example, are clearly reached in some areas and yet have a number of unreached people groups living within that large country of islands. New questions must be asked to determine what work is needed and where.

When workers accept the fact that a transition is in progress, confusion can be replaced by understanding. At the present time, the Second Era is drawing to a close, while the Third Era is under way. Excellent, life-changing work done by committed career missionaries is reaching the "Participant Stage," in which the national church can fully manage the work and invite others to join them when they want them. At the same time, bold and daring pioneers of a whole new force of workers are being

* Harry Larson worked as a missionary among the Mam Indians of Guatemala with the Central American Mission. He currently serves as Missions Pastor of Emmanuel Faith Community Church in Escondido, California.

called forth from every nation to start new initiatives for God. Five intentional steps can help reduce the difficulties of living in such a critical stage.

1. Continue to support and honor the veteran missionaries who are finishing up the Second Era task

It is extremely distressing for faithful, lifelong missionaries on the field to hear about new "movements" at home and to be made to feel that their ministry is no longer valuable or valid. Division can arise in the local church when older Christians feel that "their missionaries" are being considered second class workers in the missionary enterprise. Well-meaning ambassadors for hidden people groups have sometimes left this impression.

It is precisely because faithful veterans have labored long at the Second Era task that some of the resources can now be allocated to new frontiers. The vast wealth of experience from missionaries' years of service is a valuable training asset for new workers. Continuing to support and honor those who have served through "the heat of the day" is essential.

2. Educate the sending church about the nature of the transition

When local churches are taught some basics of missions history and strategy, they can appreciate the value of the past and the requirements of the future. They can see that while there is a place where "nationals can do the job better" in established fields, at the same time, there is a need for "a whole new missions force" in the as-yet-unreached fields. What an incredible day for sending churches as the churches that were established in the First and Second Eras now become senders themselves and as the new missionary force has the opportunity to become an integrated, international corps.

3. Allocate new resources and missionary personnel to pioneer work

Even while honoring and supporting those who are finishing the Second Era task, there must be inten-tional appropriation of new funds and new forces for the task remaining. Missionaries retiring from a field will naturally be tied to the people they have given their lives to reach. They will be cognizant of the needs and will want to see people recruited to take their place. However, the task will not be finished simply by continuing to staff missionary posts that were created 50 to 100 years ago.

4. Share new vision with present missionaries

When missionaries come home on furlough, often the first thing they want to consider is additional study. They are anxious to know the results of new research and often contribute to such research from their field experience. Part of the sending church commitment should be to share current insights and strategies with these partners and offer additional training wherever possible. Few missionaries who are exposed to these insights are not excited by them.

5. Maintain a strategic balance among different types of missionary work

When sending churches and agencies do not intentionally consider their plans and goals, they will drown in a sea of conflicting voices. There is no one "right" way. Our God is a God of variety and individuality. He will lead each group to organize its involvement in world outreach in unique ways. Still, it is essential to act intentionally and strategically. Churches that want to be attuned to what the Spirit is doing today will ask themselves these questions and plan accordingly:

- Are we praying and seeking the Holy Spirit's fresh guidance in our missions program?

- Are we satisfied with what we currently give to Third Era pioneer work among unreached people?

- How much, if any, of our *new* resources should we be budgeting for Second Era work?

- Does God want to make us a "Third Era church" through "adoption" and "engagement" of an unreached people group? *

---

* "Adoption" in this sense refers to the commitment by a congregation to pray for and support efforts to reach a specifically named, unreached people group. "Engagement" is the actual establishment of an effort to reach the group through the appointment and sending of missionaries.

These are some of the questions we should be asking ourselves and praying about. Our Father's heart is moving all of history to its climactic conclusion.

This age will not end with a whimper, but with a bang! Let's tune our heartbeats to our Father's and get on with the Great Commission task!

17. *Why is an understanding of transition periods critical for church mission committees and others involved in supporting the missionary task?*

_____

_____

_____

_____

Movements

The visionary men God used, their influential writings, and some of the movements they helped engender are summed up in Figure 5-4. This table, while not comprehensive by any means, does help identify clearly each distinct period.

ERAS OF MISSION HISTORY	FIRST ERA (1792 - 1910)	SECOND ERA (1865 - 1980)	THIRD ERA (1934 - Present)
EMPHASIS	Coastlands of unreached continents	Interiors of unreached continents	Hidden and unreached peoples
PIONEERS	William Carey	Hudson Taylor	Cameron Townsend Donald McGavran
WRITINGS	*An Enquiry Into the Obligation of Christians to Use Means for the Conversion of the Heathens*	*The Call to Service* *China's Spiritual Needs and Claims*	*Tribes, Tongues, and Translators* *The Bridges of God*
RELATED MOVEMENTS	Haystack Prayer Meeting Society of Brethren	Cambridge Seven Student Volunteer Movement Laymen's Missionary Movement Women's Movements	Student Foreign Missions Fellowship Urbana Conventions Adopt-a-People A.D. 2000

Figure 5-4. Three Eras of Protestant Missions Showing Emphasis,
Pioneers, Writings, and Related Movements

Each period has generated movements which have fueled the specific missions thrust with personnel, prayer, and financial support. Student movements have been of particular importance in producing recruits for mission work. Men's and women's movements have been a key in generating prayer and financial support as well as personnel. In this Third Era, the Holy Spirit is also raising up movements along strategic lines. Both the culmination in A.D. 2000 of the second millennium since Christ gave the Great Commission and an achievable unreached peoples target are generating a spontaneous worldwide crusade for the completion of the task.

Student Movements

Throughout Protestant mission history, student movements have been tremendously important. Students are the prime human resources for most enterprises. They are at an age when they are making career and other major decisions with lifelong implications. It is no surprise, then, that the Lord of the Harvest has consistently raised up movements to challenge students to consider the high calling of missions. Much of this work has been done in unobtrusive, low profile ways as students have gathered together to pray and study God's Word. Occasionally, this steady work of the Spirit takes on a more prominent aspect, as in the case of InterVarsity's student missionary convention, which regularly draws 20,000 participants to the University of Illinois' Urbana campus. The following sections excerpt and summarize a portion of a book by David Howard entitled *Student Power in World Missions*.

The Haystack Prayer Meeting*

The student missions movement in the First Era is identified with an event which has become known as the "Haystack Prayer Meeting." Samuel J. Mills, a young man who was converted during the "Great Awakening" which began in 1798, was instrumental in this event and in the movement that grew out of it. Howard describes that important meeting:

On the North American continent the beginnings of overseas interest on the part of the church can be traced directly to student influence, and more precisely to the impact of one student, Samuel J. Mills, Jr. (1783-1818). Born in Connecticut as the son of a Congregational minister, Mills was brought up in a godly home. His mother reportedly said of him, "I have consecrated this child to the service of God as a missionary." This was a remarkable statement since missionary interest was practically unknown in the churches of that day and no channels (such as mission boards) for overseas service existed in America. Mills was converted at the age of seventeen as a part of the Great Awakening that began in 1798 and touched his father's church. His commitment to world evangelism seemed to be an integral part of his conversion experience. From the moment of conversion, on through the years of his study and for the rest of his public ministry, he never lost sight of this purpose.

In 1806, Mills enrolled in Williams College, Massachusetts. This school had been profoundly affected by the religious awakening of those years, and devout students on campus had a deep concern for the spiritual welfare of their fellow students. Mills joined with them in their desire to help others. It was Mills' custom to spend Wednesday and Saturday afternoons in prayer with other students on the banks of the Hoosack River or in a valley near the college. In August, 1806, Mills and four others were caught in a thunderstorm while returning from their usual meeting. Seeking refuge under a haystack, they waited out the storm and gave themselves to prayer. Their special focus of prayer that day was for the awakening of foreign missionary interest among students. Mills directed their discussion and prayer to their own missionary obligation. He exhorted his companions with the words that later became a watchword for them, "We can do this if we will."

---

* Howard, D. M. (1979). *Student power in world missions* (2nd ed.) (pp. 71, 73-76, 89-98). Downers Grove, IL: InterVarsity Press.

Bowed in prayer, these first American student volunteers for foreign missions willed that God should have their lives for service wherever He needed them, and in that self-dedication really gave birth to the first student missionary society in America. Kenneth Scott Latourette, the foremost historian of the church's worldwide expansion, states, "It was from this haystack meeting that the foreign missionary movement of the churches of the United States had an initial impulse." *

The exact location of the haystack was unknown for a number of years. Then, in 1854, Bryan Green, one of those present in 1806, visited Williamstown and located the spot. A monument was erected on the site in 1867. Mark Hopkins, who was then president of the American Board of Commissioners for Foreign Missions, gave the dedicatory address in which he said, "For once in the history of the world a prayer meeting is commemorated by a monument."

The Cambridge Seven

As the Second Era began to gather momentum, students at Cambridge University in England were stirred to consider the plight of the unevangelized through a one-week visit by the evangelist Dwight L. Moody. Students committed their lives to Christ, and many volunteered for missions, causing applications to the Anglican missionary society to increase dramatically. Interest was also drawn to the new mission founded by Hudson Taylor for the evangelization of inland China.

During 1883-84, a group of outstanding students, some of whom were converted through Moody's ministry, volunteered to serve with Taylor's mission. Sensing a unity of purpose and outlook, these seven traveled extensively throughout England and Scotland following graduation, visiting campuses and churches. David Howard comments:

> Their impact for missionary work was far beyond the few months of time they invested in this tour. In February, 1885, the seven sailed for China, to be followed in subsequent years by scores of students who, under their influence, had given themselves to Jesus Christ to reach other parts of the world.

The Student Volunteer Movement (SVM)

The Second Era also received the blessing of the Student Volunteer Movement, largely among American students. The impact of this force for world evangelization cannot be overestimated. The powerful and eloquent writings of the movement's leaders are still bearing fruit with students today. David Howard writes:

> In the history of modern missions, probably no single factor has wielded a greater influence in the worldwide outreach of the Church than the Student Volunteer Movement. The names of its great leaders—men of the stature of John R. Mott, Robert C. Wilder, Robert E. Speer, to name a few—stand high in the annals of the foreign missionary movement. Its watchword, "The evangelization of the world in this generation," was so profoundly influential in motivating students for overseas service that John R. Mott could write, "I can truthfully answer that next to the decision to take Christ as the leader and the Lord of my life, the watchword has had more influence than all other ideals and objectives committed to widen my horizon and enlarge my conception of the Kingdom of God."

In the summer of 1886, at the invitation of Dwight L. Moody, 251 students gathered at Mt. Hermon, Massachusetts, for a month-long Bible study. There was a great stirring among the students for foreign

---

* Latourette, K. S. (1950). *These sought a country* (p. 46). New York: Harper & Bros.

missions, and 100 volunteered for foreign service. During the 1886-87 school year, Robert C. Wilder and John Forman traveled to 167 different schools to share the vision for world evangelization. Over 2,000 students volunteered for foreign missions.

In 1888, the movement was formally organized. It focused its activities on college campuses through speaking tours, literature, and every four years, a massive student missions convention. Thousands of volunteers pledged their lives to foreign mission work. The movement peaked in 1920 with the convention in Des Moines, Iowa, which hosted 6,890 delegates. In subsequent years, however, the SVM began to decline due to liberal influences, and by 1940 it had turned its focus to social and political issues. Nevertheless, by the most conservative estimates, the movement produced at least 20,500 volunteers who reached the foreign field through the mission agencies which had emerged to channel them.

The Student Foreign Missions Fellowship (SFMF)

Concurrent with the emergence of the Third Era, the Holy Spirit raised up another student movement. The Student Foreign Missions Fellowship was organized in 1938 under student leadership, and chapters were formed throughout the United States. When the InterVarsity Christian Fellowship (IVCF) arrived in the United States from Canada in 1945, the SFMF merged with that organization as their "missionary department." As with the SVM, one of the SFMF's objectives was to hold periodic international student missions conferences. The first one was held in Toronto in 1946 and the second, in 1948, at the University of Illinois' Urbana campus, where it has been held ever since. Fueled by returned veterans from World War II, the SFMF sent more students overseas in missionary endeavors during the next two decades than during any other comparable period in history.

The turbulent decade of the 1960s, with its anti-establishment philosophy, deeply affected students of that generation. Seldom have missions been looked on with more disfavor. By the 1970s, however, students began to take a more positive view towards reform from within the system, and a renewed interest in missions resulted. This shift in attitude is evident from the records of the Urbana student missionary conventions. In 1970, 7% of the delegates signed decision cards to volunteer as missionaries. In 1973, 28% pledged to go if called. In 1976, 50% signed decision cards, and the percentage has not dropped since that time.

The student movement in the Third Era has many expressions. While well established organizations like IVCF and Campus Crusade for Christ have actively realigned much of their emphasis to Third Era objectives, newer organizations patterned after the SVM have emerged. Caleb Project, for example, developed traveling teams to mobilize college students to concern for the unreached. Each of these organizations has had an important part in continuing to spread the gospel.

18. Why are student mission movements strategically essential to the missionary task?

_____

_____

_____

While the impact of student movements on the three eras of Protestant missions is incalculable, other movements have also fueled the enterprise in their own way. Although not as eminent in mission history, they are worthy of consideration.

Men's Movements

In 1906, under the inspiration of former leaders of the SVM, the Laymen's Missionary Movement was founded during a prayer meeting commemorating the one hundredth anniversary of the Haystack Prayer Meeting. The organization called for men to band together in congregations to "work with the pastor in enlisting all members and adherents in the intelligent and adequate support and extension of missionary work." * The movement sought to be "an inspiration rather than an administration," desiring to present an adequate missionary policy to influential groups of men as well as exploit methods of missionary finance which had produced the best results. As the organization's first secretary, J. Campbell White wrote:

> The Movement stands for investigation, agitation, and organization; the investigation by laymen of missionary conditions, the agitation of laymen of an adequate missionary policy, and the organization of laymen to co-operate with the ministers and Missionary Boards in enlisting the whole Church in its supreme work of saving the world.

Within a few years of its inception, the movement had been instrumental in organizing thousands of men as active promoters of missions in their congregations. The movement quickly spread to England, Scotland, Germany, and Australia. Hundreds of thousands of dollars were raised during the two decades of the group's existence for the support of the thousands of volunteers who were going out.

19. What was the primary focus of the Laymen's Missionary Movement?

_____

_____

_____

Women's Movements

The incredible losses suffered by both sides during the American Civil War forced women into roles they had generally not exercised before that time. They ran businesses, banks, and farms and founded women's colleges. From the end of the war in 1865 into the next century, they also played a major role in the missions movement. During this period, over 40 women's mission agencies were formed which promoted and supervised the work of over 100,000 women's missionary "societies" in local churches. Each missionary society was dedicated to prayer and financial support of missionary work.

The women's movement of the Second Era peaked in 1910. In that year, there were 44 women's mission boards open to single women interested in a missionary career. By then, mission leaders of stature such as Hudson Taylor and Dwight L. Moody were publicly acclaiming the effective contribution of women missionaries to world evangelization. Single women had not always been accepted by standard denominational and faith missions. The change in policy by many of these mission agencies, due to the recognition of the legitimate and competent work of women on the field, may have contributed significantly to the decline and eventual disappearance of women's mission agencies.

---

* White, J. C. (1992). The Laymen's Missionary Movement. In R. D. Winter & S. C. Hawthorne (Eds.), *Perspectives on the world Christian movement: A reader* (rev. ed.) (p. B91). Pasadena: William Carey Library.

20. What roles could lay movements play in the Third Era?

_____

_____

_____

_____

Current Movements

Along with a strong student movement, the Third Era is being characterized by worldwide movements based on strategic considerations. Two primary motivating factors are driving these movements:

- The identification, "adoption," and "engagement" of the remaining unreached people groups for evangelization in a drive for "closure" of the Great Commission.

- The celebration of the second millennium approaching in A.D. 2000.

These movements are not bound exclusively to the Western world. The Two Thirds World missionary force has been strongly impacted by Third Era missiology, and thousands of unreached peoples have already been targeted by non-Westerners with the hope of planting the church within those groups by the year 2000.

Adopt-a-People

The primary distinctive of the Third Era is the identification and planting of the church among the remaining peoples of the earth where that has not happened. The task is quantifiable, and leading missiologists such as David Barrett, Patrick Johnstone, and Ralph Winter have attempted to establish what the number of remaining people groups is. While there is still no clear consensus, the discussion has brought into clear focus the fact that there is a *significant* number of such groups, perhaps as many as 12,000.

How can they be reached? One by one. Churches can take the initiative in "adopting" people groups. Mission agencies can then help the adopting churches and/or others "engage" these groups for evangelism. Efforts are being made to track through a centralized computer database the groups that need targeting and those that have been targeted. This information is then provided to agencies and congregations through a computer "bulletin board." This way of "organizing" the task remaining has caught the imagination of mission leaders throughout the world. During the Asia Missions Congress (Seoul, Korea, 1990), Asians acknowledged their responsibility for "adopting" 3,000 groups. Latin Americans have carried out their first continent-wide consultation (Costa Rica, 1992) to divide up and begin "engaging" their share of groups as well.

A.D. 2000

Approximately 2000 years ago, Christ issued the Great Commission that converted His disciples into apostles. Over the centuries, hundreds of plans have been formulated by God's people for completing the task, none of which has yet reached that ultimate conclusion. The close of this millennium has spurred a new series of global schemes for world evangelization. Over 80 organizations have launched initiatives to complete the work before 2000 A.D. An important difference between these and other plans is that for the first time ever, these organizations are making a significant attempt to *cooperate* in achieving their common objective. A consultation held in Singapore brought together the key mission agencies of the entire world. Mechanisms were established for keeping in touch, and cooperative agreements were initiated between similar ministries such as radio broadcasters and research databases.

Specialized ministries for the fostering of *partnerships* have also emerged to help "broker" relationships. In some cases, up to 30 distinct agencies are now collaborating together to reach a specific people group. International alliances such as the World Evangelical Fellowship are also effectively providing a global network for churches as they pursue the goal of world evangelization. The theme, "A church for every people by the year 2000," has struck a responsive chord in God's people around the globe.

21. *What is distinct about current mission related movements compared with former movements? What is similar?*

_____

_____

_____

_____

Some missiologists assert that the Third Era will not be followed by a "Fourth Era" since, by definition, the Third Era is the "what is left" era. If Third Era missionaries can indeed plant a cluster of reproducing churches in every people group on the face of the earth, the Great Commission goal of "all nations" will have been met. This is the *strategy of closure* which is propelling many of the movements in this era. It is the hope of every "world" Christian that this completion of the Great Commission task will usher in Christ's kingdom in power and glory. There is still much to do, however, before the assignment is completed. "Ask the Lord of the harvest, therefore, to send out workers into His harvest field" (Luke 10:2).

Summary

The three eras of Protestant mission expansion help trace the systematic expansion of Christianity during the past 200 years. The lessons of each era provide unique contributions to subsequent eras. We have now entered the Third Era of missions history and have the advantage of being able to learn lessons from the past in pursuing the completion of the Great Commission.

The lives of the pioneers of the Protestant missions movement provide both inspiration and priceless insights into the nature of the task. William Carey fathered the movement; Hudson Taylor mobilized it towards the interiors of the darkened continents; Cameron Townsend brought attention to the thousands of tongues and tribes around the world; and Donald McGavran clarified the concept of people groups and paved the way for systematic church growth around the world.

The Holy Spirit has always raised up movements which have provided the resources for each of the eras. Student movements have been of particular importance in providing personnel, while men's and women's movements have given tremendous prayer and financial support. The Third Era of missions is characterized by a global movement which is focused on identifying and partitioning the task among Christians around the world. It is the hope of many that this strategy of closure will usher in Christ's return in glory and power.

Integrative Assignment

1. *Contrast and compare the three eras of modern missions by pointing out their differences and similarities. Then list what you feel to be the most important lessons or principles we can learn from studying these eras.*

2. *Write a short inspirational paper utilizing lessons from the lives of the pioneers of the mission eras as your main source.*

3. *What will be the end result of the great missions fervor which has arisen during the current stage of the Third Era? Write a descriptive paper of what you expect from the year 2000 and beyond.*

Questions for Reflection

1. *God raises up movements at strategic points in mission history to channel personnel, prayer, and financial resources into the Great Commission task. Do you feel compelled to become part of today's mission movement? Why or why not? Talk to the Lord about this and let the Holy Spirit guide you.*

_____

_____

_____

_____

_____

_____

2. *You have now completed your study of the first volume of **World Mission**. In what areas have you been most challenged so far? What have you learned that you need to apply to your life? Record your thoughts.*

_____

_____

_____

_____

_____

_____

Subject Index

A

Abrahamic Covenant   1-3, 1-13, 2-1 – 2-9, 2-11 – 2-12, 2-14, 2-17, 2-28, 3-1, 3-8 – 3-9, 4-3
AD 2000 Movement   5-25, 5-30
Adam and Eve   1-11 – 1-13, 1-16, 2-1
Adopt-a-People   5-25, 5-30
Africa Inland Mission   5-6
Alcuin   4-14
Alfred   4-16
American Board of Commissioners for Foreign Missions   5-2, 5-27
Anglo-Saxons   4-13 – 4-14, 4-19 – 4-20, 4-22
Antioch church   3-14, 3-17, 4-1, 4-8
Apostles, response to Great Commission   3-12 – 3-13, 3-15, 3-30, 4-1
Arians   4-9, 4-11
Asia Missions Congress   5-30
Augustine   4-13

B

Babel   1-16, 2-1
Baptist Missionary Society   5-14
Barbarians   4-11 – 4-15, 4-23, 4-31
    See also Celts, Goths
Barnabas   3-14 – 3-15, 3-17
Barrett, David   5-30
Barth, Karl   1-19
Bede   4-19
Benedict of Aniane   4-17
Benedictines   4-12, 4-16
Bernard of Clairvaux   4-19
Bible, role in evangelization   1-2 – 1-9, 1-24
Biblical mandate   1-3 – 1-4
BOBO theory   4-6
Boniface   4-13 – 4-14
Boxer rebellion   5-18
Bubonic plague   4-19 – 4-20

C

Caleb Project   5-28
Cambridge Seven   5-25, 5-27
Campus Crusade for Christ   5-28
Carey, William   5-2, 5-6, 5-9 – 5-14, 5-17, 5-25, 5-31
Carlisle, Thomas   2-25
Carolingian Renaissance   4-14, 4-19
Cassian, John   4-9
Catholic missions
    See Roman Catholic missions
Celts   3-14, 4-4, 4-7, 4-9, 4-12 – 4-14, 4-19
Charlemagne   4-14 – 4-17, 4-19
Chiang Kai-shek   4-22

China Inland Mission   5-6, 5-16 – 5-18

Christ
    "all peoples" perspective   3-4, 3-6 – 3-9, 3-21, 3-30, 4-1
    and Abrahamic Covenant   1-13, 2-6 – 2-9
    and Great Commission   3-6, 3-9 – 3-11, 3-19, 4-4
    and Jonah   2-25
    as Messiah   3-1 – 3-6, 3-21, 3-23, 3-27, 3-30, 4-1
    as Son of Man   3-3
    example of identification   1-6 – 1-7
    role in kingdom of God   1-13 – 1-15, 3-24 – 3-28, 3-30
    role in salvation   1-20
    victory over death   3-24 – 3-25, 3-27, 3-30, 4-1
    victory over Satan   1-13, 3-24, 3-26 – 3-28, 3-30, 4-1
    victory over sin   3-24, 3-26 – 3-27, 3-30, 4-1
Christianity
    effects of   4-24 – 4-26, 4-31
    expansion of   3-15 – 3-17, 3-30, 4-1 – 4-2, 4-4, 4-6 – 4-16, 4-18 – 4-24, 4-31, 5-31
Church
    characteristics of   3-19 – 3-20, 4-25
    indigenous   3-20 – 3-21
    role of   3-17 – 3-21, 3-28 – 3-30
    See also Christianity
                Evangelization
Church Growth Movement   5-10, 5-22
    See also Evangelization, of people groups
Church Missionary Society   5-3
Cistercian revival   4-17
Closure   4-26, 5-1, 5-30 – 5-31
Cluny Reform   4-17
Colomban   4-13
Conferences   5-8, 5-10, 5-28, 5-30
Constantine   4-7, 4-10, 4-14, 4-17, 4-19
Council of Jerusalem
    See Jerusalem Council
Crusades   4-7, 4-18 – 4-19
Culture, and gospel   1-5, 1-7, 2-2, 4-11, 5-21

D

Dark Ages   4-2, 4-14 – 4-15
Dawson, Christopher   4-16, 4-22
Diaspora   2-27, 4-3
Diocletian edicts   4-10
Disciples
    preparation for Great Commission   3-6 – 3-9, 3-30
    See also Apostles

E

East India Company   5-11, 5-14
Edinburgh Conference   5-8, 5-10
Ellul, Jacques   2-25
Epochs of mission history   4-2 – 4-4, 4-7 – 4-8, 4-10 – 4-12, 4-14 – 4-16, 4-18 – 4-23, 4-31, 5-1

Author Index